C I T Y

# CITY EDITOR

By STANLEY WALKER

City Editor, New York Herald Tribune
Author of "The Night Club Era"

*With a Foreword by*
ALEXANDER WOOLLCOTT

THE JOHNS HOPKINS UNIVERSITY PRESS
BALTIMORE AND LONDON

Originally published in hardcover by Frederick A. Stokes Company,
New York, 1934
Johns Hopkins Paperbacks edition, 1999
9 8 7 6 5 4 3 2 1

The Johns Hopkins University Press
2715 North Charles Street
Baltimore, Maryland 21218-4363
www.press.jhu.edu

**Library of Congress Cataloging-in-Publication Data**

Walker, Stanley, b. 1898.
    City editor / by Stanley Walker.
        p.    cm.
    Originally published : New York : F.A. Stokes, 1934.
    Includes index.
    ISBN 0-8018-6292-2 (alk. paper)
        1. Journalism.    2. Journalism—New York (State)—New York—History—20th century.
3. American newspapers—New York (State)—New York—History—20th century.
4. Newspaper editors—New York (State)—New York Biography.    5. Journalists—New York
(State)—New York Biography.    6. Walker, Stanley, b. 1898.    7. New York herald tribune.
I. Title.
PN4784.C62W3    1999
071'.471—dc21                                                          99-15162
                                                                        CIP

A catalog record for this book is available from the British Library.

*To*

GRAFTON STILES WILCOX

# FOREWORD

IN this volume are set forth the moody reflections of a city editor, the most resourceful and stimulating newspaper man to fill that post on a New York daily since the late Charles Chapin was shipped off to Sing Sing for the murder of his elderly wife. Chapin was the acrid martinet who used to issue falsetto and sadistic orders from a swivel chair at the *Evening World* in that now haze-hung era when Irvin Cobb was the best rewrite man on Park Row and I was a Christian slave in the galleys of the New York *Times*. In the small morning hours when we reporters would brood over our sorrows while consuming sirloins with fried potatoes at Jack's, we liked especially to dwell on the oft-told episode of the youngster sent by Chapin to interview a cowboy who had eloped with the ranch-owner's daughter. The runaways were traced to a shabby lodging house off Union Square and when the inquiring reporter intruded blandly on their clandestine bliss, the cowboy tossed him down stairs and added to that virile gesture of dismissal the convincing threat that if the reporter ever again tried poking his ink-stained nose into their private business, he would experience all the pangs of buckshot in the seat of his pants. The reporter crawled to the nearest telephone and confessed his defeat to Chapin. The big chief remained undaunted. "Look here," he said, "you go back and tell that bully he can't intimidate me."

The reporter who sees his city editor knock off work at six o'clock, after assigning him to sit all night on the chill steps of a hospital waiting for some stuffed shirt to die or to run his legs off all over the rain-drenched Bronx on the trail of a stolen necklace, is bound to cherish at such times much the same feelings about his boss as does the doughboy out cutting wire in no-man's-land while his captain snores in a lousy but enviable dugout further back. When one of these buck-privates of journalism is being snubbed by the doorman at the Union Club, or helping the homicide squad unpack the trunk in which a corpse has been left until it has become noticeable, he thinks of a mere executive as one too sheltered from the scuffle of newspaper work to be entitled to speak about it with authority—feels about him, indeed, much as the Tommies in a certain British regiment felt about the Colonel who, at a courtmartial, accounted for their defeat by telling of the rigors of the post where they were stationed. It had given the Colonel himself a disabling cold in the head. Egad, gentlemen, a chap had to sleep night after night with nothing between himself and the damp ground except a thin native girl.

But, just as the college undergraduate begins in time to think of the faculty as something more than malicious conspirators against his peace and leisure, so in the long perspective afforded by retirement to less exigent forms of journalism, I now see the city editor and the staff drawing closer together. I see them merge. Now, in my dotage, I realize that the captain and the men share a common lot and that victory is possible only when neither lets the other down—when the men, on their side, give every ounce of devotion and when the city editor, on his, stands always on guard, protecting the reporters not only from the occasionally infuriated citizenry but from the endless imbecilities of the high command.

Stanley Walker is and for some years has been the city editor of that ascendant amalgam known as the *Herald Tribune*. If I am justified in my impression that he is the most notable ciy editor of his time, you need look no further than these pages for the explanation. They are so obviously the work of one with an avid interest in the craftsmanship of his trade, one who further is insatiably fascinated by its material. That material is the changeless and ever changing Bagdad which is the territory of his staff. To Walker it is all new and endlessly entertaining. Probably only a fellow from the hinterland would find it so in such full measure. It is no accident that *The New Yorker* is edited by a native of the startled town of Aspen, Colorado, and that the city editor of the *Herald Tribune* is a stray from Lampasas, Texas.

Here are set down his cogitations on such professional questions as "Who Murdered the New York *World?*" or "Are Women Newspaper Men?" or "Why was Herbert Bayward Swope?" The discussion of these and kindred topics always stirs my old and vain regret that although all the arts are benefited by a running fire of comment from the newspapers, the newspapers themselves remain uncriticized. A weekly which devoted a department to such criticism of the dailies, a department designed to keep tabs on the newspapers just as sternly and just as exhaustively as the *Times,* let us say, keeps tabs on the theatres, would work wonders for the press in New York. The fitfully recurrent feature in *The New Yorker* called The Wayward Press (the one signed Guy Fawkes and written as a rule by Robert Benchley) might of course be called a step in the right direction unless step be too vigorous a word. Perhaps toddle would be better. I have in mind a far sharper and more unremitting fire and I know of no one better fitted to conduct it than Stanley Walker.

This book of his will be valuable in all the swarming schools of journalism. It might profitably be read by the thousands of students who intend entering newspaper work and most of whom will eventually tap on Walker's door only to be informed that, even if Richard Harding Davis should come back to life and offer to work for $15 a week, he could not be squeezed into the already bloated staff.  In this book such postulants will find much to give them pause.  If it can turn them away—if anything can turn them away—they will, I suppose, be no great loss to a trade which, all in all, is more fun than any other.

ALEXANDER WOOLLCOTT.

# CONTENTS

# CITY EDITOR

# AUTHOR'S NOTE

WHENEVER newspaper men get together they argue about the fine points of their craft, its ethics, its philosophy, its history, and its great heroes. Persons who never saw the inside of a newspaper office often ask questions, wondering whether a paper is produced by machinery or by some sort of black magic. Young men and women, puzzling over their futures, seek to learn whether newspaper work is worth doing. What I have attempted here is an answer to some of these questions—an informal survey of present-day journalism in America, from the viewpoint of a man on the city desk of a metropolitan paper. In my fifteen years in New York newspaper work, the last seven of which have been passed as city editor of the *Herald Tribune*, I have seen many changes, encountered many strange and charming people, and accumulated, no doubt, a vast number of prejudices. I think, however, that I have retained all that unaccountable affection for the work which I had when younger, and that this affection has increased with the years. I love its people and its traditions. It is, to me, the greatest business on earth. In what follows I have wanted to be fair but plainspoken; no one, it must be, ever can succeed completely in being either.

S. WALKER.

# CITY EDITOR

## HARD, SOFT, AND MEDIUM

THE acrobatic city editor of fiction always has the adjective "hard-boiled" before his title; it seems as inevitable as "waiting" automobile, "nearby" drugstore and "hurrying" pedestrian.

The boss of the city room is supposed to be a rather learned but consistently brutal curmudgeon, as insensate to the more mellow aspects of life as a Mergenthaler linotype, the possessor of deep inside information which if divulged would make the blood run cold, and the recipient of psychic tips which enable him to humiliate his less fortunate rivals.

He invents strange devices for the torture of reporters, this mythical agate-eyed Torquemada with the paste-pots and scissors. Even his laugh, usually directed at something sacred, is part sneer. His terrible curses cause flowers to wither, as the grass died under the hoofbeats of the horse of Attila the Hun. A chilly, monstrous figure, sleepless, nerveless, and facing with ribald mockery the certain hell which awaits him.

Actually the city editor, who is responsible for the work of the reporters and rewrite men in covering the news of the city and surrounding territory, appears to be very much like other men. He suffers from migraine and buck fever. He has his moments of fumbling and fright; he knows that no matter how good he is, he is not quite good enough. He knows that no amount of effort, even with a brilliant staff, can make the picture of his city, as mirrored in the

news, as complete in its moving lights and shadows as it
should be to approach perfection.  He knows, no matter
how well-ordered his news-gathering machine may be,
that on some days beats will be scored against him.  He
knows frustration and bewilderment.  He also, unless he
lacks imagination, has a whale of a good time.

Like other men, he fears, not hell, but the coming of the
day when he will be through—the day on which he himself, or his employers, will realize that the touch is not as
sure as it was, that something has happened to the vital
spark which makes all good newspaper men what they are,
that the two splendid weapons, judgment and memory,
have somehow become rusty and useless.  This crack-up
may come with rather surprising suddenness, as the realization sometimes comes to a prizefighter that he has no more
fights remaining in him.

What is left?  There may be some job around the office
where the strain is less, where there is little or no responsibility, and where the man's experience may be useful.  Or
maybe there's a copy-reading job open in Albany, or an
easy political post in Washington.  Again, he may put on
his hat and go out into the street to join all the other dere-
licts who have been shriveled and battered in the quick
passing of the ruthless years.

Some of these wornout gaffers pass their old age boring
helpless listeners with tales of how good they were in the
days when there were giants in journalism.  Others putter
around in gardens, and the great stories of yesterday, which
once were so urgently important and so exciting with life,
now seem dim and pale.  The memory of the throbbing
office—the incessant ringing of the telephones, the daily
attempts to keep the office boys awake, the clean inky
smell of the fresh edition just off the press, the practical
jokes on the office half-wit, the crusade for some cause
which at the time was like another Holy War, the parade
of freaks and fakers and mountebanks, the complaints and

libel suits, the reporters who got drunk and couldn't write their stories, the campaign to get a $5 a week raise for a deserving reporter with a wife and too many children, the pictures with the wrong captions, the tense speed of election night, the patient drive to instill a few sensible "don'ts" into the heads of the young men—all grow indistinct and without meaning.

And yet, while he is at it, the city editor has one of the best jobs which journalism has to offer. He can mar his paper, or help make it great. There are dull stretches, but usually there is not time to do all the things that cry for doing. The job is run by organization, but it must be, in some aspects, unconventional, for news itself is unconventional. The opportunities for kindness or cruelty, high professional competence and stupidity, are almost without limit. There are, also, sweet satisfactions.

Men who have run the city desk on newspapers have come in widely different make-up. Some have been inclined to snarl or lose their tempers; others are thoughtful, polite or even soft. Some drive themselves without mercy, and seem to stand it through the years; others, more's the pity, are lazy, poorly informed and ineffectual. However, the fictional conception of the city editor, despite the occasional character suggested by one of the more famous bosses, is generally wrong.

Most city editors are curiously anonymous; their names are known to few outside of newspaper offices. They do their work without bluster or ostentation. For example, in New York the city editor of the *Times* is the gentle David Joseph, who has been known to write poetry; the city editor of the *Sun* is the unfailingly reasonable and thoughtful Edmund Bartnett, who studied for the priesthood; and the city editor of the *World-Telegram* is the serious-minded Burnett Olcott McAnney, who is so polite that when he gives an assignment to a reporter it seems he is doing all but apologize for troubling him.

This is not to suggest that there have not been two-fisted, roaring, tough Simon Legrees; there have been, and their like will come again. But the growth of urbanity has made inroads on the temperament and manners of the city desk. Sometimes, it may be, there is too much politeness and consideration. The moderns may be at times too soft for the good of the business. The "good fellows" can overdo it.

The classic example of the cold, efficient, city editor is, of course, the late Charles E. Chapin, who died in 1930 in Sing Sing Prison, where he had been sent after he had shot and killed his wife, Nellie Beebe Chapin, as she lay asleep in their hotel room in New York. Today, men who develop traits and methods similar to his are said to be marked with "the Chapin stigmata."

He was rather generally hated in the office of the *Evening World,* which he ruled with more power than most city editors have, but his professional ability was respected, and with good reason. The oldest story of him is of how Irvin S. Cobb, then on the staff, heard that Chapin was ill and looked up from his typewriter to remark, "I trust it's nothing trivial."

Some of the survivors of the Chapin days on the *Evening World* still speak of him with mingled awe and hatred. Up to the time of his death in 1934, Lindsay Denison (sometimes spelled Lindsey Dennison and with many other variations), who was an outstanding reporter and rewrite man under Chapin, could not hear the mention of the malevolent man's name without glowering, working his jaws and muttering hoarse imprecations.

Chapin had a cold, objective attitude toward his own work. Nevertheless, his viewpoint had more than a little sound sense to it. He said of newspaper men: "They give all that is in them to the service of their employers and when they are old and worn out they are cast adrift like battered wrecks. Some find a brief haven in an obscure political job, to be again turned adrift with the next administration. I shudder at the thought of what may come to them after that. The luckier ones die young. Few remain actively in harness as long as I did."

Perhaps it was the dread of being cast loose in his old age which caused Chapin to beg his few well-wishers not to attempt to obtain a pardon for him. They probably could have freed him. He was a most docile, helpful and industrious prisoner, and his garden at Sing Sing was a spot of beauty and peace. Just before he died Warden Lewis E. Lawes visited him. "Do you want anything?"

"Yes," said Chapin, forthright to the end. "I want to die. I want to get it over with."

It is probable that Chapin was slightly deranged even before he killed his wife. He was a sadist, though he punished himself as much as anyone else. Of himself he said:

"I was boss of the office for more than twenty years and most of the men on the staff worked shoulder to shoulder with me for periods ranging from five to twenty-five years, and few ever resigned, although there was not a man among them who would not have been welcomed in almost every other newspaper office in the city. You constantly heard of crack men leaving good jobs to work under Chapin, but you seldom heard of one leaving Chapin unless he was fired. And in all those twenty years I never saw or spoke to a member of the staff outside the office or talked with them in the office about anything except the business of the minute. I gave no confidences, I invited none. I was myself a machine, and the men I worked with were cogs. The human element never entered into the scheme of getting out the paper. It was my way of doing things. That it was not a bad way is proven by the fact that I stayed in my job for twenty years and was the highest salaried city editor on earth. I used to fire the boys for being late, or making up bum lies, or falling down on a story. But I never fired a man for being drunk or getting in a personal jam."

Chapin as city editor fired 108 men. He had one of the most brilliant staffs ever assembled, but he did not hire cubs, as some of the other papers did, and train them. He let the other editors do the training, and then he would offer them so much more money that they would jump to the *Evening World*. Of this system, Frank Ward O'Malley said: "Charlie Chapin always had his eye open for talent so thoroughly recognized that it was simply smeared with fame by the time Charlie began to send letters and personal couriers with the request that the talent 'drop in some day and talk things over.'"

He had no patience with amateurs, incompetents or bunglers. He knew his job and expected the men to know theirs. He could spot a four-flusher at a great distance, and he prided himself on the variety of ways in which he fired men. Once a reporter was late telephoning a story. Chapin barked at him: "Your name is Smith, is it? You say you work for the *Evening World*, do you? You're a liar. Smith stopped working for the *Evening World* an hour ago."

A reporter who was late for work told Chapin a complicated story of having scalded his foot in the bathtub. A few days later Chapin fired the reporter, explaining, "I would have fired you earlier but I wanted to see how long you could keep on faking that limp." A young man asked Chapin "what to do next" while he was covering a big fire. "Go pick the hottest place and jump into it," advised the tyrant. Sometimes, however, he fired people without meaning to. The old-timers could tell when a "firing" was real and paid no attention to the other kind. One younger man took Chapin at his word when the great man told him he was fired, and did not report at the office next day. He received a telegram from Chapin saying, "If you are not back at work by Thursday morning, you are fired."

It was difficult to fool the old man. Once the Criminal Courts reporter missed a ferry from Staten Island and telephoned the office from the ferry house at 9 A.M., reporting that he was on the job at the courthouse. "Cover the flood," ordered Chapin. "What flood?" "There must be a terrible flood at the Criminal Courts building," said Chapin. "I can hear the boats whistling."

Chapin was a good but cantankerous judge of writing. He once fired a man for using the word "questionnaire," which at that time had not been admitted to the dictionary. On another occasion a reporter, writing of the finding of a body floating in the East River, referred to "the melancholy waters." "Pretty good phrase, that," said Chapin. He was overheard; thereafter, for days, the Harlem River, the Gowanus Canal and Spuyten Duyvil all developed "melancholy waters." Chapin issued a warning that the next man who used the phrase would be fired. A young reporter, Dwight Perrin, who later became city editor of the *Tribune* and after that assistant managing editor of the St. Louis *Post-Dispatch,* had not heard of the warning, and the next day his first story was of a suicide whose body had been picked up in the Hudson. Perrin started his article, "The melancholy waters of the Hudson—" Chapin was furious. "You're fired," he said. " 'Melancholy waters'! Now, look here, in all sense how could the waters of the Hudson be melancholy?"

"Perhaps," suggested Perrin, "it was because they had just gone past Yonkers."

"Not bad," said Chapin. "You're hired."

His nature was inexplicable. He hung a "Do not Disturb" sign outside the room where his wife lay murdered. While in the Tombs he criticized violently the way in which the newspapers had handled the stories of his crime. "What's the newspaper business coming to?" he wanted to

know.  Once, when his perspicacity had caused the arrest
of Gaston B. Means on a murder charge, he rubbed his
hands together; some one remarked that he seemed to be
feeling his oats.  "Why shouldn't I be happy?" asked the
spirit of sweetness and light.  "I've started a man on his
way to the electric chair."

Chapin had known bitter poverty in his youth.  He
worked himself up by sheer nerve and ability, asking no
favors and giving none.  Whatever may have been wrong
with this creature, so hard and so twisted, he was profes-
sionally competent, and probably would be today if he
were alive and sitting at the city desk of a metropolitan newspaper.  Quite possibly, viewed as a machine, he
was the ablest city editor who ever lived.

Of another stripe but the same period was Arthur
Greaves, who was city editor of the *Times* from 1900 until
his death in 1915.  Greaves could be hard-boiled and hard-
hitting, but ordinarily he was amiable.  Newspaper men
respected Chapin and hated him; they respected Greaves
and loved him.  His period on the city desk of the *Times*
was one of the greatest for that newspaper.  The almost
legendary Carr V. Van Anda was managing editor.  Ex-
pansion of news-gathering facilities was going ahead
rapidly.  There was much intelligent selectivity; enterprise
was sought always; a "beat" meant more than it usually
means today.

Greaves was born in Wales and came to America in
1871.  He went to school in Hartford, Conn., sold papers
on the street, and at the age of 13 studied stenography.  At
16 he was secretary to the president of the Fitchburg Railroad at $35 a week.  He quit and went to work as a re-
porter on the Boston *Globe* at $7 a week.  He joined the
*Times* staff in 1888 as a reporter, and three years later he
went to the *World*.  He was one of the best reporters in
the city; his knowledge of shorthand made him valuable
at important trials and hearings, and in covering the doings

of Theodore Roosevelt, who was baring his teeth and growling at Police Headquarters. Greaves's shorthand notes were sometimes useful in convincing Roosevelt that he had not been misquoted—one of the common complaints of the future President when he realized that what he had said might not have been politic.

After Greaves became city editor of the *Times* he headed the staff of reporters which that paper sent to political conventions. He remained, even on the desk, a good reporter. He understood all the difficulties, and was agreeable to work for. An illuminating anecdote is of a reporter, sent out on a story by Greaves, who did not report back to the office that night, or the next day, or for two whole years. One morning the long-absent reporter came into the office, determined to apologize to Greaves and, if possible, to get his job back. The reporter was sitting by the city desk when Greaves came to work. Without showing the least surprise, Greaves said pleasantly: "What the deuce are you doing here on your day off?" The man was back at work the next day. Greaves never mentioned the two years' absence.

Instead of scarifying a man with abuse, Greaves was a master of the gentle rebuke. He once suspected a ship news reporter of spending very little time on the job, and of devoting most of his talents to selling real estate in the Rockaways. One day when the reporter telephoned to report that he was at work, Greaves asked casually if he would stop by a certain steamship office, collect a parcel for him and bring it immediately to the *Times* office. The reporter confessed that he was not at the barge office, but at the Rockaways. "I thought so," said Greaves. That was all. He felt that the exposure of the fraud would be sufficient punishment and warning for the time being. This method usually worked.

Among newspaper men the old New York morning *Sun* is regarded as one of the eternal glories of journalism.

In its most glamorous era, its local news was in charge of George Barry Mallon as city editor and Selah Merrill Clarke, the beloved "Boss" Clarke, as night city editor. They formed a team which worked together in sympathy, without friction. The paper they helped produce may not have been as great as sentimental old codgers think it was, but it was undeniably good.

"Gentle George" Mallon, who had a face like the topographical layout of Ireland, was distinguished not only by his education and professional ability but by his friendly, soft-spoken manner. He made thousands of friends. During his régime the *Sun* became like a gentleman's club. Among the men on the staff during his time, and to whom he served as guide and adviser, were Samuel Hopkins Adams, Will Irwin, A. E. Thomas, Albert W. Atwood, Robert Welles Ritchie, Henry James Forman, Edward W. Townsend, who wrote the "Chimmie Fadden" stuff, and Frank M. O'Brien, who later became editor.

There are few stories about Mallon. He was not the sort of man about whom legends of brutality or freakishness or startling coups grow up. He was city editor from 1903 until 1912. He left to become literary adviser of the Butterick Publishing Company. From the end of the war until his death in 1928 he was in charge of publicity and advertising for the Bankers Trust Company. As president of the Dutch Treat Club he continued his associations with writers, artists, editors and playwrights. He was a graceful and witty speaker, and became a conspicuous citizen of New York.

Of different cast was the night man, "Boss" Clarke. Stories about him are endless. He was night city editor from 1881 until 1912, so long, indeed, that it seemed that no one else ever had held that job or would ever hold it. He died in 1931. In his old age he passed his time reading and making sun-dials for his neighbors. In the long years of his retirement he was not forgotten by

his old colleagues, nor were young men allowed for long
to go ignorant of the reputation that Clarke had, which is
now firmly embedded in tradition, of being the best han-
dler of news that the business ever saw.
Clarke was dignified, modest to the point of eccentricity,
amazing in his knowledge, friendly, but never a mixer.
His memory was remarkable. He had a gift of knowing
instantly the right word. His deft touches lifted stories
out of the ordinary. He never hesitated; when he wrote a
headline it was a *Sun* masterpiece. He handled the living
language, and was not afraid to use a word or a phrase
merely because it was unusual. His pencil slew a million
clichés.
He never lost his enthusiasm. He always got excited.
He would pace up and down in front of a telephone booth
where a rewrite man was taking a story, and finally would
jerk open the door and demand, "Well, well, what does he
say?" When a fire engine went past he could not relax
until he had located the fire.
"Boss" Clarke was a large man with a drooping, slender
mustache, frosty eyes and an abrupt manner which was
likely to terrify a young reporter. He smoked a pipe with
a long, curved stem. He used to get up twenty or thirty
times a night, push his glasses on the top of his forehead
and walk the length of the city room for a drink of water.
In his spare time he would puzzle over intricate mathe-
matical problems, make tiny designs on paper and then
throw them away. He would lay aside everything to read
the comic sections. He was never five minutes late or
early, reporting for work at 5 P.M. and remaining at his
desk by the window on the second floor of the old *Sun*
building at 170 Nassau Street until 1:30 A.M. He always
carried an umbrella. He knew the city thoroughly, but
no one seemed to know what he did when he was not
working. He never married.
He was embarrassed but pleased when the staff gave him

a new pipe. In 1917 the Sun Alumni Association gave a dinner in his honor, but Clarke didn't attend. He barricaded himself in his home in Brooklyn, disconnected the telephone, and sent this message: "If I had a forehead of brass, I could go to a dinner in my honor, but I don't see how a common, decent man could do it, do you?"

Memory, on a job like his, always pays dividends. One night, twenty-five years after the Beecher-Tilton trial, a death notice reached his desk. Clarke said to a reporter: "Look in the file of February 6th or 7th, 1875, and I think you'll find that this man stood up and made an interruption. Write a little piece about it." The dead man had been a juror at the trial. The files confirmed Clarke's memory.

Again, after the death of Russell Sage, a reporter obtained information purporting to disclose the contents of Sage's will. In outlining the story to Clarke, the reporter mentioned the name of his informant. Clarke said: "We won't print the story. Dig out the files for June, 1899, and somewhere on the front page—I think it will be in the third or fourth column, on the first or second of June —you'll find a story telling that this man was sent to Sing Sing for forgery." He was right as usual.

When Sage was dying, the reporter assigned to the death watch returned to the office, said that Sage's physician had said he was an old friend and college classmate of Clarke's, and to "tell Selah that if there is the slightest change in Mr. Sage's condition I will call him personally on the telephone."

"He always was a damn liar," said Clarke. "You go back to the house and sit on the doorstep."

He was a thoughtful gentleman. One of the *Sun's* best reporters covered the flashy wedding of a stage beauty and a society sportsman. The ceremony had been performed by a comical Tammany alderman. The reporter wrote a gorgeous, whimsical story, or so he thought. "Just the facts of the marriage, please," said the Boss, handing the copy back to the reporter. "The two most important events in the life of a woman are her marriage and her death. Neither should be treated flippantly."

On another occasion a *Sun* reporter happened to see a fat policeman chasing a tramp at the Battery. The policeman slipped with a splash into a large puddle and the hobo escaped. No mention of the incident had been made at Police Headquarters, but the reporter came back and wrote one of those rather windy, amusing *Sun* stories.

"It's an amusing story," said Clarke, "but they read papers at Police Headquarters and this policeman may be put on trial for not reporting the escape of the tramp. Suppose we drop this classic on the floor."

Some wild men, men given to quixotic practices, have sat as city editor in the more refined Eastern cities, but most of the more fabulous characters appear to belong to the West. There was, for example, Josiah Mason Ward, who, as a young man in San Francisco, is credited by Gene Fowler, the bawdy Herodotus, with being "the man who showed Mr. Hearst how to be Mr. Hearst." Ward reached his full blossom in Denver, as city editor of the Denver *Post*, that raucous sheet owned by F. G. Bonfils and H. H. Tammen. From 1897 to 1912 this irascible, pudgy, wheezing, red-faced, snorting, hard-drinking, erudite and goatish genius made a reputation which is still remembered throughout the land by ageing reporters and copyreaders who once worked with him in Denver.

Ward, when the divine madness was upon him, would wave scissors, and his shrill voice would soar up the scale. His own handwriting was as indecipherable as Horace Greeley's, but he was a stickler for typographical accuracy. He cursed reporters who misspelled names—not merely cursed them but flew into violent rages and made highly personal remarks about the brains, the ancestry and the probable sex aberrations of the offenders.

Part of his genius as a city editor lay in his remarkable hunches. He would tell a reporter to go out to the stockyards at the south end of Denver and see what he could pick up. Just as the reporter got there the stockyards would go up in smoke. Or he would send a reporter to a certain street corner and tell him to wait there until something happened; the reporter, after waiting ten minutes, would be rewarded by having one or more men murdered before his eyes. The *Post* was famous for its eye-witness stories. He allowed reporters great leeway in writing their stories, which helped make the *Post* the highly profitable enterprise it was.

Ward was a high-powered scandalmonger, scenting scandal in circumstances which on the surface might seem perfectly innocent. His conception of a first-rate sex story was implied in his favorite order: "God damn it, give me something with lace on it."

He had a terrible temper, and was unreasonable, but five minutes after reviling a reporter Ward would buy him a drink. He is said to have kept a cub reporter, Bobby Beers, around as a sort of whipping boy. After a stormy session with Bonfils, Ward would waddle into the city room and fire Bobby Beers. Sometimes Beers would be fired four or five times a day, but it never worried him. He would go out and have a few drinks and come back to work. Ward would have been most remorseful if Beers had taken any of these discharges seriously.

In his early San Francisco days, when he was city editor of the *Examiner,* Ward printed a shocking, libelous story concerning a divorce case. The man in the case marched into Ward's office, brandishing a revolver and screaming threats couched in words which only James Joyce appears able to get into print. Ward said: "Wait a minute. This is a hell of a way for a man to die—without a drink. Won't you let me have just a short time before you shoot me?" The agitated Lothario agreed and they went next

door to the saloon. They ordered whisky and the bartender set the bottle on the bar. Ward raised it as if to pour
a drink, then suddenly whirled and walloped the would-be
killer across the bridge of the nose with the bottle. The
man sank to the floor. Ward took the revolver away from
him, pocketed it and said, "Come on, old man; let's have a
drink on this." They had many drinks. Before the day
was over they were drinking not only to the health of the
woman in the case but to each other's health. It was the
start of a fine, pure friendship.

For some reason difficult to fathom, the most romantic
and talkative reporters in America, it appears, either work
in Chicago or once worked there. They dilate upon
the outlandish practices of Chicago newspaperdom, of
Homeric feats of reporting which resulted in epoch-
making "beats," of stealing pictures, snipping telephone
wires and outwitting the enemy. Wherever they discuss
these exciting matters they always mention the name of
Walter Howey, who cut a wide swath in Chicago newspaper work. Howey for several years has made his headquarters in New York, where he is head of Hearst's picture
service, an expert on engraving processes, and editor (by
telephone) of the Boston *Record*. Many years have passed
since his astonishing Chicago days. When he was making
history he was both brilliant and wild.

After working on papers in Fort Dodge and Des Moines,
Iowa, Howey headed for New York, but lack of money
forced him to stop in Chicago. He went to the office of
the *Daily News* and asked Henry Justin Smith for a job.
Smith said they could use a reporter who knew the town,
and asked if Howey was familiar with Chicago.

"Sure, I know it like a book," said Howey.

"Well, how long would you allow to get from here to
the intersection of Jackson and Washington Boulevards?"

"About ten minutes."

Howey saw Smith's look of surprise and added: "I'm a pretty fast runner, you know."

"Well," said Smith, "you run down there and call me up when you arrive. If you can do it in twenty minutes I'll give you the job."

Outside, Howey approached the nearest policeman, asked where Jackson and Washington Boulevards met, and received the sad information that those two thoroughfares never met. Howey went back and confessed to Smith, who gave him a note which landed him a job on the Chicago *City Press,* a cooperative news gathering organization.

Howey was returning from his first assignment, a trivial hearing, on the afternoon of December 30, 1903, when the manholes in his path began to spout fairies and knights in armor. "We're getting away from the fire," explained a knight, "and came underground from the theater." It was the Iroquois Theater fire, in which 602 persons died. Howey called his office and then went to work. He purchased the rights to the sole use of a telephone for $5 and began getting facts. It was the biggest news story in all Chicago's history, and Howey was the first man on the spot. He distinguished himself. Of this he says:

"It shows how lucky I was. I was always lucky. Jobs, stories and everything fell into my lap. I never was really clever."

Howey worked on the Chicago *American,* the *Examiner,* the *Inter-Ocean,* and in 1908 became city editor of the Chicago *Tribune* under the great and well-loved James Keeley, who began life in the slums of the Whitechapel district of London, and who died in 1934 after serving for years as a vice-president of the Pullman Company. On the *Tribune* Howey became famous for his reckless energy, stunts of colossal impudence, and stories which seemed to be almost the fruits of divination.

A robber boarded a mail car, stuck up the clerks, took $1,000,000, stuffed it into a suitcase and when the train

slowed down at the Englewood station jumped off and disappeared in the darkness. The reporters got the facts and
went to their offices. Then a flash came in from another
part of town, five miles away, that a policeman had been
shot while attempting to arrest a man. "That's the guy!"
shouted Howey, and sent a detachment of reporters to
cover what ordinarily would have been a small, routine
assignment. It was the mail robber, all right, and the
*Tribune* reporters were able to witness the capture of the
man, by 200 policemen, and give Howey a great beat.
Later that night Howey was asked how he had guessed the
man who shot the policeman was the robber. Howey explained that, in the first meager flash of news from the
shooting, he noticed the policeman had said that the man
who shot him carried a suitcase. The editor assumed, correctly, that this suitcase carried the stolen money. Carrying such a treasure, a man naturally would shoot when
stopped by a policeman.

Later, Howey, after a tiff with Joseph Medill Patterson
of the *Tribune,* went to Hearst's *Herald-Examiner,* where
he put all his ingenuity into battling his old paper. For a
few years after 1917 he was managing editor of the
*Herald-Examiner.* The men who knew his work in Chicago, including Burton Rascoe, the critic, and Charles
MacArthur, the playwright, who worked with him, agree
that he was a tornado when in action. MacArthur calls
him the greatest editor he ever knew, and adds that, while
editor, he was the best reporter on the staff, which is one
test of competence, for too many men on city desks forget that they ever were reporters. Indeed, some of them
never were. They were mere clerks.

Howey was, and still is, temperamental, argumentative
and full of rowdy spirits. MacArthur recalls that in the
old Chicago days he and Howey used to go out together
after work, drink all night and throw cantaloupes at
strange people until 8 A.M. Back at the office, Howey,

feeling that he might be getting too intimate with his staff, would abuse MacArthur and rewrite all his copy.

It is quite possible that some of the old Howey vigor and imagination, with a touch of the "get-that-story-or-else" spirit, would be a godsend to any sedate paper which is piddling along unable to distinguish between energy and bad taste. Howey and those of his school may not have been burdened with ethics, but they were lively.

The job of city editor is a little less piratical and adventurous than in the old days. The machinery is faster. The staffs are larger, the organization more orderly. Crusading has died down, partly because readers suspect the motives of a paper which beats its breast, as they suspect a yammering bogus evangelist.

Competition between newspapers, although always present, is not outwardly the blazing vendetta that it used to be. An exclusive story, important enough now, remains exclusive only a little while, and soon means little either in circulation or prestige. And yet the man on the city desk, despite all the changes, has what is in many respects the best position in all of journalism. He deals with strange and ever-shifting material. The show has its dreary interludes, but it is never quite the same. If he wants to work, or if he really has ideas, he can find a full outlet on almost any paper. The grandstand from which he watches the parade, it must be, affords the most nearly complete and certainly the most amusing view. His power, to develop men or to injure them, is enormous, and must continue to be as long as newspapers are run according to the present system.

He may compare himself with the manager of a baseball team, impresario of a road show, the driver of a mule team, a school teacher hammering knowledge into the backwoods crackers, an overworked and underpaid hangman, the boss of a chain gang, a priest with a parish in Hell's Kitchen—in whatever fashion he tries to rationalize his position and explain why he does this and why he does that, the truth remains that his best reward lies in the knowledge that he has seen a magnificent performance of buffoons and sinners, stuffed shirts and brave saints.

"You meet such interesting people." Well, except for the bores and the swine, who sometimes hold a clear 51 per cent of the voting stock, or perhaps more, that's probably as true as anything can be in a world of yes and no, where even the Ten Commandments may be questioned on the grounds of public policy.

# FASHIONS IN NEWS

PROBABLY there can be no exact definition of news. It is more unpredictable than the winds. Sometimes it is the repetition, with new characters, of tales as old as the pyramids, and again it may be almost wholly outside the common experiences, as when a detective encounters a Chinese panhandler.

It was Amos Cummings, one of Dana's great editors (not Mr. Dana himself, as many historians believe), who gave to journalism the "man bites dog" illustration of what is news. But Mr. Cummings's aphorism leaves much ground uncovered. Not necessarily does the sharp departure from routine make news. Sometimes the opposite is true, and the normal man, one of the army of Caspar Milquetoasts, who has lived his life entirely by rote, may find, sometimes on his eightieth birthday, that his very dullness is remarkable.

News is as hard to hold as quicksilver, and it fades more rapidly than any morning glory. But, for all that, it is the best yardstick we have to hold up against the growth and decay of human lives and human ideas. It is a sounding board, employed by ordinarily well-meaning newspaper men, on which the love-calls and the prayers, the whines of meanness and the trumpets of glory, receive their test. It is cheap and worthless stuff, and it is the sinews of history.

For the craftsmen who assemble and arrange the news, it is something else; for all of them, unless they are misfits or dullards, it is like a slightly daft but compelling woman —sometimes vampire, sometimes a dancing and laughing girl, now a harridan of a wife with whom there is no peace, and again a jolly, croaking slattern. Those who have lived and fought with the flighty strumpet are never quite the same again. Even when they reach a spavined and drooling senescence, they remember her, and their sleep is troubled by visions that never can quite be recaptured— of such things as the funeral of Buffalo Bill, of the horrible day when the excursion boat *General Slocum* went down, of the incredulous look on big Willard's face when Dempsey hit him, of Darrow pleading for Bill Haywood, of Arnold Rothstein sitting in a restaurant before he went to his death, and a thousand other things which at one time, when the news was white-hot, seemed terribly important. That is why old gaffers say, proudly and sadly, "I used to be a newspaper man myself."

The handlers of the news come in many stripes, just as their news comes. Some are fast, nervous men, all pride of craftsmanship and no conscience, and others are thinkers, who sometimes wonder why they do thus and so. Few are heroes, and few expect much appreciation. When their business is praised by such a man as Lord Hewart, Lord Chief Justice of England, they are likely to dismiss the compliment with a grunt. Said Lord Hewart:

"In a country that enjoys, or has, or is supposed to have, representative institutions the newspaper is, of course, a necessity. It is not any the worse for that. But do we always think as gratefully, or indeed as justly, as we might of the amazing ability, diligence, care and learning, the wit, the humor, the skill and the versatility, the dutifulness, the courage, the conscientiousness, and the sheer hard work which go to the making of the best kind of newspaper?"

The newspaper man's thought is: "Thanks, my Lord, but the boys don't do their work half well enough." They fumble. They allow errors, some of them inexcusable, to slip by even when they feel that the machinery is as nearly perfect as it can be. They are sometimes dreadfully short-sighted; again they are careless, unfair, hampered by childish policies and outworn theories.

The best workmen learn to recognize news, of course, not by painful definition, but by intuition. They recognize it at a glance, as easily as a physician recognizes a man with a cirrhotic liver. Give a night news editor on a morning paper the gist of the ten or fifteen most important news items, and he can draw a diagram of his front page in less than two minutes. If you asked him why he had been so sure of his judgment of the relative value of the items, he would either say he didn't know, that it was merely his opinion based upon his own reactions, or he would launch into a long, halting explanation which would really explain very little.

To be sure, the judge of news values—managing editor, night editor or city editor—is often wrong, and must revise his decisions, but he would be just as often wrong if he sought to analyze carefully the social importance, the psychological effect or the disruptive possibilities of each item. The business can't be done with charts and graphs; at any rate, it never has been done that way.

What is news to the editor is news to the citizen. In its more spectacular manifestations, news may be identified as easily by the man in the subway as by the editor with the green eyeshade. It is news when Charles A. Lindbergh flies the Atlantic, and when his baby son is kidnaped. It is news when a *Titanic* or a *Lusitania* goes down. It is news when the mayor of a great city, finding himself hemmed in and facing an unpleasant doom, decides to quit. It is news when a nerveless man-hunter and his companions send a volley into Clyde Barrow and Bonnie Parker. It is news when an heir is born to a great fortune or a throne, and it is news when a Togo or a Mrs. Cornelius Vanderbilt or a James J. Corbett lies down to die. It is news when the earth shakes and cities are ruined. It is news when an Ehrlich finds his silver bullet for syphilis, and every advance in the study of the nature of cancer is news—as, some day, the conquering of cancer may provide a news story greater than the declaration of a war.

Such material obviously is news of the first rank. It furnishes the best-remembered stories. It is in this field, the field of the obvious, that most great newspapers spend most of their money and energy and professional diligence. But there is another field, a misty frontier, a journalistic No Man's Land, that lies between what obviously is important news and what certainly is not news. It is in this Gran Chaco of newspaperdom that papers make themselves foolish or brilliant; here they score their immortal triumphs and their monumental stupidities. Dealing with the imponderables, the monsters which are difficult to discern in the underbrush, calls for the most acute intelligence and the most restless imagination.

In this field lie the situations, the trends, the vague forebodings, the temper and feel of a city, the slow groundswells of opinion, the premonitions of social change, the subtle changes in manners, customs and thoughts. The time comes when a newspaper editor, with all the spot news covered, the obvious well attended to, will feel that something which may be of more genuine news interest than the entire budget of Reno divorces, the bright sayings of Max Baer, the worries of the Board of Education and the annual optimistic pronunciamiento of Charles M. Schwab. Editors have been known to interpret a peculiar pain in the left knee as a hunch that some prominent man would die in a few hours. Others observing the fidgeting of a public official at a dinner, have suspected that the man was a crook and have started investigations which resulted in shocking exposures. Hunches in the field of ideas may not smack so much of black magic, but they come from random thoughts on religious movements, foreign debt payments, the workings of communism or the dissatisfaction of large groups. Is there a wide-open fault in the structure of the National Recovery program which is clearly demonstrable and which inevitably will have definite manifestations? Then that must be watched and studied. Are the labor unions dying, or will they become stronger than ever? Such matters, lying partly in the realm of news and partly in the field of disputation and opinion, sometimes must be handled on the editorial page, but not always. They may have legitimate excuse as important news. Editors who can handle such material are few; the rapid economic and social changes of the last few years, and the constant shifting of characters and beliefs, have placed a strain upon news judgment, probably a greater strain than newspapers have felt since the World War. If ever the newspaper business called for the best brains, the best professional skill, it calls for them now.

Newspapers, it may be, need to make their editorial pages even more informative than they are today. The news columns, on many papers, are far ahead of the editorial page in giving the reader a clear interpretation of what is happening. The decline in influence of the editorial has been a subject of much tearful and jocular comment. Some of the older Jeremiahs have lamented that the public cares little about the partisan calls to arms of the modern counterparts of Greeley, Watterson, Dana and the other flagellators and molders of opinion.

It might be good for the country if a leading editorial could be regarded once more as a true fragment from Sinai; but the simple circumstance remains that it isn't so regarded. It may be that the powerful, ripping editorial will come back in style; the betting among the canny seems to be against it. One strong, terse editorial, clearing away the underbrush, illuminating a subject and expressing a definite policy, may be magnificent. If there must be other editorials, why not make them authoritative, factual, carefully analytical, without screaming, frothing or special pleading—a natural supplement to the information in the news columns? Are millions swayed when Mr. Hearst advises them in a signed editorial? Perhaps; what is more likely, they pay little attention to it.

The foregoing is not to argue that a newspaper can or should be a daily *New Republic*, a recasting of Gibbon's "Decline and Fall of the Roman Empire," the collected works of Walter Lippmann, or the forebodings of Ogden L. Mills. It is merely to suggest that the stuff of history, and the materials of today, might be treated a bit more clearly and factually.

The pedants insist that a newspaper should "have live social consciousness," that it "should take a long view of current events with the eye of the historian," while presenting "a comprehensive picture of modern civilization." Doubtless true, professor, provided you don't have to worry about the probable bankruptcy of your newspaper. And yet it is curious that even the most transparent charlatans among publishers attempt, at one time or another, to rationalize what they are doing, to invent some sort of philosophy and to argue seriously (while their own employees are stifling lewd guffaws) that their work on this earth is for the public "good." A funny business, sometimes a carnival with peep shows and flea acts, and again as solemn as an unusually high-minded session of the Sanhedrin.

A few dreamers among newspaper men persist in believing that a newspaper can be as accurate as the World Almanac, as long-headed as the ablest social planner or historian, and at the same time avoid the dead hand of dullness and ponderosity. It should, above all, be alive.

Failure of newspapers to point out genuinely significant movements until these movements had become so prominent that no one could avoid their discussion, has been the subject of complaint from critics of journalism. George Bernard Shaw dropped his cap and bells long enough a few years ago to accuse newspapers of an affliction which he

called "time-lag"—that is to say, it requires too long for
papers to wake up to facts, and a revolution may have
taken place before the press has realized that it is any more
than a few bombings, stabbings and speeches. Shaw observed that the press was tardy in recognizing the news
values inherent in the experiment in Russia. Allowing for
some overstatement which may be fallen into by vege-
tarians as well as beef-eaters, he appears to have been correct. Time-lag is a real affliction.

Another news thinker, who has his moments of authentic greatness, is Dr. Nicholas Murray Butler, president of
Columbia University. Once Dr. Butler complained, with
all good nature, that the ordinary man who reads newspapers is somewhat in the plight of the man at the sea-
shore who is fascinated by the surface undulations of the
ocean but who is unable to get any clear or sensible picture
of what the ocean is really like. Dr. Butler's myopic
bather is a lineal descendant of the unfortunate spectator
who couldn't see the forest for the trees.

Many criticisms of newspapers for failing to perceive
instantly the news value of something which is outside
the routine of fires, murders, deaths and larceny, are perfectly fair, and may be backed by volumes of evidence.
For example, one evening in 1924 Dr. Butler himself, appearing at a dinner of the Missouri Society in New York,
delivered a remarkably well reasoned and eloquent de-
nunciation of the Eighteenth Amendment.

It seems a long time ago, but the Butler speech was
made at a time when few Americans appeared to have
any genuine hope that the prohibition law would be re-
pealed before many decades had passed, if ever. Moreover, any man who spoke against prohibition thereby set
himself up as a target for the stink-bombs of the Anti-
Saloon League and the other associations of bluenoses.
Even Alfred E. Smith, usually outspoken, let years pass

without making any clear-cut statement opposing the Eighteenth Amendment.

A few of the papers recognized that the Missouri Society speech of Dr. Butler was something of vastly more significance than the ordinary after-dinner fulminations of an educator. For the most part, however, they were slow in appraising it for what it was—a masterly indictment by a far-seeing and immensely courageous man. Curiously, that speech may have been the real beginning of respectable opposition to prohibition; certainly from that night on Dr. Butler, though attacked by all the squirt-guns in the dry arsenal, grew steadily in the popular esteem. People used to smile at the sayings of the good doctor, but no more. He came to be regarded as a blown-in-the-bottle sage.

The argument, of course, is made constantly by the professors and soul-searchers of journalism that newspapers, even those of dignity, are inclined to favor the sensational but intrinsically unimportant news rather than news which has a vital relation to the welfare of the human race. Often the objectors are right, but sometimes the charges are made without looking closely into the evidence.

For example, there is the belief, held so widely that it is almost a part of the American credo, that Dr. Charles W. Eliot, president-emeritus of Harvard University, and Rudolph Valentino, the motion picture sheik, died at the same time, and that the American newspapers turned over their front pages to the news of the passing of the motion picture actor and consigned the news of Dr. Eliot to relatively obscure pages. There was supposed to have been something faintly anti-social, even immoral, in such a lopsided display.

The facts, however, put a somewhat different light on the case. Dr. Eliot died on Sunday, August 22, 1926, at Northeast Harbor, Maine. In their Monday morning editions both the New York *Times* and the New York *Herald*

*Tribune,* to mention only two of many newspapers throughout the country, gave the news of the death of Dr. Eliot the preferred position on the first page, and even a few sensational newspapers adjudged the news to be of interest. The *Herald Tribune* had a two-column headline, with a regulation photograph of Dr. Eliot with whiskers, on the right hand side of the front page. In their Tuesday morning editions the *Times* and the *Herald Tribune* each allowed a column, on the inside pages, naturally enough, for an account of the Eliot funeral plans.

Although it had been known on Sunday that Valentino was critically ill, the actor did not die until Monday, August 23, at 12:10 P.M. Some of the earlier editions of the afternoon papers still thought enough of the passing of Dr. Eliot to place the news on page one, although they merely duplicated the full accounts of the morning papers. When Valentino died the afternoon papers, with perfectly sound judgment, removed the Eliot item to an inside page and let the news of the more recent death occupy the preferred spot on the front page.

The tabloids, of course, which were never renowned for their restraint, indulged in a magnificent orgy of stallion-like headlines, sobbing chronicles of the life and death of the actor, and as many photographs of the hero, alive and dead, as the traffic would bear. It was as if the death of Valentino must mean the abandonment of all hope by American womanhood. The tabloids, for all their sensationalism, were justified in their news play of the death. If they had any doubts about its news value, they were sure they were right when they observed the grotesque scenes at Frank E. Campbell's undertaking temple, where hordes of pushing, hysterical women sought one last look at the classic features of the amiable Italian.

And yet, somewhere in the Eliot-Valentino legend, there may lie an issue. Suppose Dr. Eliot and Valentino had died unexpectedly, at the same hour, and the newspapers had found themselves confronted with the necessity of deciding which was the more important as news. It is probable that most of the so-called respectable newspapers of standard size would have given them about equal prominence on the first page.

However, a good argument could have been made by a conservative newspaper for regarding the death of the actor as of the greater interest, even of the greater importance. Dr. Eliot had not been active in the affairs of the world for a good many years, and most people, particularly the younger generation, thought of him, if they thought of him at all, merely as an old gentleman with sideburns who once had selected a five-foot shelf of books. On the other hand, Valentino had made himself into a symbol of something or other. This circumstance might have seemed deplorable to an editorial writer who had long ago seen his own well-springs of romance dry up, but, deplorable or not, it was true.

Indeed, the tabloids and sensational papers have had a good effect upon the rest of the press, forcing them to print more photographs and more news of interest to people—not what some Olympian may think ought to interest the people. Likewise, in most cities where Mr. Hearst has a newspaper, the opposition paper or papers tend to become better. The Hearst paper might not be a great paper, but usually it prevents the others from becoming insufferably stodgy and lazy. Mr. Hearst has performed meritorious service in jolting his rivals out of a lethargy which often is a part of their natures.

Another common complaint against newspapers, particularly against the more wide-awake ones, is that they are unduly sensational in their handling of crime news—that such items, as frequently presented, may be an incentive to crime, that they present a picture of civilization which is out of focus, and that they are evidence of a desire to pander to the cheap surface emotions of the herd mind.

Much of this is arrant balderdash. The truth is that the more complete, factual and mercilessly accurate the account of a crime, the better the newspaper.

In the first place, crime news is not solely the concern of low-grade morons. It is of just as much interest and importance to the most respectable and highly intelligent people. This interest may be justified, if necessary, on the ground either of social significance, community safety, entertainment, or sheer curiosity.

If the youth of the country, reading the facts of the St. Valentine's Day massacre in Chicago, is tempted to purchase machine guns and begin firing, then there is little hope for American youth. One might as well have argued the stories of prohibition graft should not have been printed, on the ground that it would give some people an idea of how to make easy money.

In some instances it has been shown rather conclusively that a few books and motion pictures, which have made heroes out of gangsters, have furnished the suggestion which impelled an already emotionally unstable youth to commit some dreadful crime. Most criminals who blame a book, a picture or a newspaper, however, do so merely to divert attention from their own cussedness and lack of balance and to gain public sympathy. Was Nietzsche to blame for the monstrous Loeb and Leopold crime? Hardly. When the whole records of the twisted personalities of these two fiends were brought out in court, poor old Nietzsche could plead a pretty convincing alibi.

Almost always crime news—complete and even blatant —is necessary before any serious move for reform is ever attempted. A false sense of civic pride has caused many newspapers, particularly in towns where the booster spirit is rampant, to ignore or "play down" crime news which they fear will give the tender, growing community a bad name. Even Chicago is extremely sensitive about its reputation as a shooting preserve for hellions, and the citizens of Memphis choke and turn purple when the city's high homicide rate is mentioned.

Without publicity it is doubtful if Alphonse Capone ever would have been sent to prison. It is axiomatic among all intelligent criminals that all publicity is bad publicity for them. The accounts of Capone's activities and the explanations of his intricate system of racketeering, set forth sometimes rather flamboyantly, to be sure, made the man a high and shining mark of evil—so challenging to law and order that it is said Herbert Hoover himself, while President, set in motion the machinery which finally brought the great entrepreneur low.

This is not to suggest that the newspaper men who wrote of Capone's doings were consecrated to the public service or were burning with a holy, crusading zeal. They were simply news men who appraised the Capone empire as a paradise of absorbing news stories. Few news gatherers seethe with indignation at the sight of evil. They take little punishment in the psychic regions. They can't afford to. The newspaper man who takes the moral lessons too much to heart is likely to shake himself to pieces, or even to turn editorial writer.

The most telling criticism of the usual handling of crime news by the American press (the British press, by the way, is incomparably worse, despite the common Yankee belief that all English newspapers are as dignified as Queen Mary on parade) may be made on the grounds of craftsmanship. That is to say, the American police reporter often produces dreadfully incompetent work; to disguise his failure to obtain details, he fakes, sobs and gasps to produce a spurious effect, hinting at sinister mysteries which do not exist and building up horrendous, ghostly criminal overlords who, when examined realistically, turn out to be flyweight Jesse Jameses.

The tabloids and the more sensational press are the principal offenders against the realistic treatment of crime news, but the others are far from perfect. It should be possible for any newspaper to print the straight, simple and sometimes moving details of a crime story, without losing any of the entertainment value. A story of a murder or a robbery, even when embellished with photographs of a cigar-smoking gun moll with her legs crossed, rarely suffers from too many cool, honest facts.

Among the best examples of crime stories since the war have been a few which drew their strength from their unabashed and unadorned detail. Sometimes they lay a bit outside the usual conception of "spot news." There was, for example, the painstaking, unemotional report of the woman probation officer who investigated the background and ups and downs of Celia Cooney, the original bobbed-hair bandit who, with her husband, terrorized Brooklyn shopkeepers in the middle 1920s. Mrs. Cooney's girlhood had not been passed with what is usually called the advantages. Indeed, it had been pretty tough. The New York *World* obtained the text of the report on her life and printed it under a separate headline, without comment. It was infinitely more interesting than one of those amazing layouts of composite pictures which Bernarr Macfadden used to run in his tabloid New York *Graphic,* and it was as matter of fact as a treasurer's report.

Another excellent example of effective, unusual treatment was offered by the New York *Times,* when Richard Reese Whittemore and his associates in crime were rounded up by the New York police. The bold deeds and rather extraordinary attainments of this aggregation of murderers and thugs were shocking enough, even on the surface, to make news of the first rank. It is said that Adolph S. Ochs, publisher of the *Times,* had been puzzled and annoyed by occasional hints that Jews were showing an increasing aptitude for the more spectacular and sinister crimes, and that he, a Jew, ordered a complete inquiry into the Whittemore gang. A group of reporters were set to digging into the past of the men, including genealogy, race, religion, home environment, schooling and every other personal detail. It made a fascinating exhibit, and the story ran for columns. It was worth every line on its news value.

Those who sneer at crime news forget that this type of material has an eternal appeal to readers, and that some newspapers have distinguished themselves in their attitude toward it. Some of the more startling crime stories in the last fifteen years—the deeds and execution of that gifted robber and gunman, Gerald Chapman; the strange Hall-Mills murder in New Jersey, which ranks high in the list of great mysteries; the grisly love story of Judd Gray and Ruth Snyder—have brought out the strength and weakness of the news judgment of newspapers.

Of course there have been instances of a newspaper mistakenly trying to keep a story alive long after its readers are tired of it. It required a long time for the tabloids, in particular, to realize that the marital and other adventures of Edward W. Browning, the New York real estate dealer known lovingly as "Daddy," and of Leonard Kip Rhinelander, who married a quadroon and then tried to get out of it, were no longer exciting. And the second investigation of the Hall-Mills murder, which resulted in a long trial, was a costly and futile undertaking, instigated by a tabloid.

Few students of the trends in news coverage of recent years have given credit to the changes, sometimes almost imperceptible to the general reader, which may be laid to the influence of the news magazine *Time* and to the *New Yorker*. These weeklies, although different in appeal, nevertheless have demonstrated what some people suspected all along—that facts, marshalled in smart, orderly fashion, can be charming. The enormous amount of honest research which goes into the making of *Time* might be studied by all newspapers; even its stylistic inventions

("Impatient last week was wiry, horse-faced Foreign Minister Joseph Doakes") have affected the writing in many
papers, sometimes but not always for the better. Its logical arrangement and classification of news is uniformly
admirable. Its publisher, Henry R. Luce, and his right-
hand man, John S. Martin, are essentially newspaper men
of the highest professional skill.

The *New Yorker,* which has been enormously successful, has demonstrated that a smart, casual style, coupled
with a sophisticated viewpoint, does anything but repel
the reader. This weekly is the product of the peculiar
genius of Harold Ross, a veteran reporter who, before becoming interested in magazines, worked on newspapers in
many parts of the country. He gives the impression,
which is deceptive, that he is scatter-brained. Actually he
is a shrewd merchant of news. He prints "Profiles" which
sometimes are models of the art of biography. The "Roving Reporter" feature often is brilliant and timely and
would not be out of place in the news columns of any daily
paper. Moreover, the *New Yorker* is admirably conscientious in checking its facts and in getting the minute, revealing details. It has made money by treating its readers,
not as pathological cases or a congregation of oafs, but as
fairly intelligent persons who want information and entertainment.

Many of the modern experiments in "going back of the
news," or of digging up material which under old-
fashioned definitions might not be considered news, have
had brilliant results. One day, a few years before the repeal of the Eighteenth Amendment, Geoffrey Parsons,
chief editorial writer of the New York *Herald Tribune,*
received a letter from a citizen of Decatur, Indiana,
remonstrating in a well-mannered fashion with the paper
for its anti-prohibition editorials. The writer argued that
the newspapers in the larger, wet cities did not realize that,
in many small towns, there was an overwhelming senti-

ment in favor of the dry law, and that the law was fairly well observed. At the suggestion of Mr. Parsons, the *Herald Tribune* sent Alva Johnston, an exceptionally well-equipped reporter, to find out what the Indiana town was really like. The next week his five-column account of the life of the town, its drinking habits and its social customs, was printed in full. It was one of the finest of all news stories; moreover, it was a sociological document with implications of national importance.

In its broad outlines news changes little, but in appearance and in emphasis of treatment it constantly changes. Most of the larger newspapers pay less attention to trivial fires, accidents and brawls than they once did. On almost all fronts there has been a gain in all the qualities that make for intelligent presentation of what the world is like.

Labor news has improved. It does not consist, as much as it used to, of blackjackings, little riots and the bluffs and chicanery of labor leaders and associations of employers. Now more attention is paid to the basic questions—unless, of course, as in the Gastonia troubles of 1929, some dramatic incident of violence lifts the situation out of the ordinary considerations of an industrial stalemate. The reports of Louis Stark of the New York *Times,* who covers most of the labor news for that paper, have been models in the reporting of that type of material.

The improvement in the reporting of legal actions, of scientific advances, of medical and religious news, has been apparent in the better papers. The reporter who doesn't know a tort from a subpœna duces tecum has no business covering the courts of law. The man who covers religious news need not be an ex-clergyman to have a sound knowledge of theology and the trends in the various denominations. Some of the men writing financial and business news—and this field has expanded immensely—bring to their tasks a keen insight into what their stuff is about. Even the Washington news, always the despair of managing editors, has shown a clear improvement in quality and completeness. Bias is less pronounced. What the newspapers may have lost in vigor by embarking on fewer crusades they have gained in fairness and confidence.

The call now, perhaps, is for even more fairness and impartiality, for an even more alert appraisal of what is happening and what is about to happen, for even more cold realism, and possibly for a broadening of interests. It may be that tomorrow newspapers will discover that there are types of news somewhere in the clash of people and ideas, which will be as revolutionary, and as profitable, as James Gordon Bennett's hunch that people would read news of society and sports.

# NOTES ON A NOBLE CALLING

THE ordinary American newspaper reporter, not many years ago, in the O. Henry era and later, was identified in the popular mind as a low and irresponsible rake with misshapen and unnatural images in his head, a flask of gin on his hip, scant carfare in his pocket, dandruff on his coat-collar, a leer in his eyes, and headed straight for Hell or Seattle. He might be well educated, but he was frittering away his time. He might have his moments of charm, but he was regarded as essentially a wastrel and, given the opportunity, a Grade-A guttersnipe. His dreams, when genius kissed him, might carry to the stars, but his feet were in the mire in some back alley.

What now? Thanks to the motion pictures, a few plays, and the antics of a handful of the gentlemen of the press in real life, the popular conception of the news-gatherer seems, if anything, a shade more scrofulous than before. Today the reporter is supposed to smash all furniture in sight when invited to a home. He prefers to climb the chandelier before beginning an interview with the Chairman of United States Steel. He gets his greatest scoops while sleeping off a drunk in some boozy haven in the red light district. He writes best on twelve Scotch highballs. He insults everybody in earshot and is rewarded handsomely for his bad manners. He is happiest and most heroic when he has been thrown down a flight of stairs. He has one wife whom he rarely sees and always mistreats, an ex-wife in Peoria who has never been able to collect alimony, and a honey in Brooklyn Heights who regards him as a misunderstood Zola. Quite a lad.

The picture is awry. Take the members of the staff
of any respectable newspaper, or even the staff of a paper
which is not so respectable, dress them up, put them at a
dinner table opposite the board of governors of the
Racquet and Tennis Club, and observe the contrast. The
club members, no offense meant, might as well be dele-
gates to a hardware convention in Des Moines—solid men,
but lacking a certain urbanity and zip.

It is told of the late Frank A. Munsey that, soon after
he had bought the New York *Sun,* he saw a distinguished-
appearing stranger leaving the editorial offices and walking down the corridor leading to the street. Mr. Munsey
stopped in his tracks and gazed, intently and admiringly,
at the retreating figure.

"Who is that man?" he asked a nearby word-painter.

"That is Reggie Wilson, a reporter on the New York
City News Association."

Mr. Munsey went to the city editor.

"Hire Wilson," he advised. "He is exactly the type of
man we want on the *Sun.*"

In this manner Reginald A. Wilson, a handsome, pre-
maturely gray Canadian, joined the morning *Sun* staff.
He remained with the property, through mergers, until
his unexpected death years later on the station platform at
Albany. Mr. Munsey, whatever his esthetic faults may
have been, liked clean things. Wilson was only one of an
endless list of personable, competent, intelligent gentlemen
who have served newspapers all over America as reporters.
Such men need no defense. They never did. They have as
much contempt as anyone for the slovenly workman, the
grafter and the cad. They practice a high art, and an
honorable one.

The trend toward a higher type of reporter began long
ago. The better newspapers always have shown a prefer-
ence for decent, educated men. But for a long time the
congenital loafers and the rum-pots continued to debauch

themselves and hamstring their papers. The job was to clear them out. The change, even since the war, has been astounding to those who have seen it at close range.

The habitual drunkards, along with an array of other misfits, have been driven out, and they have been replaced, for the most part, by younger, better educated and more enterprising men. Somehow it isn't fashionable any more, or even very amusing, to be gone on a drunk for a week when important news is breaking—or even unimportant news. Not that the modern reporter is a fanatical abstainer. Ah, dear Bishop, not at all! Reporting never was a profession for bigots. No more, drunk or sober, is ignorance a cause for boasting by a reporter.

The business (if it is a business) calls for the best. Sometimes it mistreats its best, starves them, and then throws them into the ashcan. More often it deals with infinite justice and consideration, and even goes out of the way to avoid unfairness. The job of reporter has heart-warming compensations. Sometimes it pays a living wage. Sometimes it is "a stepping stone to better things." Again it is a satisfying career in itself.

The subtle attraction of newspaper work for a young man is not new. Laugh at the printer's ink love-call, but it's real. The better papers always have encouraged the cub. In three months, usually, it would become apparent whether the youngster had any marked talent for the work. Some of the neophytes would fail. Others would go ahead and make names for themselves which are remembered today wherever newspapermen talk of the glories of the past.

The pull to the young man seems stronger today than before. Twenty and thirty years ago only three or four men a day would apply at a newspaper office in New York for jobs. Now it is a dull day when a dozen don't apply, and sometimes there are as many as fifty. The unemployment situation is responsible for part of the increase, of course, but not all of it. There were almost as many in 1928 and 1929.

Are these young men deluded? Many a newspaper man of ten, fifteen and twenty years' experience will tell the newcomer that it is all a thankless, profitless enterprise. The glamour, they say, is phoney at bottom, and in a few years the young man will become a cynic, appraising the world and his fellows with disillusioned eyes, even with bitterness. The oldsters may think they believe this, but, if they are worth their salt, they are either spoofing themselves or they should be in some other business.

The truth appears to be that most of the veterans are as fully alive to the romance and fascination of newspaper work as any cub; more, they are just as gullible, just as full of hero-worship. At the advanced age of 40 they will swallow strange potions and prostrate themselves before strange gods. When a reporter says, "I've seen a big ship go down before," or "This is a fair obituary, but I liked best the one I did on Chauncey M. Depew," or "I can't see much point to this murder; you see, I covered the Rosenthal killing," it is, perhaps, time for him to leave the city room forever.

It is a shame that, out of the thousands of potentially able recruits, so few can find a place where they will have a chance. Many of the younger men who have joined the staffs of the more solvent papers in the course of the last few years have served creditably. Usually they know more than the older men knew at their age. The fledglings often flabbergast their elders with their erudition—a scholarly but lively sense of words, a sound background in history and economics, the ability to translate or even to speak two or three foreign languages, a comprehensive knowledge of literature, and sometimes a definite expertness in art and music.

All the young man needs, granted he has a natural feeling for the work, is experience, and he can obtain that quickly. Such a man is likely to outstrip the reporter of the old school in a few years; he carries too many guns, and, if his legs are good, he can make the older man appear ridiculous. Of what avail is dexterity at the tricks of the trade, and a mass of scattering information picked up through the years, against a combination of genuine education and unlimited energy? The old reporter is in the position of an outworn champion pugilist: his only hope against the youngster is to outbox him, and the day comes when he can't do that.

Suppose a young man has an opportunity to start work on a newspaper. What can he expect? Assume that he brings to the job a thorough equipment. Assume, moreover, that he has some sympathy for the roaring comedy and the tragic foolishness of the human race, that he has a restless and searching mind, that he soaks up smells and information and significant trivia alike from the policeman on the corner and the bibliophile in his study—that is to say, assume he shows a clear talent for newspaper work.

Such a young man will find, for all the occasional dreary interludes, that he has been plumped down in the midst of the liveliest and most amusing of worlds. It is, for him, like attending some fabulous university where the humanities are studied to the accompaniment of ribald laughter, the incessant splutter of an orchestra of typewriters, the occasional clinking of glasses, and the gyrations of some of the strangest performers ever set loose by a capricious and allegedly all-wise Creator. The faculty at this fount of knowledge is so grotesque that the young man may be puzzled by the presence of mummified but helpful gnomes, slinking or boisterous yes-men, and thwarted old desk-thumpers.

Teach him anything? They can teach him almost everything. And he is being paid—not much, but something—for attending this place which is part seminary, part abattoir. If, after a few months, he doesn't enjoy

it, he should quit. The show may be better next year, but
he wouldn't appreciate it.

This is not to imply that newspaper work is not a serious
undertaking, with a high public responsibility, and that a
newspaper office should not be operated as efficiently as the
peculiar nature of the materials will permit. No business
on earth calls for more thought, or, to the pious, prayer.
No one can make it entirely honky-tonk, or entirely count-
ing house. But, if it has any life, it must be at times a
pasture where salty, jocose spirits lift their hooves and
bray. Every office needs at least one man who, though a
competent workman, understands that existence is primarily a droll affair, with the horse laugh predominant not
only to the grave, but after the will is read.

For purposes of keeping up morale and teaching the car-
dinal truths of life, any large paper could afford to hire, at
princely salary, such a man as Gene Fowler, the former
Denver and New York reporter who turned to writing
books and motion pictures; or Joel Sayre, a wandering
behemoth who went to Hollywood. Both men—Fowler,
the playful Hamlet who could bend an icepick double with
one hand and for whose safety scores of prizefighters,
wrestlers and underworld characters would give their lives,
and Sayre, the puckish ribcrusher from the jungle who can
sing old songs for twelve hours without repeating—were,
and are, excellent and learned reporters, but their value to
a paper in what might be called a priestly capacity would
be incalculable. As balloon-prickers, daubers of stuffed
shirts and philosophical pranksters such men are worth any
dozen efficiency experts. There are few things so soul-
cleansing as the sound of the seat of a chair giving way
while the synod is in full cry.

The young man fresh to journalism will find, sometimes
to his astonishment, particularly if he is a high-born child
used to coddling, that he is called upon to perform tasks
which entail almost endless drudgery—a searching for de-

tails of the most picayune sort. He must learn names and middle initials. He must know his town and its people. He must attend dull luncheons, dinners, board meetings and charity affairs. He must learn that it is possible to make at least ten mistakes in a ten-line obituary, all of them unpardonable. He will, innocently, commit crimes which make him fit fodder for the gibbet. He must learn the monotony of waiting for something to turn up, or fidgeting in the ante-room of the office of some wealthy bounder who has intimated that he may have an important statement soon.

He must learn that a few butlers are inclined to be somewhat aloof, and to console himself with the thought that he wouldn't want to be a butler. He must learn not to ask the city editor how to get to Canarsie. He must learn that the loudest-mouthed man in the office is probably the most incompetent, and that he probably won't be there long, and to discount his lectures on news values and methods, and his thoughts on why Joseph Pulitzer was not a real Liberal. He must learn all the "don'ts" and a million boring things that go to make up professional technique. He must learn, if he doesn't already know it, to avoid adjectives and to swear by the little verbs that bounce and leap and swim and cut.

What then? The young man, even if he has shown unusual aptitude, isn't paid much. The starting weekly pay, on most of the larger papers, may be $15, $20 or $25. Suppose the young man in six months or a year demonstrates that he has the qualities of an excellent newspaper reporter. He thinks he deserves a raise, and he is right. When he fails to get it he wonders whether he hasn't made a mistake. Since the beginnings of the depression in 1929 hundreds of young men have been held back because the newspaper publishers, far from raising the pay of anyone, were trying to save money. Not always has this been true; even in the worst years a few newcomers to the business have gone ahead rapidly.

Ten and fifteen years ago the outstanding reporters in New York could expect to receive from $100 to $200 a week. Those figures are considerably lower today. Six years ago the average salary for New York reporters was between $60 and $65 a week. Now it is $50, or possibly a dollar or two less. The young men in law, in medicine, or in Wall Street, likewise have found their pay decreased —if, indeed, they had any pay at all.

Most sound newspapers, and most sound newspaper men, have weathered the depression so far, right side up. The newspapers today, as always, want results, which may be a way of saying that they need reporting. The papers need fresh material, fresh treatment—even revolutionary ideas of news coverage. The managing editors and city editors cry always for better stuff. The way ahead for the young man, as well as the old, is surely as hopeful, or as dismal, as it ever was.

The more influential papers have improved. They print more news. They are fairer. Their interests have broadened enormously. Almost everything which interests any considerable group of people is news today—old furniture, bridge, flycasting, the incidence of multiple births, and even the doings of tropical fish. Reporters have almost unlimited opportunities to develop specialties. To be sure, the fundamentals are the same: get all the facts and write them clearly. Women, wampum and wrongdoing are always news.

After a short time the young man may find that he likes to report crime and police news, although most young men, more's the pity, appear to feel that this branch of reporting is distasteful. Others will become interested in municipal affairs, and will gravitate in their assignments toward City Hall or the State House. Others, with a liking for economics and finance, will find their place under the financial news editor. Still others will exhibit a knack for difficult and unusual interviews (the interview, excepting possibly society news, was perhaps the greatest invention of James Gordon Bennett) and will pass much of their time in the boudoirs of garrulous crones with memories, in old men's homes and down the bay to meet the more vigorous and breezy specimens.

Another group, always small, will be able to cover anything on the face of the earth. These rare and brilliant workmen, to whom the whole world is a pathetically defenseless oyster, are the hope of the papers. They have legs, wind, imagination, knowledge, a sleepless curiosity, and they can write the blunt Saxon tongue.

Get ahead in the business? There is no way of stopping them. These men become the greatest foreign correspondents, the great Washington correspondents, and the men who are sent first by the newspapers and the wire services whenever there is trouble, anywhere from China to the Balkans. God help them if they become upstage! They might as well go into radio, where exhibitionism pays, for the spoiled man likely will find himself assigned to Tombs Court—a good assignment, but only a soldier can take it after he has tasted the fleshpots. There must be no prima donna.

Room for ambitious local reporters is larger now than at any time since the war. For many years, after the public had come to think of the whole world as part of its own backyard, the front pages were full of cable news, and it required some appalling local catastrophe, such as the ejection of Judge Ben B. Lindsey from the Cathedral of St. John the Divine or the sighting of the first robin on Long Island, to cause much attention. For a time, in New York, not even the news of half the local and suburban homicides was printed in the leading papers. Today all homicides are printed, as religiously as the social notes, unless crowded out by exigencies of make-up. The trend, unmistakably in New York, is toward complete local coverage. Not all the peace conferences, and all the New Deals, can quite dull the mind of the reader to what is happening in his own home town. The space devoted to local news in most New York papers has increased 50 per cent in the last fifteen years.

The tragedy of many young men is that, once they have attached themselves to a payroll, they recoil shyly from mental effort. They stop learning. Between the ages of twenty-five and thirty a newspaper man should be at his best; what he acquires after that is valuable, as experience, mellowing his temper and making his judgment more acute, but the man in his twenties usually has a driving flame which is never quite recaptured. Few reporters, starting newspaper work past thirty, can hope to master its complexities.

Does the business kill its best men? Sometimes, but it is more likely that the test lies in the man, that each man carries his guillotine or his wreath of laurel in his own typewriter. Some are dead, or burned out and useless, at twenty-five. Others, like Frederick T. Birchall, for years the peppery acting managing editor of the New York *Times,* can go back to reporting when past sixty and win the Pulitzer Prize for foreign correspondence. The survivors are few, but on occasion the old champions do their stuff with surpassing brilliance.

Mr. Birchall, in common with a few other experienced technicians in news-gathering, is possessed not only of unfailing energy but of a keen desire to know what lies behind a situation. Such men, as the saying has it, go back of the news. Failure to seek out the underlying, and often most important news, is the principal weakness of the younger crop of reporters—not all of them, but so many that it is saddening. It was so long ago. Of the four who wrote of Jesus, John was the only one who showed signs of being a lively, inquisitive reporter.  He wanted to know things, and he asked about them.

The complaint is made against the modern reporter that he does not go to all his sources, that he won't dig, and that he is too easily content with a collection of perfunctory statements which obscure the issue more than they reveal it.  Probably there is some truth in this, although the old-time bloodhounds were not as magnificent as legend sometimes makes them seem.  Facilities for getting at the truth, even through a barricade of press agents and lobbygows, are better now than in the golden days when such men as Lincoln Steffens fancied they were on the inside of devious, horrendous labyrinths of politics and corruption. Every paper of size has at least a handful of men who, to the indictment that they are lax in ferreting out the hidden facts, can plead a stentorian "Not Guilty!"

Young men can be ruined, and so can old men.  City editors and managing editors sometimes must be blamed. Unsympathetic handling, a long period of slighting or persecution, can do much to hobble the spirit of a reporter. There is very little of this sort of thing.

Booze, despite the beneficent repeal of the Eighteenth Amendment, still spoils reporters who, without the bottle, might be worth keeping.  Excitement, irregular hours of work, and the pulling and hauling of various emotions which beset the young men, are responsible for breakdowns, often manifested in heart disease or tuberculosis.

Marriage ruins other men.  It is true, and a bit sad, that the laudable ambition to marry often leads a newspaper man into such a maze of difficulties that he loses his hair, his digestion and his ability to work.  A few seem to thrive on the connubial existence, and they appear happy in their suburban homes, with their automobiles and their droves of children.  But it is a tough assignment for most.  The nature of a newspaper man's work keeps him from home until unheard-of hours.  His wife, though she may be sympathetic, doesn't always like it, and comes to regard his work as a stupid and probably rotten enterprise.

There has been proposed a cure for most, or all, of the drawbacks which beset the grand but dubious old profession of reporting. Soon after Franklin D. Roosevelt went to the White House, a group of newspaper men began forming what came to be known as the Newspaper Guild. This organization represented the first widespread articulate movement on the part of newspaper men to protect themselves from the ups and downs of economic change. The Guild became strong, though many of the ablest newspaper men, who regarded themselves either as individualists or as professional men, refused to join.

The Guild began with a rather nebulous idea of some sort of collective action by reporters and other editorial workers to obtain such boons as a minimum salary, a fixed period for the promotion of beginners, an agreement under which notice and pay should be given in the event of the discharge of an employee, and some plan for the security of aged workers. The Guild also sought a five-day, forty-hour week, which, on most newspapers, was granted before the Guild had been recognized by the publishers. The five-day week presents difficulties in covering stories which run for a long time, but they are not always serious.

The program of the Guild raised old questions. Wouldn't it have been more sensible, as strategy, for the reporters to have sought increased pay, to which many of them were clearly entitled, before asking for the five-day week? Moreover, it developed that many reporters were not so enthusiastic about the five-day week after all; they asked to be permitted to work overtime for extra pay, pointing out that they need the money and that, besides, the extra day means nothing to them.

One wing of journalists has long favored affiliation with the American Federation of Labor. Thus, if the printers called a strike, the reporters might go out in sympathy, particularly if they had a contract which expired at the same time.

The union movement may work some day for the greater glory of journalism, but it seems more probable that it will alienate the sympathy of the more conservative members of the press. By proposing a set of handcuffs for the men who do the hiring and firing, it may eventually hurt the workers themselves. Should a reporter be paid $35 a week simply because he has been working for a newspaper for one year, or for two years? It is an eternal truth, though perhaps unfortunate, that some men are worth only $30 a week, no matter how long they work—but they are still useful.

The tendency may be to pull down the pay of the more highly-paid reporters, many of whom deserve more than they get, to raise the pay of those at the bottom. Thus it is possible that the average pay in New York will be around $35 or $40 a week, and if a man expects more than $60 he will have to take up some other business or water the elephants on his two days off. The men may learn, also, that the services of a great many of their numbers are far from indispensable. The publishers, if so minded, can always plow under one-third of the crop.

Publishers come in gaudy and inexplicable patterns. Some are friendly peasants at heart; others appear to feel that God has called them to their high estate. But most of them are decent, and always have been decent, to their reporters, even at times when their newspapers were in sad financial distress. Editors all over America have said to reporters who have had a long and wearing grind, "Take two or three days off and rest up." There has been little brutality. Any attempt to smooth out the hard places deserves sympathy, but unionism has always seemed alien to the spirit of the news worker.

The best reporter is cut from the same cloth as the great ones of ten, fifty or a hundred years ago. He may be a

scarecrow or an Adonis, an old Groton alumnus or a former office boy whose folks live in Hell's Kitchen, an earnest
Jew from Riga or a wild, poetic Irishman whose parents
came from County Clare—whatever he is, if he belongs to
the top flight, he is an admirable person, living in a fine
tradition, who deserves the best things in an uncertain and
comical world.

It is doubtful if he wants to ally his calling with the
labor unions. If he is really a good reporter, he remembers
a truth picked up quickly along the way by all observant
news-gatherers: Don't bet on clergymen or labor leaders.

# COVERING NEW YORK

NEW YORK has everything. It affords the newspaper man an ever-changing spectacle. Its hanging gardens are said to be superior to those of Babylon. Its honest, staid burghers are cut in the pattern of their counterparts in any humdrum community. Its rackets probably are as brutal as those of Marseilles, and more devious and varied than those of Chicago. Its vice has made it spoken of as if it were competing with the iniquities of Port Said and Harbin. It is deliriously beautiful, and ugly as a mildewed toad. Somehow, the city cannot be slandered, and anything that may be said of it in praise or abuse is more likely than not to be true. It has very little civic pride in the sense that other towns, with their boastings and sensitiveness to criticism, are proud. A community conscience doesn't exist.

The big town is Rome, Paris, Jerusalem, Berlin, with traces of Dubuque at its dullest and Dodge City at its most uproarious. It is the city of yes and no. It attracts great lawyers, not always the best. It draws outstanding surgeons and physicians, but not always the most competent. It is supposed to draw the cream of the theologians, educators, reformers and assorted thinkers, but it doesn't always. It is duck soup for medicine men and three-card monte adepts. It is said to draw the ablest newspaper men, and it draws some good ones, but there are others just as good in Chicago, St. Louis, Kansas City, Baltimore and even in the bayou and desert towns on little struggling sheets. The city has political leaders who can't sign their own names; it has others who relax by reading the Greek classics. It has had lifeguards who couldn't swim, and subway conductors who lectured before learned societies on early Irish literature.

A newspaper, in theory at least, is supposed to present an accurate reflection of what the town is like. The job is so big, and so complicated, that some newspapers naturally have concentrated upon an appeal to certain groups and have not bothered with attempting complete coverage. The better papers try to give at least a summary of what is going on, a fairly faithful mirror of what the city is like. The picture, at best, always has been a hit and miss daub, a cock-eyed etching. The heart of the magnificent city remains elusive.

And yet, today, New York certainly is as fascinating, and as productive of news, as it ever was. Fifteen years ago, before most of the mergers, the morning newspapers, the *Herald, Sun, Tribune, World, American* and *Times* set apart each night an average of eighteen or twenty columns of space for local news; today the New York *Times* and the New York *Herald Tribune* may devote from twenty-five to forty-five columns to the same class of material, and on some nights Mr. Hearst's *American* will have almost as much local news space. Fifteen years ago a morning newspaper might have only forty local items day after day; it is not unusual now for a paper to have 100 local items, some of them illustrated with photographs which would not have been attempted even ten years ago. Fifteen years ago all society news and the obituaries could be printed on the same page; now at least two pages are required on such papers as the *Times* and *Herald Tribune*.

For the coverage of the news of New York and vicinity the city desk of a newspaper is responsible. Most papers charge to the city desk all the news as far north as Albany in New York State, all of New Jersey and Connecticut. The job, essentially, is one of machinery. The whole task of gathering news has been speeded up and systematized, which does not, or should not, mean that the papers are all the same, that they are lifeless, or that enterprise and imagination cannot produce exclusive and brilliant results. The problems of covering the happenings in New York and vicinity are not radically different from those in any other town, even the small towns. The principal difference is in size and methods of selection. The structure is always similar. Memphis has its large Negro population; New York has its Harlem, the greatest Negro urban center on earth. On all the fronts which produce news—politics, city government, police, courts, crime, finance, art, music, the theater and personalities—New York is simply an exaggerated, blown-up country town. But in New York much more relatively trivial news may be thrown away.

In New York the city editor and all his colleagues will find that it pays to know a great many people. This is true in all cities. Does the Dallas editor find it useful to know Artie Compton, manager of the Adolphus Hotel? Then the New York editor should be on good terms with David B. Mulligan, manager of the Biltmore. Can the Chicago newspaper man walk along Michigan Boulevard and pick up or absorb stories and ideas? So in New York a newspaper man can roam Broadway or Fifth Avenue and obtain a feast of nonsense and news. Likewise, in New York as elsewhere, the newspapers and the alert men on their staffs have their friends, rooters, and spies, men and women who inform them, often for no reason except good will, of extremely important news. Tips from friends sometimes are better than all the machinery ever devised.

A tubercular tramp newspaper reporter, headed for Denver, once dropped this solemn pearl: "Kid, don't ever be mean or snooty to anyone. Not even a streetwalker. You may need her help sometime. Some day, a chance in a thousand, she may give you a great story." The frayed rod-rider may have been excessively romantic, but he spoke the truth akin to the Kiplingesque advice to be on speaking terms with the great gray apes of the hills, because no man knows when he will need an ally.

Once there was a mystery in the death of a beautiful woman whose body had been picked up on the sands. Murder was suspected. No paper could find her picture. Late at night a blowsy derelict came by a newspaper office with her photograph and, mentioning the name of a man on the paper, said: "I'm leaving this for him. He did a fine thing for me once." The unidentified courier left in the drizzle without giving his name or asking compensation. He said it wouldn't matter. And the newspaper man for whom he had left the photograph was puzzled. "I can't imagine who it could have been. I can't recall offhand ever having done a kind deed for anyone. But it's nice he thought I did."

News may swell in with the winds. It may come from an alcoholic hunch. It may result from a letter or a mysterious telephone call. A friend of the paper may bestir himself to turn tipster. A paper without friends is as lifeless, and as helpless, as a man without friends. These well-meaning citizens are sometimes nuisances, and must be throttled, even as in the smallest towns, but often they do produce news.

Mostly, however, the gathering of news in New York is directed by a well-organized, coldly planned machine—a machine which strives to be as exact and scientific as possible in handling material which is of necessity fluid, evanescent and incapable of accurate prediction. The city editor and his assistants read all the newspapers and magazines. At any rate, they are supposed to. They continually clip items from their own and other papers which contain a hint of a news story, or which suggest that something interesting may occur a week from next Tuesday. There is a filing system of such items, known as "futures," so that every day an envelope containing possibly 100 clippings or memoranda may be drawn out, looked through and used as the basis of assignments to reporters. The city desk has the task of keeping a complete calendar not only of what probably will happen, but what by any conceivable chance might happen.

Moreover—and this is of tremendous value in a city such as New York—there is a compact card file of the names, addresses, office and home telephone numbers of perhaps 1,000 men and women who may be needed by a reporter or rewrite man who is working on a story. These cards sometimes carry such notations as: "If he can't be found, call Herbert Bayard Swope," or "Don't call after midnight; it makes him sore as hell and he won't talk anyhow," or "If not at home, have him paged at the bar of the University Club," or "He will pretend to be angry, but can always be flattered." A grand dossier, fit for the Pinkertons.

Any large newspaper needs a fairly large corps of reporters, for sometimes the investigation of the background of one apparently unimportant situation may require the attention for hours of three or four men. Much of the most pressing work in New York can be done by telephone, but sometimes fast leg work is essential.

The number of reporters, including all classifications, on a New York newspaper ranges from about twenty, which is regarded as a small but often adequate staff, to the seventy or more men which the New York *Times* is able to throw out on assignments of all sorts.

Sometimes mere numbers are of little use. Indeed, members of platoons of news hawks have been known to trip over the feet of one another. For complete coverage, of course, a large staff is essential, but day by day a somewhat smaller staff can do the job as well or better. Exceptional results often are a matter of speed. Sometimes the infantry may win; again, the cavalry and the airplanes will come out first.

The routine, official New York news, in addition to the

news of many luncheons, dinners and conventions, is covered by the New York City News Association, an organization of which all the principal papers are members except the tabloid *Mirror* and the *Morning Telegraph* (horses and Broadway). This news is carried instantly by printing machines into the offices of the member newspapers and to the Associated Press. The morning papers pay a little more than $400 a week each and the afternoon papers more than $300 a week for the service. Directed by the able William G. Henderson, a veteran newspaper man who knows New York thoroughly, City News covers City Hall, the Municipal Building and city departments, State and Surrogates' Courts, the Federal Building, Police Headquarters, the Court of General Sessions and District Attorney's office, the Magistrates' Courts in Manhattan and the Bronx, ship news, and all accidents, fires and sudden deaths.

Of New York's five boroughs, Manhattan, the Bronx, Brooklyn, Queens and Richmond (Staten Island), the City News concerns itself only with Manhattan and the Bronx.

The association employs about sixty persons. It has been regarded for more than two decades or more as being virtually indispensable for the safe covering of routine news. The association always distinguishes itself in reporting election returns, a feat which, if undertaken by the individual newspapers, might result in endless confusion and delay.

The theory back of the organization is that the newspapers, by pooling their resources, may have protection. For example, the West Side Magistrate's Court is covered for City News by Arthur Corrigan, seasoned and reliable reporter, and few newspapers bother to send their own staff men there unless a case arises in which they are particularly interested. Without City News, each paper would be forced to have a man in the court, and on some days the news wouldn't be worth the expense.

The City News confines itself solely to gathering facts and transmitting these facts speedily, in concise form. Its reporters must avoid stylistic folderols, all attempts at decoration. Additional checking, development, and rewriting will be done in the various newspaper offices to suit special needs or policies. The association at one time or another has had in its employ some of the best newspaper men in the country—W. Axel (Baron) Warn, of the New York *Times;* Richard Reagan, of the New York *Herald Tribune;* Lester B. Stone, now secretary to Mayor F. H. LaGuardia; James Corrigan, now dead, the beloved Sinn Feiner who covered the Federal Building in his old age; Waldo Walker, circulation manager of the New York *Times;* Christy Bohnsack, who became director of the municipal radio station and who was famous for years as an arranger of receptions, dinners and parades; John Regan, who still goes down the bay to meet the ships for the City News, and an endless roster of other men, some now buried and forgotten and others going ahead in business, politics, or journalism. Most City News reporters seek something else after a few years, or even after a few months. The work is hard, the pay limited and the product entirely anonymous. Work with the organization furnishes excellent experience; sometimes, sadly, it is the refuge for the reporter who is never going anywhere.

Similar to the City News is the Standard News Association, a privately-owned organization directed by John Eddy, a former Hearst man, to which any newspaper may subscribe. Standard News covers New Jersey, Westchester County, Long Island, Queens, Brooklyn and Staten Island —that whole inchoate sprawling area which lies outside the range of the City News Association. Considering the size of its territory the Standard News does a competent job. It misses a lot of news, but it surprises with its occasional speed and alertness. Fast, hard-hitting rewrite and desk men in the central office in New York take the news by telephone, whip it rapidly into shape, and the stories are

in the newspaper offices in much less time than it takes a
cub to spell Rabindranath Tagore correctly.

It would be possible to get out a presentable newspaper
without hiring a single reporter, relying solely upon City
News and Standard News for local coverage. Four or five
fast rewrite men would be needed, and that's all. Indeed,
several papers at one time and another, hard pressed for
capital, have come very near doing this. Such a paper,
however, could not long compete in its local news with
papers which not only covered the routine but which employed men enough to develop items of especial flavor or
merit—items which lie entirely outside the cut-and-dried
functions of the news associations.

Out of an apparently inconsequential paragraph in the
report received from a news service some one on the city
desk may find a name, or a suggestion, which may be investigated and developed into an article of such interest
that the other papers should put their flags at half-staff.

It might be feasible for the New York newspapers to
abolish both the City News and the Standard News Associations without causing themselves more than temporary
inconvenience. These organizations had much more reason for operating in the days when there were many more
papers than are published today, and the cost to each was
less. As each old paper died, or was knocked on the head,
the cost to each remaining participant in a local news service arrangement automatically became higher.

Abolition of the whole system surely would make for
freshness and competition. Some items would be missed,
but others, and perhaps better ones, would be drawn out
of what is already a poorly-charted news field. A morning
paper, now paying more than $400 for the City News,
could hire twelve or more reporters—who need jobs, God
knows—to take up the slack if that news service were
stopped.

Except in a few spots, the larger papers already have the

news covered by their own men, and the services are only added insurance. In the suburbs, most papers have correspondents who can be relied upon to protect them. If one or two more papers should fail, or be merged, the argument for the stoppage of these local news service will be stronger.

The world-wide news services, the Associated Press and the United Press, are in the opinion of some editors of little use to the city desk in New York. Great, possibly, on a disarmament conference, or an earthquake in Japan, but not so good at home. Their local so-called "feature stories" are occasionally bright, but too often unrevealing. The Associated Press, in particular, has come a long way from the pioneer wisdom of the sainted Founding Father, Melville E. Stone, who was not wisecracking when he indicated in his dead-pan fashion that readers wanted information, which is to say, plain facts. After that, he said, advise them. Then entertain them. A carnival does neither.

The United Press, which is better than it once was, also is guilty of a needless straining for effect. Now and then, valuably enough, one of the news services will send through a bulletin announcing that a person of prominence is dangerously ill, or even dead. Except for these occasional signposts of Charon's shipping schedule, the A. P. and the U. P. are not considered by some editors indispensable so far as the covering of New York news by New York papers is concerned.

In New York, more than anywhere else in America, the handling of local news has been split into many departments. Some departments are supervised by the city desk, but others contribute to the worries of the managing editor, who is the directing, executive officer of the paper in its handling of all news. The sports department, of course, is so important that it must exist as a separate entity from the city desk. The society department requires peculiar experience and specialized knowledge. Unless it is watched carefully, this amorphous spreading of responsibility will result in a sort of inert, ponderous bureaucracy, where all the inmates know everything and do nothing. Ordinarily, the more direct the control of the city desk over these specialized departments, the better the news coverage.

Something mysterious often happens to a man, or even a woman, when placed in a special department on a newspaper. Too many of them immediately fancy themselves experts, their minds closed to everything except one tightly circumscribed assignment. They foolishly begin to shut out all the rest of the world and to ignore news. These reporters, who have been assigned to special and important phases of news, should be among the most valuable newsgatherers. Sometimes they are, but often they turn out to be wasted. Many appear to regard their special assignments as pensions, or as rarefied contemplative work entailing no vulgar grubbing for old-fashioned news. Misled wanderers of this stripe must be talked to, sometimes rebuked, and even fired. Somehow it appears difficult for these precious ornaments to understand that they are still in newspaper work. Fortunately, enough of them retain a nose for news to justify the department system.

There have been heartbreaking instances of this metamorphosis from plain reporter to hoity-toity specialist. The fashion editor is out of town when the time comes to write of the fashions in the Easter parade. The sports reporter is not sure whether Babe Ruth's bellyache is serious, and in any event must go home to dinner. The art reporter has been giving Diego Rivera's stuff the up and down all afternoon and is too tired to cover an auction of $100,000 worth of art in the evening. The so-called Broadway or theatrical reporter is tied up with a Sunday story, and would rather be let off the obituary of David Belasco. A financial story has broken, but the earnest young man in whose field it ordinarily would fall has been working since morning, and has an appointment for dinner and bridge. The aviation expert is writing a Sunday review of the history of flying since the Kitty Hawk days of the Wrights and can't possibly find time to handle the story of the killing of seven in an airplane crash.

Somehow, however, the news is handled, usually by working reporters who take all news in their stride and do not fancy themselves pampered specialists. To be sure, the smart newspaper men never forget that they are reporters, and that the paper is published primarily, not to keep them on the payroll, but to give the readers the news. Specialists such as Maury Paul (Cholly Knickerbocker) of the New York *American;* Eugene Lokey, of the financial news department of the New York *Times;* Ward Morehouse, Broadway reporter for the *Sun;* Michael V. Casey (real estate) and John E. Kelly (marine news) of the New York *Herald Tribune,* among many others, often have remembered that a story is a story.

Much of the blame for the occasional lapses of the experts, of course, lies with the chief complainant, the city desk. The city editor often has assumed that because he said to a man, "From now on you are to cover all religious news, from Bishop William T. Manning to the visiting yogis," he should have no more worries about the news of the comings and goings, the ups and downs, of the gentlemen of the cloth. A dangerous assumption. New dominies, with flabbergasting news, will arise on the morrow to require special handling. The city desk is never let off anything, and it shouldn't be.

For all the shortcomings, the best New York newspapers are the best in the country, even in their treatment of purely local news. For one thing, in New York a mass of nonsense and piffle, which might be important in a smaller town, may be ignored. The city is so big, with so much news, that the newspapers rarely send a reporter to the weekly lunch of the Rotary or the Kiwanis club, which would be covered without question in a smaller town.

Moreover, there is probably less of a slavish attitude by newspapers in New York than anywhere else, except possibly Chicago and Baltimore. A reporter or an editor may tell a known faker or pest to go to hell and get away with it. Even better, he may tell an insinuating advertiser, or any one of the inevitable horde of charlatans and special pleaders, how to find the door to the elevator. By and large, New York newspaper men are freer from annoyance than the men in smaller cities. Within the limits of reason and taste, they may speak freely, act honestly, and take care of news problems according to their best professional judgment.

The city is whatever one wants to make it. Experiments are tried, but the basis of news coverage changes little. Papers still keep death watches on the doorsteps of prominent citizens who are expected to die. Occasional crusades—few of them very serious any more—are started and dropped. Now and then Wall Street kicks up. Anniversaries come and go. We lay a wreath, plant a tree. Justice Joseph Force Crater is still missing. A police commissioner tells his men to get results, or something dreadful may happen. When a story breaks, the only way a paper can find facts is to call out the reporters and go after it.

As in battles, the principle of covering the more important news in New York ("Get there fustest with the mostest men") is about the same as it was fifty years ago. The paper which knows the most about the city, and handles its facts most intelligently, fairly and attractively, is the best paper—certainly as a local newspaper.

Judges, reformers, evangelists, fads, crime waves and mayors come and go in a many-colored parade, a parade which is always a little different but which marches to tunes familiar to the men at the listening posts.

In New York, taking one day with another, the most fruitful news field is the municipal administration. City Hall, even when all news is in the doldrums, must be watched. At the beginning of 1934 a reform-fusion administration went into power. Tammany, for four years at least, appears crippled and starved. Mayor LaGuardia, a sort of political Toscanini, who is master of his trade but is of such uncertain temperament that no man knows whether to expect an embrace or a bomb, began making more news than any Mayor since the war. The newspapers had to call upon their reserve strength to cover the flurries of reform and reorganization, and the excitement stirred up by a new broom.

It is curious that the administration of James J. Walker as mayor of New York furnished so little news. James had a way of charming his newspaper friends, of beguiling them with "off the record" revelations, so that much news of actual administrative happenings never saw print. Not until Samuel Seabury, as counsel for a legislative committee, began digging into the appalling mess, was there much recognizable news of the first rank.

O'Brien, probably the most unfortunate man ever to be mayor of New York, had a heart of gold but he was a fumbler. He made little news. He was afraid of the press. He distrusted newspaper men, who, he suspected with some justice, regarded him as a well-meaning but inept politician with an undershot jaw, a clean soul and a gift for interminable prolixity both in speeches and conversation. He was started to defeat by the newspaper men who employed the lethal device of quoting his utterances verbatim.

The new champion, LaGuardia, knows politics as few men understand that tricky game. He can be cunning, polite, evasive, insolent, playful, and forthright to the point of brutality. He is unpredictable. Some newspaper reporters and editors swear by him; others fear, from experience, that he might at any time be grossly unfair. He will bite in the clinches. He has, on more than one occasion, fancied that some newspaper man was out to "get him" and has complained to the man's employers—always a foolish gesture on the part of any public official who is dealing with honest newspapers and honest reporters. Many have been guilty of this error, including Herbert Hoover.

One school of thought holds that LaGuardia may spoil his best record any day; another believes that there is no end to what he may accomplish for the city, and no limit to his own political future. He found the city in an appalling financial condition. Thanks largely to his stamina and ingenuity, the city's credit recovered. Whatever becomes of him, local politics and the New York City government—that assortment of die-hard Republicans, the snarling, bitter Tammany veterans, the high-minded but ordinarily futile Independent Democrats, the fast-withering Socialists, the hopeful City Fusion Party, and all the other seesawing groups—must continue to make news.

The city is brimful of news—news of ideas, of people, of petty feuds and high aspiration. Doubtless New York has never been covered thoroughly, intelligently, and with the sense of proportion that it deserves. The magnificence of the city calls for better coverage than it receives even from the modern high-geared machinery. It should be the paradise of the newspaper man. Nowhere is the performance louder, funnier, or with more provocative, mysterious overtones.

Whatever happens, whatever systems may be evolved for the chronicling of the doings of the city and its millions, a man on the city desk will pick up the latest edition of a rival paper and groan, "Good God! How did they happen to beat us on this?" New York is a good newspaper town. It will be as long as the boys are fighting.

# THE QUICK AND THE DEAD

WHY does a great newspaper die? Why does another one continue at a steady plodding pace, year in and year out, with little change in circulation, revenue and influence? And why do others spring up and succeed sensationally in a field where the wise men said there was no chance? There are a million answers to these questions, many of them wrong. The answers are inextricably mixed up with personality, political policy, social philosophy, psychology, and trends of economics and business, and pure luck. Some papers die when they might easily have been kept alive; others flourish contrary to all the rules of newspaper science.

Since the war the business of owning and operating newspapers has been a saturnalia of quick mergers, sudden death and phenomenal growth. Many a paper which had a strong following at the time of the Armistice is forgotten now except by readers with long memories. The chains have expanded. Except for the local news, a paper in New Orleans may be substantially the same as a paper in, say, Kansas City. Critics of newspapers complain that the syndicates and the news services have given the American press a dull uniformity. This charge, with a few exceptions, is true enough but it does not necessarily mean the end of enterprise. Moreover, the reader of even a small paper probably gets more for his money than he once got.

Doubtless the most significant trend in American journalism since the war is exemplified in the rise of the *Daily News,* the New York tabloid, which some people even to this day insist, with strong reasoning, is not a newspaper at all. On the night in 1919 when the first issue of the

puny, mewling, impudent sheet reached the other newspaper offices, there was considerable interest in what the
newcomer would be like.  The idea of a tabloid had been
discussed frequently; indeed, it had been tried at one time
and another, rather half-heartedly.

In the office of the New York *Times* the editors, reporters and rewrite men were discussing the infant—and a
pretty terrible looking product it was.  Everybody except
Carr V. Van Anda, the managing editor, was contemptuous of this brash, sickly child of the Chicago *Tribune*.  Mr.
Van Anda, a man of great foresight in such matters, told
his associates: "No, I think you are wrong.  This paper
should reach a circulation of 2,000,000."  In 1934 the
*Sunday News* passed 2,000,000; the daily doubtless can
reach that figure soon if the proprietor and Max Annen-
berg, the circulation manager, really want it to.  Its profits
in 1933 amounted to $3,300,000.  June 26, 1934, the *Daily
News* printed the following editorial, which tells of its
history from *The News* viewpoint:

### HAPPY BIRTHDAY, DEAR NEWS,
### HAPPY BIRTHDAY TO YOU!

We're fifteen years old to-day—the *News* is, we mean.

It was fifteen years ago to-day—June 26, 1919—that the
first issue of this newspaper came out of the old Evening Mail
Building at 25 City Hall Place, since torn down.  It came off
rented presses; a goodly number of copies were presented to the
public free; there was some doubt as to whether this paper,
modeled in those days on the successful *Daily Mirror* of London, could make the grade in the New York newspaper field.

That doubt has been largely laid to rest, if we may say so.  The
paper began to succeed almost from the first.  It has gained
steadily in both circulation and advertising, until—we rap on
wood—it now has more of both than it ever had before.

In April, 1921, we moved to 25 Park Place, where we had
our own presses and consequently put out a better job of print-

ing. But the building was uncomfortable. Early in 1930, we moved into the new News Building at 220 E. 42d St.

The News Building has been called a beautiful piece of architecture. It is. But its beauty happened only incidentally. The main object was to build a building which would serve in the best possible way as a modern newspaper plant. Raymond M. Hood and John M. Howells, original-minded architects, who designed the building, kept this prime object in mind all the way through. The vertical stripes which make the building stand out are the result of using different colored bricks to set off the windows.

The setbacks in the News Building are the result of the zoning laws. But for the zoning laws, we'd probably have built a boxlike building to have more office space. Which leads us to believe the zoning laws are a good thing; they give big buildings' neighbors more light.

About the time we occupied the new building, the depression ceased to be a joke. So did renting office space, of which The News Building had plenty. There was a $4,000,000 mortgage on the building, and this mortgage became a nightmare to us because of the steady downward trend in general business. Whenever we got hold of some money, we put it on the mortgage, until the mortgage was all paid off—which is a great relief.

Why did *The News* succeed? Of course, at the start there was the usual caviling, about how this new paper was the stenographers' delight and the gum chewers' dream, and got its circulation by means of contests.

We aren't running any major contests now, haven't for sometime. Not that we wouldn't run one if we could think of a good one; but the circulation and advertising have kept up just the same.

We might point to our policy as a reason for *The News'* success. But if a paper's readers don't know what its policy is, it does seem useless for the paper to try to tell them. It would be a work of supererogation, we should think, to repeat that we're in favor of the Roosevelt and LaGuardia Administrations up to now, and that we think the United States should have a navy second to none.

One item in our success to date, we believe, is the fact that we have always tried to give all *The News* employees reasonably good working conditions. We may be kidding ourselves, but we think most of them are reasonably well satisfied. Anyway, they deliver good work.

How about the paper's future? People grow up, grow mature, grow old, and die. So do newspapers. We don't know whether we've reached our peak, or whether we'll grow stronger yet. Nobody can tell.

One idea we have adopted, though, in an attempt to counteract the aging process in this shop. Our key men have been asked to spot considerably younger successors and help train them—whereas in most business houses the King is forever looking apprehensively over his shoulder at the Crown Prince, and hates to think of a successor.

This scheme has worked out astonishingly well so far. The key men have taken to it enthusiastically, their present reward being longer vacations. So maybe *The News* can minimize the crippling effect of aging executives hanging onto their jobs and fighting off any new blood that tries to muscle in with fresh ideas and viewpoints.

That is a good editorial, and a perfect example of the prose style of *The News*—simple, unaffected, friendly, as if the paper were saying, "Well, pal, I'll tell you how we feel about things."

*The News* has some exceptionally competent editors, including Harvey Deuell, Frank Hause and Frank Carson, and one of the liveliest and best-paid staffs ever put together in New York. It put the five-day week into effect long before the other papers. It is, as the happy birthday editorial says, a good place to work. But why has it been so successful? The editors insist that it is because it bears the imprint of the man they believe to be the ablest publisher of all time, Joseph Medill Patterson, the same man whose soundness was suspected in the long ago because he had Socialistic leanings and fooled around with writing plays and pamphlets. Robert R. McCormick runs the

Chicago *Tribune;* Captain Patterson is the brains of the whopping offspring in New York.

*The News* formula has worked on that paper, but when Captain Patterson tried to apply the same idea in starting the weekly magazine, *Liberty,* he was not so successful. Into that little magazine went $14,000,000. The diagnosticians over at *The News* say that Patterson is greater than Northcliffe because his mind is, actually, the public's mind, while Northcliffe's was what he thought the public's mind ought to be. Moreover, it is a notorious fact that the voice of the people is the Voice of God. *The News* holds to the belief that more information of significant interest to the public can be obtained by listening to street corner patter than by covering the deliberations of a world conference at Geneva.

It is argued, moreover, that the policy of *The News* is the greatest compliment ever paid to the intelligence of the public. *The News* writes up, not down, to its readers. The editors admit that the educational equipment of the public might average that of a 14-year-old, but they insist that the legions of hoi polloi are enriched by all their experiences and that their intellect is the average of that of the editors who convey the news to them.

*The News* has had a few shibboleths. In its early days, with an account of a shooting, it would print a small picture of an automatic pistol ("gat" or "roscoe") with the peremptory caption, "Stop Selling These!" It favored more playgrounds, and fought to put baseball diamonds in Central Park. Most of the time, however, there is little trumpeting for a cause. Captain Patterson's chief idea is simply to get out a paper that a lot of people will read and enjoy.

*The News* operates on the psychological principle that, no matter what his background or education, a man is governed by his emotions. The editors doubt, and with good reason, that it is possible really to edify or improve any considerable mass of people. Therefore they give the readers plenty of personalities and pictures. When the idea of the NRA came along, Patterson, instead of publishing it as an abstract economic document, translated it as simply as possible into terms of jobs and dollars.

Human frailties are dealt with tolerantly. Indeed, Captain Patterson is said to feel that he himself is the possessor of several human frailties. When the late John H. McCooey, Democratic boss of Brooklyn, made a State Supreme Court Justice of his son, John H. McCooey, Jr., who up to that time never had been regarded as another Cardozo, all the other papers were somewhat indignant. *The News,* however, asked in effect, "What could be more natural than for a father to give his son the break?" What, indeed?

The photographs reproduced in *The News* are uniformly excellent, sometimes magnificent. They are well selected with an eye to dramatic or human appeal, and they show up on the printed page distinctly. Indeed, all the way through, *The News* is a remarkably fine typographical job. Its influence has led other papers to pay more attention to pictures. It may also have lessened the old tendency of some of the other papers to fly off the handle now and then and actually bait their readers.

In its handling of news, the Patterson tabloid is much less razzle-dazzle, much more conservative and factual, than it used to be. By 1934 it was neither conservative nor wild —just a jolly, rollicking brother of all humanity. It does not pretend to be a complete newspaper. It prints what interests the editors and throws the rest away.

The principal criticisms, from a professional standpoint, which may be made against *The News* are that it sometimes seems unduly biased in some of its news stories; that it has spent money on news sources in ways which would not be sanctioned by Holy Church; that its banner headlines have been highly misleading and some of its news stories based merely upon rumors which a little investigation could have shown to be unfounded. However, these criticisms have much less point than they had a few years ago.

*The News* in many respects has grown up. Its reporting of crime news has improved enormously, particularly in the rather important matter of authenticity. Its sports pages are among the brightest and best to look upon. Whether brilliant or not, the idea upon which the paper is founded certainly works. Ten years ago the term "tabloid reporter" was a sort of epithet, like calling a man "Judge" during the Seabury inquiry into the lower courts. The employees of *The News*, loyal and generally competent, have removed some of this opprobrium.

The other New York morning tabloid, *The Mirror,* is built upon a pattern similar to *The News*, but, except for the fact that it carries Walter Winchell's daily treasure house of gossip and flabbergasting information, and the sports comment of Dan Parker, it has little in it that isn't done better in *The News.* It is too bad that *The Mirror* feels it must print strained and often inaccurate stories, although it is seriously handicapped by a lack of news services and by the further circumstance that, although it has attained what ordinarily would be considered a splendid circulation, more than 500,000, the advertisers don't seem to like it.

*The Mirror,* in the beginning, was Hearst's half-hearted challenge to *The News;* A. J. Kobler, who runs the paper, may yet make a go of it. Its features are half-baked and thin. Emile Gauvreau, a peculiar genius with a gift for tabloid news, is Kobler's editor, but even he has not been able to threaten the leadership of *The News.*

Gauvreau for a time was the brains of Bernarr Macfadden's evening tabloid, the *Graphic,* that fabulous sheet founded by the great muscle-flexer and carrot-eater in 1924. It lasted, to the amazement of one and all, until its bankruptcy in 1932. For a time the circulation mounted

alarmingly.  Gauvreau wrote a memorandum and posted it
on the bulletin board:

"The circulation of the *Graphic* has reached the point where
it is tearing the guts out of the presses.  This has resulted from
my policy of sensationalism.  Any man who cannot be yellow
has no place on the staff."

In the great days of the *Graphic* it introduced the composite picture, part photograph and part nightmare, a
bastard art form which reproduced the editor's conception
of what took place.  It was completely lacking in integrity.
This synthetic art was used to illustrate the bedroom horse-
play of Edward W. Browning, the real estate operator who
married Frances Heenan, known to this day as "Peaches,"
and the grotesque love story of Leonard Kip Rhinelander
and his quadroon bride, the sad-eyed Alice Jones.

Macfadden gave out an interview in 1929 expressing his
ideas of journalism.  He said:

"Every time anyone wants to condemn a story for its frankness they call it a sex story.  That is no criticism at all.  There's
nothing wrong with sex stories.  No romance ever existed that
wasn't a sex story.  No marriage is ever performed that doesn't
involve a sex story.  It is only prudery that points a forbidding
finger at sex.  You can't do anything about such an attitude.
You can only lift sex to its proper dignity.

"Newspapers of today are too mechanical, too cold.  They
are not getting enough of the real color of life into their make-
up.  Many of them assume an ominous, forbidding tone that
keeps them fenced off from the actual feelings of their readers.
Many editors set themselves up on a pedestal high above their
readers.  They seem to confer with Almighty God every day.
The people are afraid of them.  They ought to come down off
their pedestals and get on the same level with the public."

The truth seems to be that although Macfadden may
have been an expert on sex in the raw, spinach and cold
baths, he was hardly an expert in newspaper technique.

Toward the end, the paper seemed to struggle for a time to be conservative, to emerge from the red light district of journalism—but cautiously and gradually, so that no one would be aware of the reformation until it had become a fact. It was no use. Macfadden went back to the more familiar world of magazines, of nude bodies and clean minds, and meatless beef stew. He couldn't even make his sex authentic.

Of course, to newspaper men at least, the passing of the *World* and the *Evening World,* as such, was the tragedy of the post-war period of newspaper life. The *World* died in 1931, by court order, and though its end at that time was inevitable, the event was more shocking than the death of any great personage could have been. Why did it die? Probably because of many reasons.

The *World* flourished on the high public spirit and the professional competence of old Joseph Pulitzer, and long after his death the paper was sustained by the impetus of his personal genius as a newspaper proprietor. When that impetus ran down, the end was in sight. There were three sons—Joseph Pulitzer, Jr., publisher of the enormously successful St. Louis *Post-Dispatch;* Ralph Pulitzer, who was proprietor of the *World,* and Herbert Pulitzer, who paid little attention to the actual conduct of the business. Joseph, with his hands full in St. Louis, did not feel that he should attempt to pull the New York properties out of their difficulties.

What of the other brothers? They were amiable, well-educated men, and Ralph at least made a serious attempt to master the complexities of publishing a newspaper. It is the custom to blame them for the failure of the *World,* and even to suggest that somehow they shirked a moral obligation. However, there surely is one point that should be remembered: its sale hurt Ralph Pulitzer more deeply than it hurt anyone else. He was always uniformly considerate of the men who worked for the *World,* even at the end.   It may be that he lacked a certain talent for running a newspaper, as some men have no talent for killing bulls, or managing a hotel, or designing a cathedral.

James W. Barrett, the city editor of the morning *World,* says in his book, "The World, the Flesh and the Messrs. Pulitzer": "I don't exactly blame anybody. . . . Still, thinking it over, I can see that the Pulitzer brothers were at fault.   When it had become perfectly clear that none of them had brains enough to run the plant except at a loss, they might have let somebody run it who knew how."

Franklin P. Adams, the columnist, who had been with the *World* for more than nine years, conducting his "The Conning Tower," contributed a chapter to another post-mortem book, "The End of the *World.*"   Mr. Adams, regarded by some as a professional sneerer, a picker of birdshot out of packs of caraway seed, a giddy pool-player and diner-out, is in fact a shrewd and cagey observer of men and of why things are the way they are.   Said Adams:

"If I were asked to say what the *World* died of, I should say that Joseph Pulitzer created it and killed it; that J. P. gave, and J. P. took away.   There is no doubt that Joseph Pulitzer was a great journalist, nor that he had courage.   But I think that he was a man who must have been torn by misgivings as to his own power and ability; that these doubts and fears so dominated him that he was incapable of trusting anybody; and by trust I mean the last limit of trust. . . .

"Certainly it never seemed to me that, by the terms of his will, he had trusted his sons—any of them—enough to let them run his papers independently of him.   Militant for the independence of journalism, he yet forced his sons to be dependent upon him; to depend upon his independence, so that they must automatically have been robbed of any great independence of their own. . . . I think it was paternal distrust of the boys that doomed the paper, for the boys naturally found it difficult not to distrust everybody, no matter how slightly."

Adams's verdict, though it cannot cover the whole picture, probably is true. For the record, the passage in Joseph Pulitzer's will around which the court action on the sale revolved, follows:

"I further authorize and empower my executors and trustees to whom I have hereinbefore bequeathed my stock in the Pulitzer Publishing Company of St. Louis at any time to sell and dispose of said stock or any part thereof at public or private sale at such prices and on such terms as they may think best and to hold the proceeds of any stock sold in trust for the beneficiaries for whom such shares were held in lieu thereof and upon the same trusts. This power of sale is not to be construed as in any respect mandatory but purely discretionary. This power of sale, however, is limited to the said stock of the Pulitzer Publishing Company of St. Louis and shall not be taken to authorize or empower the sale or disposition under any circumstances whatever by the trustees of any stock in the Press Publishing Company, publisher of the *World* newspapers.

"I particularly enjoin upon my sons and my descendants the duty of preserving, perfecting and perpetuating the *World* newspapers, (to the maintenance and upbuilding of which I have sacrificed my health and strength) in the same spirit in which I have striven to create and conduct it as a public institution from motives higher than mere gain, it having been my desire that it should be at all times conducted in a spirit of independence and with a view to inculcating high standards and public spirit among the people and their official representatives and it is my earnest wish that said newspapers shall hereafter be conducted upon the same principles."

Thus did the dead hand of a great man tie up his properties and his children. There were long hearings before Surrogate James A. Foley, who finally gave permission to sell the properties to Roy W. Howard of the Scripps-Howard newspapers in these words:

"I hold that the trustees, as the representatives of the estate, have the power and general authority to participate as corporate officers and holders of the estate stock in the sale of the property of the company [Press Publishing Company] and that the equitable powers of the Surrogate's Court should be invoked to generally authorize them to make such a sale. I hold further that there is an implied power of sale in the will, which, in the present crisis, may be exercised by the trustees. I hold further that the proofs presented to me as to the financial condition of the Press Publishing Company, its diminishing assets and increasing loss of revenue, in its business operations, create a duty by the trustees to act for the protection of the beneficiaries of the trust."

But what killed the *World?* There was an unsuccessful business management, which not only failed to obtain advertising revenue but which imposed what probably were false economies in the gathering of news  Then, in January, 1925, the price of the morning *World* was raised to three cents, competing with the other morning papers which sold for two cents. The *World* profit that year increased $500,000, but there was a circulation drop from 404,377 to 342,928. By the end of 1926 the circulation was down to 285,882. In 1927 the price was put back at two cents, but only a small increase in circulation resulted. And the advertising was becoming thin.

There were other factors. Frank I. Cobb, the chief editorial writer, who was ready to take a position on almost any question instantly and to fight at the drop of any hat, had died. He had been succeeded by Walter Lippmann, who was scholarly, thoughtful, but not a slambang fighter. The character of the editorial page changed; some thought it better, but others missed Cobb.

The other cause for the death of the *World,* which may have outweighed all the others, was that it was done to death by termites. The management kept on the payroll during the crucial years an army of wornout veterans, of men who never had been worth their salt and who never would be. Sentiment, tradition, false loyalty, or plain softness persuaded the management to let them continue eating up the payrolls. These ancient destroyers of efficiency did their nibbling from the basement all the way up to the high gold dome. The name of Herbert Bayard Swope always comes up when newspaper men discuss the decline of the *World*. Swope is sometimes regarded, and not alone by Swope himself, as among the greatest of newspaper men. Even today he writes letters praising, with the air of mentor, the work of reporters, and he will tell a tired young editor, "My boy, you are the best bet in sight as a successor to me." What are the facts? He left the *World*, where he had been executive editor, just before the final death rattle had set in. The obsequies were left to Ralph E. Renaud, who became managing editor. While Swope was there he was in a position of tremendous authority. The imperious rattle of his heels upon entering the city room would strike terror into brave reporters; again, his bark over the telephone from the racetracks of Baltimore or Saratoga would change the make-up of the front page. Swope years ago was a reporter of great vigor and enterprise; as an editor he was, when working at it, full of fire and fresh ideas. He made much money in speculations. He won the praise of Mrs. Arnold Rothstein for his talent for picking suitable names for racehorses.

But, for all his charm and his occasional ten-strikes, he is regarded by one wing in journalism as having been strangely helpless to stop the deadly process which left the *World* a decayed, profitless shell. Could he have saved it? Maybe; on the other hand, it may be that not even the great Swope of legend, working at it conscientiously twenty-four hours a day, could have stopped that slide toward the end.

Roy W. Howard, who bought the *World* properties for $5,000,000, scrapped the morning *World* and merged the *Evening World* with his *Evening Telegram*, which he had

purchased from William T. Dewart as the first move in the
invasion of the New York field by the Scripps-Howard
chain. He held the morning *World's* Associated Press
franchise for a time, received many fantastic offers for it
from pint-size Northcliffes who would sidle up and show
him rolls of greenbacks, and then decided to drop the franchise.

The old *World* papers live today after a fashion in the
*World-Telegram,* an afternoon paper which has managed
to keep a circulation of around 400,000, and which, were
it not for the overhead in the form of notes, mortgages,
etc., would be a profitable concern. The paper today has
few traces of the individual character of the old *World*
except the daily column of Heywood Broun and the book
comment of Harry Hansen.

It seems long to have been the general opinion, among
newspaper men, that the Scripps-Howard papers throughout the country are honest, vigorous, bright but sopho-
moric. They might be well-intentioned, ready to break a
lance with any dragon, but somehow lacking in solidity
and professional expertness.

Their editorial slogan, "Give Light and the People Will
Find Their Own Way," sounds good, but in practice the
*World-Telegram* has been the chief exhorter among all the
papers in New York. It cried for Joseph V. McKee for
Mayor, then plopped to LaGuardia, then was sick when
McKee decided to run after all, and at last was mightily
relieved when LaGuardia was elected Mayor of New York.
As a journalistic product, it is alive in its news, but skimpy
and shot through with dubious semi-crusades.

Despite the efforts of Lee Wood, its dynamic and courageous executive editor, it remains a hodge-podge in its
make-up. It has one of the best staffs anywhere, but its
best men often waste their efforts on thin "feature stories"
and rather flimsy specials. And yet, for all its continual
fumbling for a coherent character, it now and then gets its

teeth into a good story, or a good idea, and goes after it in splendid style. Some of its editorials are well-documented, straightforward and actually say something. It is one of the most interesting of all papers to watch, for after more than three years it still appears not to have quite been able to make up its mind what it will be.

The *World-Telegram*, according to some seers, sought to draw its readers from those who disliked the extremely conservative *Sun* on the one hand and the highly sensational *Evening Journal* on the other. Hearst's journal is almost wholly a feature paper; it keeps a high circulation, but its advertising has given it trouble. The real enemy of the *World-Telegram*, in revenue and prestige, is the *Sun*.

The *Sun* is an independent Republican paper. For many years it has supported the Republican candidate for President, but it has thrown its support to Democratic State and city candidates, and was almost always in Al Smith's corner when he was running for Governor of New York. The *Sun* is managed and written for the most part by veteran New York newspaper men who figure that the old paper will be around for a long time. No use getting excited. Don't go out on a limb for a man who may double-cross you tomorrow. Box them, don't fight them. Get out a clean, good-looking, informative paper. Keats Speed, the managing editor; Frank M. O'Brien, the editor; Harold M. Anderson, the great old editorial writer, and a half dozen or more others have been doing business at the same stand for many years. They may be a little lame on a late afternoon news story, but the *Sun* still deserves, most of the time, the slogan which it had when little Virginia wrote in to ask if there was a Santa Claus, "If you see it in the *Sun* it's so." And yet, the permutations of newspaper business are so difficult to chart that it may have to change. Already, on many days, it has become a good deal of an advertising handbill, catering to many special groups.

The New York *Evening Post,* the paper of Alexander
Hamilton and William Cullen Bryant, was taken over in
the winter of 1933 by J. David Stern, owner of the Philadelphia *Record* and the Camden, New Jersey, *Courier and
Post.* Stern acquired the paper from John C. Martin, son-
in-law of the late Cyrus H. K. Curtis. Martin had tried
all sorts of dodges to make a go of it; for a few weeks
before the Stern invasion the *Post* had been published as an
attempt at that dream of the academicians—a high-class
newspaper in tabloid form. When Stern came to New
York he restored the standard size, fired nearly everyone
around the place, and began stripping the organization
down to the chassis. Whether he can make a go of it is
still, in the summer of 1934, an unsettled question.

Many men who worked with Stern in Philadelphia,
Camden and elsewhere swear by him; some even hail him
as one of the great minds of newspaper history. Whatever
he is, in a short time he changed what was a fairly good
paper into one of the strangest ever seen in New York.
The paper started fights, some of which resembled small-
boy crusades with wooden swords. It made a record for
quixotic hiring and firing. The staid citizens wondered
whether the new proprietor was just an ambitious carpet-
bagger or a genuine messiah.

It is one of the curious traits of Mr. Stern that the word
"liberal" appears not only in his conversation and his public utterances, but in almost every paragraph of his ringing
editorials. It will be time, some day, to get a scientific
definition of the word in the light of history and modern
trends. It has been used so much by Broun, by Roy Howard, by Hearst, by Stern, by Lippmann and others, that it
has become somewhat bewildering. Even Frank A. Munsey on occasion called out for liberalism, urged the scrap-
ping of the old political parties and the formation of a
great "liberal conservative" party, whatever that would be.
A liberal, at the latest taking of temperature, and with

only a few precincts missing, seems to be a man like this: He is not a member of the Union League Club. He likes Jews. He frowns on lynching. He is hot for peaceful picketing and bitter against cossack policemen. He is tolerant of both Karl and Harpo Marx. He wants to deport Dr. Haenfstaegl, here for a college reunion. He swears by the Bill of Rights, but is always tinkering with it, scraping and varnishing. He likes dirty books. He is a rabid individualist, stringing along with Thomas Jefferson Mondays and Fridays, and the rest of the week he is a collectivist. In short, he doesn't make sense. His label is frayed. He is a lost maverick wandering on the vast ranges of the world of journalism, politics and ideas. And he knows no brother.

The "liberal spirit" in journalism is as hard to pin down as a telephone tip from an anonymous drunk. Certainly Frank A. Munsey had moments when he thought of himself as a real liberal. Probably he wasn't, because of his background, his hard beginnings in business and his habit of mind and of living, but he thought he was. He has been dead since 1925, but some journalists still revile him. He has been regarded as many things: grocery clerk, arrogant Tory, thwarted playboy, grave-digger for great journals, stock market speculator, social climber, a flinty taskmaster given to macabre punishments for those who crossed him, and so on.

Is it possible ever to be quite fair with the memory of a man whose business dealings affected so many papers, and the lives of so many thousands of men and women? Probably not, but the things said about Munsey are not all true. Indeed, he was no sooner buried than he was denounced by jackals who had been in his personal debt. These, and others, forgot his many acts of thoughtfulness and remembered only the built-up scarecrow—the cold vampire who sucked the life from good papers and threw the bones into the ashcan.

The caricature was wrong. He was a strange man, inept in many of his human relations, but he was no monster, and to the last he had that wistful yearning for companionship that all lonely rich men feel. He was capable of great kindness. He liked newspaper work, often going to great pains to compliment a reporter on a story that had aroused his enthusiasm, though it is possible that he had no real talent for making a newspaper thrive. It may be that his chief traits were a horror of waste and a disinclination to be gypped.

He was not a great newspaper man, possibly, because he did not understand people and the hot, vibrant news of people. But he was usually right when he said that the newspaper field was overcrowded with struggling, starved sheets, and knocked one or more of them on the head. Not many men were thrown out of work; most of them were quickly absorbed. He made many mistakes. He had the tabloid idea, but let *The News* in New York go ahead and do the job.

In 1916 Munsey bought the *Sun* and *Evening Sun* from William C. Reick and associates for more than $3,000,000. He merged the *Sun* with the *Press,* which he had bought in 1912. In January, 1920, he bought the New York *Herald,* the *Evening Telegram* and the Paris *Herald* for $4,000,000 from the estate of the younger James Gordon Bennett, who had died abroad in 1918. He consolidated the *Sun* and the *Herald,* after a time, and called it the New York *Herald;* he changed the name of the *Evening Sun* to simply the *Sun,* as it remains today.

Other mergers came fast. In 1923 he bought the New York *Globe and Commercial Advertiser* for $2,000,000 and merged it with the *Sun.* In January, 1924, he bought the *Evening Mail* from Henry L. Stoddard for more than $2,000,000 and merged it with the *Evening Telegram.* He seemed obsessed with the idea of owning newspapers, and merging them. His investment in newspaper properties in New York and other cities was doubt-less more than $16,000,000.

Then came his most spectacular move. He hated waste and duplication. In March, 1924, perceiving the *Herald* and the *Tribune* were the only Republican morning news-papers in New York, and that they covered substantially the same territory, he proposed to the Reids, owners of the *Tribune* (Mrs. Whitelaw Reid, who died in 1931; her son, Ogden Reid, now editor of the *Herald Tribune,* and Mrs. Ogden Reid, now advertising director) that, "You buy the *Herald* or I'll buy the *Tribune.*" He named a figure. Mrs. Whitelaw Reid astonished him by saying, "I'll buy the *Herald.*" Mr. Munsey was right. It was a natural, successful merger of two great properties.

Before the sale of the *Herald* to the *Tribune,* Mr. Mun-sey had taken great pride in his paper, often printing signed editorials on the first page. During part of his ownership of the *Herald,* until their death, two genuinely great jour-nalists, Ervin S. Wardman and E. P. Mitchell, were on the paper. Mitchell, a master and a scholar, was still useful. Wardman was an adept at the hard-hitting and always effective repetitive style of editorial, which now might be illustrated by: "Joe Doakes was a rat yesterday. Joe Doakes is a rat today. Joe Doakes will be a rat tomor-row." Munsey admired the Wardman sledgehammer, and tried to ape it in his own calls to arms.

Somehow life was not the same to Munsey after he sold the *Herald.* For some reason buried in his inscrutable soul he had admired the old *Herald;* he even admired that crochety wine-bibber, James Gordon Bennett the younger, and some say he tried to dress like Bennett, and to be as much like Bennett in manner as decorum would permit. He looked a bit like Bennett, brushed his hair and trimmed his mustache as Bennett did, and had mementoes of Ben-nett in his office.

Did he forget something? That Bennett and his father,

the fighting Scot who was the first James Gordon Bennett, had between them discovered or invented news as news is known today—society news, sports news, the weather, ship news, foreign news, the interview, financial news? That is to say, the Bennetts were news newspapermen (there was a Mayor of New York named John F. Hylan who once referred to painters and sculptors as "art artists," which, for all the scoffing occasioned at the time he coined it, is a phrase of considerable merit).

Munsey died after an operation for appendicitis, at the age of seventy-one. Seekers for strange causes hint that death was really due to his sadness at parting with his only morning paper, the *Herald*, but Dr. Samuel W. Lambert, who handled the case, knows appendicitis when he sees it. The residue of the Munsey estate was left to the Metropolitan Museum of Art. William T. Dewart, who was one of Mr. Munsey's closest business associates and who had started his business career as a $12 a week bookkeeper, bought the *Sun* and the *Evening Telegram*, along with the Mohican chain of grocery stores and other properties, from the museum in a transaction involving about $13,000,000. Dewart then sold the *Evening Telegram* to Scripps-Howard and concentrated on the *Sun*, in which many employees own large blocks of stock.

The New York newspaper field is now pretty well stabilized, although if Munsey were alive he might be able to find many wasteful spots. The *Herald Tribune*, since it took its present name at the merger in 1924, has become a powerful paper; although Republican, it has not been afraid to experiment, as in its engagement of Walter Lippmann at the death of the *World* to write an independent editorial feature. Its news, even its political news, is less biased than it once was. Its professional standing has grown rapidly. It is famous for its typographical excellence. It seeks complete coverage without becoming a dreary catalogue. It has faults, and touches of Tory choler now and then, but it is alive. The merger of the two papers was a happy idea.

The New York *Times* remains consistently a great newspaper. For the last few years, appealing generally to the same type of reader to which the *Herald Tribune* makes its appeal, it has kept ahead of the Republican paper in circulation and total advertising. The ratio varies little over the years. The *Herald Tribune* is ahead in the high class suburbs; the *Times* leads nationally and in the city. The *Times* probably has the largest staff, and, in theory at least, the most thorough news-gathering organization ever put together. Yet it is frequently beaten.

Its sense of proportion does not always seem as sure as when Van Anda was managing editor, although Edwin L. James, the new managing editor, who had been abroad for many years, is a newspaper man of great talent and resource. The paper, somehow, has a dull feel to it, but it has brightened considerably in the last few years. The patriarch of the *Times*, Adolph S. Ochs, who made the paper as the last two generations have known it, cannot be as active as he once was. The heirs and the machinery are supposed to function when he goes.

Hearst's morning paper, the *American*, has shown steady improvement. It grabbed much of the old *World's* classified advertising. It is not nearly so harum-scarum and hollow as it once was. Its news is terse and usually accurate. It has an attractive sports section. It has Brisbane, O. O. McIntyre and Damon Runyon. It has a "brains page" which sometimes provides excellent entertainment. Its fault is a common fault among Hearst papers; its aim is diffuse, and its audience hybrid, and there is a resentment against any paper which Hearst publishes, no matter how good it is.

Outside of New York, the changes have been many, and sometimes startling. The Philadelphia morning *Public Ledger* died in 1934. Eugene Meyer, Jr., a banker with money and intelligence, is trying to make the Washington *Post* into the paper it might be. The papers on the West Coast are pretty bad; the Vancouver *Sun* gives good coverage, with much empire news, and Harry Chandler's *Times* in Los Angeles is the most substantial in California. Fremont Older, old but still fighting, does the best he can with the *Call-Bulletin* in San Francisco. Luke Lea, who tried to start a powerful chain in Tennessee and adjoining States, is in prison. Many papers have suffered horribly during the depression. In Baltimore the morning and evening *Sun* papers retain their fine reputation for courageous independence.

In Chicago the *Tribune,* in the morning field, is ahead of Hearst's *Herald-Examiner,* and dominates the Chicago territory. Robert R. McCormick, editor and proprietor, is the directing head of what calls itself, with an unblushing lack of modesty, "The World's Greatest Newspaper." The *Tribune* tells its readers that it is the world's greatest (WGN), and few of the customers dispute the boast. Colonel McCormick, a tall patriot and Red-baiter, differs from his cousin, Captain Patterson of *The News* in New York, in that he has been in the forefront of the opposition against President Roosevelt and the NRA program. The Colonel, it must be, is a Tory. Moreover, few newspaper men would argue, on a basis of strict professional judgment, that the *Tribune* is "The World's Greatest Newspaper." It is not the greatest in income, in circulation, in news coverage, in disinterested public service, or in any one of many tests which may be set forth for a great paper. Officially a morning paper, the *Tribune* in essence is an afternoon paper. Its first edition is off the press at an hour when the night shift on a New York morning paper is just coming to work; many of its features are what ordinarily would be called afternoon paper features. But it pays enormously.

Opposed to it is the Chicago *Daily News,* the leading

afternoon paper, now under the management of Col. Frank Knox. The two Colonels have been having a merry battle, with Knox calling the *Tribune's* wide circulation territory, which embraces a rich area of about 150,000 square miles, "Scatterville," and arguing with advertisers that the concentrated circulation of the *Daily News* is more valuable. Ah well, Chicago was always a city of bickering and name-calling.

Out of all this summary of newspaper trends one may find the reaffirmation of a few old truths: facts sell papers; the reader suspects the crusader whose motives he does not quite understand; clean typography and attractive make-up are always valuable; the public can't always spot a confidence man, but often it can; it is better to tell the truth, fairly and as completely as possible. But what is new in all this? Did Captain Patterson originate the philosophy of the tabloid *News* in New York? Northcliffe might claim it. So might F. G. Bonfils and H. H. Tammen, who ran the Denver *Post* in a building which had carved over the front door, "Oh Justice, when expelled from other habitations, make this thy dwelling place." The Denver boys had the credo also, "A dog fight in Champa street [in which the *Post* Building is situated] is better than a war abroad."

All the surveys in Christendom cannot answer all the questions of why a newspaper blooms, or why it sickens and fades. Some young whippersnapper with an under-done dream, or some goofy stranger who made a pile of money in the bear market, may bob up tomorrow, buy a few papers and change the whole face of journalism.

# THE MAN WITH THE GREEN EYESHADE

THE newspaper copyreader doubtless deserves better from fate than he has received. This workman, who edits, corrects and manicures the copy which flows across the desk from the reporters, rewrite men, correspondents and news services, and then writes headlines (Gale Lashes Coast As Thousands Cheer), is the unsung hero of the Fourth Estate.

He is completely anonymous. His deft touches with the pencil may raise a story out of the ordinary, but it is the handsome, much publicized reporter who gets the credit. Fancy reporters, particularly young ones who have been debauched by gazing too long at iridescent and poetic images, call him a butcher. Rarely do they thank him for improving their efforts. His job usually is monotonous. He sits on the rim of the horseshoe desk, does his stint and then goes home.

Moreover, the monetary rewards for reading copy have been relatively small. Newspapers, while honestly professing to value the services of the expert copyreader, ordinarily pay the old masters less than they are worth. The wages seem to have what is known in labor circles as a "low ceiling." A fast-blooming reporter may hope to receive $100 to $200 a week after a few years, although few of them ever get that much; no matter how able the copyreader, he can hardly hope ever to receive more than $90 or $100 a week, and that figure is paid on only a few newspapers. The average in New York today is about $50 a week.

The copy desk, in spite of the efforts of well-meaning journalistic uplifters to interest young and ambitious men in its undoubted charms, remains, in all truth, pretty much a refuge for ageing men who are no longer spry enough to get out and cover assignments. This, of course, is not universally so, nor is it necessarily a bad thing. If many old reporters, faced at last with the realization that they were unable to stand the rough and tumble life of collecting and writing news, had taken the time to learn the technique of reading copy, their old age would be much more secure. They could land on the copy desk, and do useful work, instead of whining that they had given the best years of their life to reporting and then had learned too late that there was nothing else they could do.

Copyreading is not quite an exact science, but it approaches that status at its best. It requires speed, an orderly mind, a wide background, an eye for detail and a knowledge of words. More, it requires judgment. Some of the best seem to have come by the knack in some unexplained fashion. Many a time a new man has been hired on trial, and a few nights later the head of the desk would say: "I don't know where that goofy-looking bird could have picked it up, but he's a born copyreader." Other men of sound brains may remain ignorant, and inexpert at the mechanics of the job, for a lifetime.

In 1925, in a speech to the students of the School of Journalism at Columbia University, Adolph S. Ochs, publisher of the New York *Times,* said of the copyreader and the make-up man:

It is their work that supplies and applies the test of newspaper efficiency. Copyreading and make-up are the basic principles of newspaper work and it is in this branch of the profession that the School of Journalism can best justify its existence, because it is here we depart from the purely academic and enter the practical.

Of course, the best background for the profession of journalism is a general education in history, literature, political economy, law, science and so on. But all of these studies are available in every school or college of any pretension, and while a school of journalism may specialize in them, still it is yet true that for this kind of instruction the school of journalism is not necessary for those aspiring to take up newspaper work.

But copyreading embraces the art and science of editing, and make-up the art and genius of presenting the printed word. In this work there are certain elementary principles that can be taught. There is, or should be, a code of ethics, and there are many rules and regulations that suggest themselves born of experience.

Copyreading is editing, and a copyreader is truly in the full meaning of the word an editor.

The most useful man on a newspaper is one who can edit. Writers there are galore. Every profession offers them. But the editor is of a profession apart. And it is he who should be able to apply the acid test: Is it worth printing, and, if so, how best can it be put in printable form, with its values disclosed and brought within the understanding of the reader?

The demand for editors who can edit far exceeds the supply but the demand for writers has the supply always in sight. It is true that sense of news values cannot be taught, but it may be more easily acquired by an experience in copyreading.

The copyreader really functions for the newspaper reader; for his duty is to go through the process of elimination, saving the newspaper space and the reader time. He may be described as the News Digester.

Then comes his duty in headline writing. Therein is real art. It is here that art too frequently is degraded and ability too often fails to resist temptation. There are more complaints of headlines than of text, and we are constantly hearing that the headlines misrepresent, exaggerate, have a particular bias, a wrong slant, color the news, prejudice the reader, convey a wrong impression and magnify unimportant details.

A newspaper is of the instant. The newspaper headline writer must be mentally and morally sound and detached from selfish interest or prejudicial inclinations and reach his conclusions by a process of self-effacement.

So you observe that not only quick judgment but a high order of intelligence is required in copyreading. To an extent, the very character of a newspaper is established by these head-lines.

But I must hasten to take up the matter of make-up, a function for which there is a dearth of qualified men. It is a position of prime importance, for it is here that knowledge of the mechanics of newspaper making is required. An apprenticeship in the composing room is an experience and qualification that helps to place the journalist in the front rank of his profession. The make-up is the appearance of the newspaper. It is to attract the eye, to arrest the attention of the reader. The location of items of news reflects the appreciation of their importance and is often indicative of partisanship and bias.

What Mr. Ochs said then is substantially true a decade later. His summary of the work of the copyreader and the make-up, and his estimate of their importance, remain fundamentally sound through the years. On his own paper he showed that he realized the importance of these men by paying better salaries, for the leaders of this branch of journalism who went to work on the *Times*, than were paid on any other paper in America. To be sure, the *Times* acquired some queer ones, and some who were at the end of their rope or never very keen, and some who were overrated, but the Ochs appreciation of copy-editing appeared in the finished product and in the office organization. That is, the policy made for sound craftsmanship.

The plea for more attention to the mechanics of copy-reading by schools of journalism has had very little effect. It is a dismal commentary on the schools, and on the will power and foresight of young men who hope to enter journalism, that the best copyreaders today are what might be called, without hurting their feelings in the least, "old men." In a pinch, it is usually the old fellow, with from two to five decades of experience back of him, who is called upon to handle the important copy and to write the delicate headline which is to be the paper's main show-

window tomorrow morning. He may be a bigamist, suffering from dropsy, half-drunk, and living in a mangy hall
bedroom, but, so help him, he knows what to do with a
batch of copy and some pencils.

This is far from saying that all these old workhorses
can be depended upon to do their stuff. On many
nights, in some offices, it is an even money bet that they
will not even show up for work. They are, after a
fashion, the ancient clerks of journalism, but those who
are dependable and who once really mastered their craft
can find a job even when they are dodderers.

These hoary and delightful fuddy-duddies are hold-
overs from the days when the copyreader roamed the
country like the telegraph operator or the tramp printer.
Did a copyreader find a woman in Kansas City becoming
too troublesome? Then Joe McAuliffe in St. Louis had a
job open on the copy desk. Did St. Louis grow boresome?
Perhaps Edward S. Beck on the Chicago *Tribune* had a
spot. Did he want to come East? The copy desks of the
Eastern papers were lined with old friends who had worked
from Atlanta to Seattle, and who were ready to put in a
good word.

Today there is much less of this shifting about. But few
of the really competent old-time copyreaders, unless they
have proved to be absolutely unreliable, or too far gone in
liquor and loss of memory, are worrying today about
having a job. It may be a mediocre job, but it is better
than being an old reporter who can't do anything. Indeed, some of these gray sky-writers have reformed, won't
touch a drink, and now occupy important editorial positions. The point is simply this: they had the sense to learn
their business.

Too many of the young men are impatient, and won't
stand up under the drudgery. Why should they sit at a
desk, when other young men are writing stories that carry
big black by-lines, and others are getting around, painting

the town red, growing up into special writers, dramatic critics, columnists or feature writers of distinction? Well, it is hard to blame them sometimes. If they haven't a feeling for the handling of a piece of copy, of making sense out of a difficult passage and writing a coherent headline for it, they had best do something else. But the rewards of the copy desk, for the man who likes it, are not to be dismissed lightly. He has fixed, regular hours; his spare time is his own. And sitting down at one's work is sometimes a sweet boon. Moreover, many of the higher editors are picked from the ranks of copyreaders rather than from the reporting staff.

It has been difficult, since the early days of newspaper work, to convince reporters that copyreaders can be anything except officious dummies, with a gnawing inferiority complex, who delight in ruining the best work of a reporter by cutting out the frills. There is the story of the bitter old copyreader who, reading the copy of a young and brilliant reporter, was unable to restrain his genuine amusement. With every chuckle he would mutter: "Lord, this is funny. I'll fix it." Wherewith his pencil would cut out the very phrases which had moved him to rare bellylaughs. But there is not much of this wanton destruction of great literary efforts. The pencil of the copyreader usually works for clarity, conciseness and precision. Can a sentence, even a pretty good sentence, be made shorter without injuring its meaning or its effect? Then it is up to the copyreader to do it.

Reporters could learn much from listening to wise old copyreaders. Even when they are bores, their skulls are full of the accumulated wisdom of decades. Hot-headed young word-painters have been known to fly off the handle when questioned by a copyreader on the facts of a story. This is a great mistake. If the copyreader can't understand it, how can the average reader?

Who will replace the old men? In recent years there

has been an effort, wherever possible on the larger newspapers, to induce young men, who might not have any
particular gift or inclination for reporting, to try their
hand at reading copy. The results, while not always happy,
have produced some exceptionally high-class handlers of
copy. The business needs more of them. One of the best
younger ones, Walter Colclough, fast and intelligent, was
killed by an automobile in 1933.

In theory at least the copy which reaches the desk, after
having passed the city editor or the night city editor, is
supposed to be fairly clean—that is, the names should be
right, the words spelled correctly, and the general sense
of the story should be clear and orderly. Unfortunately,
the heavy run of stuff (sometimes, for weeks, on a large
paper, 40,000 words will pass under the eyes of the city
desk each night on its way to the copyreaders) makes it
impossible for the city editor to catch all the errors, or to
see that all the prose is compact and clear. He must lean
heavily for these things on the copyreader.

Curiously, many copyreaders are not good spellers, although this should be one of the first requirements, for
some of the reporters are appallingly bad. In the course
of a week, the stories of one New York reporter showed
the following curious forms of spelling: comparabel,
ernestly, alumnium, presumabley, negligiable, caberet,
hilarous, indefinate, convelasing, accomadate, chlorines
(for chorines), alter (for church altar), concockted, oc-
curance, yoedlers, scarsity, farcial, minstrell, lieutennant,
suspence, miscellainous, interpretor, definate, inaugeration,
pidgin (for the bird), vaudville, relased, duel (for dual
rôle), befreinding, colossel, rejuvination, homecide, Star-
Spangeled Banner, Oxegen, lonly, remnents, tarter, im-
prompto, distainfully, scarsely, religeous, sympathesie,
paralized, Medetarrainean, stoke-hole (for stoke-hold),
orpheum (for orphan), cunacism, authencity, devide, af-

fabile, allegeance, boni-fide, probabally, celler, seldem, vaselating and metamorpheus.

One point of view is that such a bad speller should be fired, or hanged, although sometimes a poor speller may be an excellent reporter. There is no excuse for a copyreader who can't spell.

Another complaint against copyreaders is that they do not take pains to learn the names of persons who figure frequently in the news, and that they do not read the newspapers closely enough to acquire this knowledge. For many years the name of the late Miss Elisabeth Marbury was a terror. It seems simple enough, but all new reporters would misspell it, and there were copyreaders who went through life without having learned that her first name was not spelled "Elizabeth."

The Florence Crittenton League in New York, which cares for wayward girls, is almost universally spelled "Crittenden," even by veterans. Likewise, the Ellin Prince Speyer Hospital for Animals usually comes out "Ellen." The first name of the late Dr. Linsly R. Williams of New York, a leader of the medical profession, appeared as "Linsley," "Lindsley," "Lindsey" and "Lindsay" more often than it appeared correctly. In his younger days Dr. Williams was mildly pained by these deviations in orthography, but with mellow old age he accepted it all like a good stoic. For many years the present Mayor of New York, Fiorello H. LaGuardia, saw his first name spelled "Fiorella" probably half the time. Among steamships, the *Aquitania* of the Cunard Line frequently is spelled "*Acquitania*," just as the aquarium becomes the "acquarium." Likewise, the unlettered often take Binghamton, New York, and make it "Binghampton."

Although there is very little deliberate mangling of good stories on the copy desk, and the desk certainly improves more stories than it injures, there remain a few copyreaders, members of a strange cult, who suffer from an ailment known in the trade as the itching pencil—that is, they can't let well enough alone. They think they have to change a few words, or a few sentences, on every page, either to prove that they are working or because of some obscure inner compulsion. Such men deserve all the calumny heaped upon them by heartbroken reporters. This is not the place for a detailed manual on the art and science of the copyreader; many excellent, exhaustive handbooks already exist. In general, the copyreader should learn the full and intricate technique of his trade. He, as much as any man in newspaper work, should understand that his equipment should be all-inclusive—a nice feeling for the right word, a sense of the clear and the straightforward, a sound knowledge of the people and materials which make news, a retentive memory, a weather eye for what is libelous or dangerous, and an incorruptible mental honesty which makes it impossible for him to be unfair. His sense of taste, whether he has been able to formulate a code or not, should be quick and sure. Besides knowing not to use "gut" and "flay" unless he means it, he might even learn the difference between "ramshackle" and "dilapidated," and between "replica" and "reproduction."

Students of the workings of newspaper offices constantly argue that more attention should be paid to the copy desk, and that the good copyreader should be paid a salary commensurate with his importance and his intelligence. All true, but experience has shown that it is difficult to organize and hold a competent and well-rounded group of copyreaders. Even today, when men hang on to their jobs with more tenacity than in the 1920s, strange faces appear at the copy desk, work a few months and then disappear, sometimes for better jobs and sometimes because they were not up to the standard. A few of the old wheelhorses, always reliable and workmanlike, hang on through the years.

Of the Old Guard of copyreaders, many are dead, some

in retirement, and a few are still at work in all parts of the country. Dorsey Guy, in his youth a handsome Baltimore man about town, later one of the gentler and more attractive Broadway characters, ended his days reading copy on the *Herald Tribune,* and died of cirrhosis of the liver. Charles Wear, distinguished for his unfailing courtesy and his stammering, wasted away after the death of his daughter while he was on the copy desk of the New York *Times.* Larry Covington, the Kentucky gentleman who was for years on the old *Sun,* dropped dead in a motion picture theater. James V. Linck, who had worked in St. Louis, New York and other places, and who was hot-tempered, friendly and a rapid workman, died after an operation. "Judge" Petty, one of the fixtures of the old Bennett *Herald,* who worked with his hat on, died on his farm in upstate New York. Charles Wright, also of the old *Herald,* ended his days on the *Times;* he was a man of exceptional competence. Phil Fowler, who knew how to read copy, and who had the most startling vocabulary of biting, highly descriptive terms of abuse ever known, went out into the night during the last years of prohibition and none of his old friends ever knew what became of him.

Dan Phoebus of the New York *Times* saved his money and is in comfortable retirement, toying with mechanical gadgets which always fascinated him. William Wilson, who used to report some evenings for work at the *Times* wearing a frock coat, because his eminence among the Masons required him to attend many funerals, is retired; if there ever was a copyreader with more erudition, his like has not been seen in recent years.

Ira Crist, who in his younger days roamed the country, has for many years been telegraph editor of the New York *Herald Tribune.* Allan Holcomb, who once worked on the Denver *Post* under Bonfils and Tammen, is head of the copy desk of the *Herald Tribune,* and is a master at handling copy. Logan Mueller, who has worked in many

towns, and who shares with the late "Judge" Petty the
feeling that he should wear his hat while working, also is
on the *Herald Tribune*. Chris Hawthorne, a playful and
scholarly raconteur, worked for many papers, and after
being with Hearst for years, went to the New York *Evening Post*.

Owen Oliver, who, as a young man, roomed with two
other great men, Victor Murdock and Brand Whitlock, in
Chicago, and who probably is the best story-teller of all
the Homers ever set down at a desk, remains on the New
York *Sun*. In his younger days he occasionally sought the
bottle; he handled the copy for the *Herald* on the night
that Harry Thaw killed Stanford White, received a bonus
the next day for his work, though he could not recall having been in the office on the night of the shooting. Thus
do reflexes sometimes work. Oliver, a constant cigar
smoker, was bewildered when Frank A. Munsey bought the
*Herald* in 1920 and merged it with the morning *Sun*.
Munsey had a rule against smoking. There was no rule
against holding a cigar in the mouth, however, so to this
day Oliver does his work while clenching an unlighted
cigar in his teeth.

There are many others. They helped make all manner
of papers, and they came in odd lots. Some sampled the
grape too much, and either died or reformed; others got
pleasure out of translating Greek or going fishing. By and
large, they were perhaps the most cynical set of men in
the newspaper business; a reporter must indeed be disillusioned to compare with the old copyreader who has
been fired out of caprice, or for inadvertently writing the
wrong headline, or for letting a libelous item pass through
his hands.

One of the greatest of them all was little Edward De
Courcy Logan, who died in 1933, while head of the sports
copy desk of the *Herald Tribune*. He was a quiet, gallant, kindly and remarkably well informed man who had

worked in Buffalo, St. Louis and in many other cities. His dry wit, known to only a few, was of a rare blend. He passed his vacations revisiting Civil War battlefields. He had a bad nose, which gave his speech a nasal quality, and other ailments plagued him from time to time. A year or so before his death he was in a hospital in Brooklyn, recovering from an operation for strangulated hernia, a serious business.

One afternoon the great Australian racehorse, Phar Lap, touted as the most phenomenal racer ever seen, died unexpectedly in California. George Daley, sports editor of the *Herald Tribune,* who not only is an expert on horseflesh but who has an almost fatherly love for the nags, received a bulletin announcing the passing of Phar Lap with a feeling of profound shock. In the first moments of tragic realization, when the world seemed to be crumbling about him, Daley grabbed the telephone and called Logan. The nurse propped up the frail old copyreader and handed him the telephone.

"Yes?" said Logan.

"Eddie!" whinnied Daley, the distraught worshipper of the bang-tails. "Eddie! Phar Lap is dead!"

There was silence. Then came Logan's thin voice: "Well, George, if the boys are sending flowers, count me in."

# THE MAN WITH THE CAMERA

THAT motley aggregation of impudent and flattering camp-followers, the photographers for the newspapers and the picture services, must be ranked with the top flight of newspaper men. They are vastly more important to their papers today than ever before. From the crude old Brady pictures of the Civil War to the high-speed, action "flash" of today, the art has come a long way. The telephoto invention and the fast airplane have speeded up distribution enormously. Mechanical improvements have made possible more and better pictures, with clearer reproduction. Pictures may make a paper, or throw over it a dreary pall.

Another big war, according to what appears to be a widespread and fearful feeling, may be expected at almost any time. When and if it comes the news photographer, along with the reporter, will have a chance to perform startling deeds of daring and brilliance, perhaps more than in any other holocaust. Many of the pictures taken during the last war, among them the gripping collection arranged by Laurence Stallings, were excellent—terrific in their appeal to the eye and the emotions. In the next war the photographs should be infinitely superior. Whether the battle is in the trenches, at sea or in the air, the opportunities for pictures of tremendous news and historical significance will be without end.

The young man of today, who may be experimenting with the latest technical advances in the photographic art, or perhaps making a living taking pictures for his paper of cornerstone layings, big-wigs at the speakers' table, Sunday school parades and that sort of pedestrian material, may find, if war comes, that he will be catapulted suddenly into the middle of it—to view a naval battle from an airplane, to catch the burst of artillery fire or the cloudy roll of gas, or to use his wits in getting pictures of the unpredictable revealing incidents which any war produces.

The country is full of amateurs whose hobby is either "still" photography or the taking of motion pictures. Some of these amateurs no doubt would make valuable news photographers, and from their ranks, it is quite possible, may come useful recruits in the next great conflict. For the young man in journalism, if he has a liking for photography and the patience to study its technical processes, there are few fields more promising or profitable than the close study of the news as it is handled in pictures.

In the last few years photographs have become increasingly important; even the New York *Times,* always slow to change, each year uses more and more pictures in its week-day editions, although rarely is the front page invaded. If a young man has a bent for news pictures, and a knack for sensing the sudden dramatic situation, he can make for himself a busy, highly satisfying career. Pretty good reporters can be picked up in almost any city, at any time; the really good photographers are rare. And yet the psychological appeal of the news story and the news photograph is essentially the same—it informs and sometimes entertains.

The business, now highly specialized and alert for the latest improvements, is not only more efficient than ever, but it is more respected. Illustrated newspapers once provoked Wordsworth to exclaim with poetic petulance, "Avaunt this vile abuse of pictured page! Must eyes be all in all. . . !" Once the illustration was regarded as vulgar sensationalism; now it is not only proper but necessary. It was a little startling in 1857 when *Harper's Weekly* announced, "The proprietors beg to state that they will be happy to receive sketches or photographic pictures of striking scenes, important events, and to pay liberally for such as they may use."

In 1897 William Randolph Hearst, with characteristic enterprise, chartered a special train to carry pictures of the Corbett-Fitzsimmons fight at Carson City, Nevada, to his San Francisco *Examiner*. The stunt added thousands to his circulation; the regular mail train was so far behind the Hearst special that when his rivals obtained their pictures, it was too late to use them. Since then the great picture agencies have grown up. In the last few years the Associated Press, once concerned solely with news, has developed a remarkably speedy service. The competition for fresh pictures is fully as keen as for the latest news. The cost is terrific. Getting the pictures of the German flyers on the airplane Bremen at Greenly Island cost the Acme service $18,000.

The New York *Daily News,* the tabloid, which has added great impetus to the art of newspaper photography, and which has remarkably fine reproduction facilities, was glad to pay $1200 for a photograph of the sinking of the steamship *Vestris*—one of the great news pictures of all time, which had been taken by one Hansen, a pantryman who happened to have a little vest pocket camera with him and who had the foresight to attempt a picture while the deck was tilting for the final plunge.

The growth of the news reel also has helped. The reel men, with sound apparatus, are still handicapped by their necessarily cumbersome equipment, but even so, they perform wonders. A talking motion picture of a politician, a preacher or a current hero often determines how the public will feel about him. The citizen comes away from the news reel saying: "I suspected that he was a faker. Now I know it." Or the reaction may be the opposite. A newspaper photograph can't talk, but it can convey a powerful impression. Part of Herbert Hoover's loss of popularity might be traced to the circumstance that, in almost all his photographs, he appeared lumpy, flabby and ill at ease.

It has been the custom of newspaper reporters to assume a superior attitude toward the photographer. In all truth there have been photographers whose manners were a bit dubious, whose education was not worth mentioning, and whose sense of the proprieties might have been cause for grave head-shakings. Some of the word-painters have even resented photographers calling themselves "newspaper men." Worse, they have declined to eat at the same table with them. There is less of this arrogant attitude than formerly; the sooner it ceases entirely the better it will be for everybody, especially the reporter. For the man with the camera has found his spot in the profession. He may have to be tough, but he can't be snubbed or ignored.

The news photographers are the liveliest and the most patient of newspaper men. Often, in covering routine, they must take personal risks which the reporter would not have to take more than once or twice in a busy lifetime of chasing news. How often they will risk their necks to obtain one good picture!

Unlike the practitioners in the more hallowed branches of journalism, the photographers have no particular code of ethics. They are individualists, wolfish sometimes, and as jealous of each other as the competing ladies at a gladioli exhibit, or the jittery houris in a house of call. Even the boys who are not so good in catching a horse with four feet off the ground, or a parachute jumper half-way down, will purr when complimented on a picture of the reposeful skyscrapers of lower Manhattan, and will sulk if told that some one else made a better picture.

As a rule, photographers are assigned to go out and take a certain picture to fit a news situation. If they can't get a "pose," then they are expected to get some sort of "shot." The point is, the picture must be taken. Sometimes they must use subterfuge, and forget whatever vague

code of ethical practice they may have had in their minds.
The photographer finds that he must be aggressive, sometimes offensively so; he must know the power of cajolery,
and the endless uses of tact.

If the man is good, he has a lively sense of the dramatic.
He knows that a horse in action is better than a
horse standing like a statue. He knows that Babe Ruth,
furiously striking out in a pinch, is of much more visual
interest than when relaxed, or even thinking at top speed.
Suppose snipers shoot at a man and the bullet is stopped
by a watch; a picture of the dented watch may be better
than the picture of the man. In New York's shocking
"baby massacre" a few years ago, in which a bullet killed
a child riding in his carriage, there were no photographers
present, as it was one of those unannounced flare-ups of
gang warfare. The best picture taken was of the empty
baby carriage, showing clearly, with mute appeal, the bullet hole in the center of the top.

Always the ambitious photographers, some of them foolish, take ridiculous chances to get novel pictures. A few
years ago Col. Charles A. Lindbergh was taking off from
Roosevelt Field. Pictures had been taken from all angles—
good shots, but none of them unusual. One young man
decided to take a head-on picture of the take-off; he got
in the path of the onrushing plane, got his picture and
flung himself aside just as the plane roared past. Spectators thought at first that it was an attempt at suicide. It
wasn't. The man merely wanted a better picture.

Even with the gradually increasing friendliness in the
attitude of the public toward photographers, the men are
still hampered by rules which prohibit the taking of pictures in certain places, particularly courtrooms. Few
judges will stand for pictures to be taken in court and they
have the unquestioned power to hold in contempt any man
who violates the rule. Other judges, however, sometimes
take the position, either because they really mean it or

because they are publicity-seekers, that in an important case it may be for the public good to have as many photographs taken as may be wanted. Full, pitiless publicity sometimes can be justified, even in pictures.

Many corporations, as well as individuals who may have reason to fear unfavorable publicity, are notoriously camera-shy. Railroads dislike photographs of train wrecks, although photographers have a much easier time with this type of assignment than they once had. The heads of aviation companies still squirm when a grisly photograph of a charred plane wreck is printed. Riots, and disorders arising from labor troubles, sometimes are difficult to photograph. In this connection it might be pointed out that photographs, although if they are not faked they do not exactly lie, may yet give an unfair or distorted impression of what was happening. For example, there have been complaints for years from well-meaning citizens that the New York police had on occasion been unnecessarily brutal in breaking up Communist riots. Photographs at times have seemed to bear out this charge. Granting that the police sometimes were rough, and that they had been provoked into losing their tempers, the fact is that the Communists have mastered the fine art of falling and screaming at just the right time, so that often a Communist who is doing no more than throwing a fit, or putting on a yowling act, appears in the photograph as the victim of a brutal attack by the cossacks.

The more intelligent gangsters, criminals and members of the underworld are usually skittish, except for the occasional exhibitionist. Jack ("Legs") Diamond often shielded his face from the camera men, but when in the mood he allowed dozens of pictures to be taken, sometimes with the request that he be made to "look nice." Many photographs were taken of Al Capone when he was in his glory, but he threatened to kill a group of photographers who were trying to take his picture as he was

being led off by Federal officers for the journey to the penitentiary.  There are very few pictures of Johnny Torrio,
Capone's old boss, in existence.  Larry Fay, New York
racketeer, didn't mind having his picture taken.  Many of
the Western desperadoes, like their counterparts of another era, like to pose.  Clyde Barrow and his cigar-
smoking girl friend, Bonnie Parker, both of whom were
killed, took their own pictures and distributed them to the
press—a thoughtful gesture which should be appreciated
by newspaper readers everywhere.

The elder J. P. Morgan never could reconcile himself to
the news photographers.  Whether he regarded them as
invaders of his privacy, or whether he feared his nose
might not show up well in the picture, he remained
camera-shy to his death.  The present J. P. Morgan for
many years disliked photographers, and even now he could
hardly be called a camera-hog, but there are many excellent photographs of him.  Likewise, although he is aloof,
he will often talk frankly and pleasantly with reporters.
The most startling picture ever taken of Mr. Morgan, of
course, was in the summer of 1933, when he was testifying
in Washington and a midget from the circus was suddenly
plopped on his lap.  The Senators who were conducting the
hearing were outraged and demanded that the plates be
destroyed.  Mr. Morgan's advisers, however, with a neat
sense of public relations, realized that this one silly picture
would create more good-will for Mr. Morgan than any
100,000-word statement.  The picture was reproduced
everywhere.

John D. Rockefeller long disliked having his picture
taken for the newspapers.  The first photographer to break
down the aged oil man's reserve was Jack Price, formerly
of the old *World,* whose tact, suavity, honesty and professional competence are traditional wherever newspaper men
have had a chance to know of him.  Price convinced
Rockefeller that he would receive dignified handling.  John

D. Rockefeller, Jr., has allowed many photographs to be taken of him, in many circumstances. None of them ever harmed him. Also when he encounters reporters he is uniformly friendly in his demeanor.

During the last months of his brief term as Mayor of New York, John P. O'Brien, the last forlorn hope of Tammany, became extremely camera-conscious. Mr. O'Brien is a well-set-up, healthy American citizen, with admirable human traits, but it so happens that a capricious Creator gave him a face which combines the more distinctive features of all the Irish politicians who ever lived, especially in the region of the lower maxillary. The photographers would wait until O'Brien had stuck out his really remarkable jaw, opened his mouth and started to speak; then they would snap him. A dirty trick. He ordered that no photographs be taken while he was speaking, which made things worse, resulting in some fascinating masterpieces of photography. The poor fellow, naturally friendly as a mastiff and talkative no end, became afraid to open his mouth without ducking.

Among the bitterest of the modern camera-haters (daguerreophobes) is a member of the most-photographed family of all time, Franklin D. Roosevelt, Jr. Although a young man, he insists upon his privacy. In April, 1934, while he was a Freshman at Harvard, he was sitting with some friends watching a wrestling bout in Philadelphia. Donald Corvelli, a photographer for the *Public Ledger,* took his picture and started for the door. The President's son set upon him and smashed the camera, but Corvelli saved the plate, and the picture appeared throughout the country. Jim Londos (Christopher Theophilus), the Greek Adonis, who saw the encounter, advised young Roosevelt not to go in for wrestling, although he had done a fairly good job on Corvelli. The photographers can be brash to the point of exasperation, but any thoughtful public relations counsel will advise against roiling them. Usually they will get the picture anyhow.

Another shy public figure is Fritz Gissibl, leader of the Friends of New Germany. A House sub-committee, investigating Nazi propaganda, was holding a hearing in the Bar Association Building in New York, in May, 1934. Gissibl was in the lobby talking to his colleague, Dr. Ignatz T. Griebl. Carl Gaston, photographer for the New York *Post*, took their picture.

"You've got a hell of a nerve!" shouted Gissibl. "You know you had no right to take a picture here." Dr. Griebl also was upset, and cried, "Come on! Don't let him get out of here! Start a fight! Break the camera! We'll get that plate!"

The two friends of New Germany lunged at Gaston, who was rescued by spectators. The committee ordered Gaston to destroy the plate. Feigning disappointment, Gaston drew a plate from the camera, surrendered it, and walked out, but he carried with him the exposed plate tucked in his coat. His paper printed the picture in its next edition. It might be argued that the photographer was 'unethical; on the other hand, it might be argued that Gissibl and Dr. Griebl lost their tempers over what was really a rather trivial affair, and that it would have been far better for them if they had followed the advice once given the late Ban Johnson by Judge Kenesaw Mountain Landis and kept their shirts on.

Even such a man as former Senator James A. Reed of Missouri, generally beloved by newspaper men, has been known to flare up. George E. Cauthen, a photographer for the Kansas City *Journal*, took a picture in the court house where the murder trial of Mrs. Myrtle Bennett was being held in March, 1931. Reed slapped the photographer, who was commended editorially for not striking back.

The aircraft industry, which has shown a much more

friendly attitude toward photographers recently, has had
a hard time with its publicity and its pictures.  It is
difficult for such an industry to realize that the whole
truth, even if told with a damaging picture, is better than
trying to suppress the facts.  In November, 1931, a plane
of the United Air Lines crashed near the city airport at
Salt Lake City, Utah.  Noble Warnum, a photographer
for the Salt Lake *Telegram,* appeared soon after the crash,
in which the pilot had been killed.  A mechanic stood by
the wreckage, waving a stick as Warnum approached.
Warnum took the picture.  The mechanic took the plates
from him.  There have been other instances of this sort
of interference.  One of the first things often done by
company employees is to paint over, or scratch out, the
name of the company on the plane.

In February, 1933, there was an airplane crash at the
city airport at Richmond, Va.  G. M. Bowers, assistant
director of public works of the city, prohibited photographers from taking pictures on the ground that it would
be bad publicity for the airport.

Aviation has produced many striking photographs.
Often they are full of splendid and terrifying action.  A
few years ago Captain Frank M. Hawks, speed flyer,
crashed near Worcester, Massachusetts, and was badly
hurt.  Paul W. Savage, a photographer for the Worcester
*Evening Gazette,* saw the accident, took a picture of the
flyer pinned in the wreckage, and then helped in the rescue
work.

One of the best of all news photographers is Martin J.
McEvilly, picture chief of the New York *Daily News.*
He wanted a picture of Colonel Lindbergh at the controls
of a plane in flight.  He managed to get a seat in a twelve-
passenger Fokker that Lindbergh took up at Roosevelt
Field soon after his return from France.  He concealed his
camera until the plane was well up, then he brought it out
and took his pictures.  Lindbergh didn't know of the pic-

tures until he saw them in the paper.  Later, after Lindbergh had married Miss Anne Morrow, McEvilly tried to
get a picture of the couple.  He pursued them to Maine
by seaplane, motorboat, fishing schooner, automobile and
train, spending large sums of money, but it was of no use.
Sometime later they agreed to pose for photographers at
Mitchel Field.  McEvilly, one of the most ingenious of
them all, once surprised Gene Tunney, soon after the pugilist's marriage to Miss Polly Lauder, while Tunney was
standing, in a smoked-glass disguise, on the railroad station
at Damariscotta, Maine.  Tunney threatened McEvilly,
who calmed the fighter by saying, "Mr. Tunney, take your
hands off of me!"  Ordinarily Tunney is thoroughly oblig-
ing.

Alfred E. Smith, one of the most photographed Americans, is regarded as usually agreeable by photographers,
although he often turns them down when they want what
Smith calls "baloney pictures."  While Governor of New
York he inspected the foundation of the new State office
building at Albany.  The photographers appeared.  "Well,
boys, what do you want me to do?" asked the Governor.
"How about laying some bricks?" suggested a photographer.  "Nothin' doin'," said Mr. Smith.  "No baloney pictures around here.  People know I'm no bricklayer.  What's
the use of tryin' to kid 'em?"

This sensible attitude, in later years, saved Mr. Smith
from being put upon by photographers who wanted to
take pictures of him sampling beer or performing other
undignified and sometimes commercial antics.

Whether right or wrong, it often is necessary to resort
to trickery, not only to take photographs but to speed the
plates on their way to the news rooms.  Only rarely do
these dodges harm anyone.  At the Democratic National
Convention in Chicago in 1932, in the excitement which
came when California switched to Roosevelt, the police
ordered all doors to the stadium locked to prevent anyone

from entering. Meanwhile pictures were being taken. Picture service managers were frantic to get the plates to the telephoto and to the airports. An Associated Press photographer went to a telephone booth and ordered a private ambulance to come to the stadium, park outside and send in the stretcher with attendants to pick up an injured person at a designated spot. The ambulance men were allowed to enter, the photographer put his plates in a blanket and out they went, like a patient on the way to a hospital.

Trickery, however, can have its flarebacks. There have been many bloody and revolting photographs, some of them too strong for most newspapers to stomach. Few papers print pictures of bodies of persons strung up by mobs; only a few printed the photographs of the seven who were killed in the St. Valentine's Day massacre in the garage in Chicago. Perhaps the most awesome, or the greatest, depending upon the viewpoint, was the picture which the New York *Daily News* obtained and printed, showing Mrs. Ruth Snyder in the electric chair at Sing Sing Prison. She had been convicted with Judd Gray, her paramour, of murdering her husband. The picture was taken by an imported photographer from Chicago, the city of muscular journalism, who had a specially-devised camera strapped to his ankle. He obtained entrance to the death house as a newspaper man and a legal witness, after Lewis E. Lawes, the warden, had put all present on their honor that there would be no attempt to take pictures. It was a good shot, only a little blurred and out of focus, but it covered the whole front page of the tabloid in its later editions the next morning. It sold papers. It stirred comment, and aroused no end of discussion on what the world, and journalism in particular, was coming to.

The tabloid's editors, and Sid Sutherland, the reporter who covered the story and arranged the coup, defended the taking of the picture. It was, as a stunt, magnificent.

It could be argued that the picture was news to which the public was entitled. Do people wonder whether capital punishment is right or wrong? Well, this picture tells what capital punishment is like. Again, it portrays, better than any words, the pay-off of the wages of sin. Certainly it could be defended, and it was. But there was another side. The more conservative papers, none of whom would have printed the picture if they had got it, pointed out the violation of confidence, the obvious pandering to the morbid mind, and the general lack of taste of the whole proceeding. Any good sophist could file an interesting brief upholding either point of view. However, it is doubtful if the *Daily News,* confronted with a similar situation today, would attempt such a feat. It would be carrying enterprise pretty far north.

The Ruth Snyder picture, moreover, is regarded by the men who take news pictures as perhaps the most damaging blot upon their professional history. Their attitude—and it isn't all jealousy—is that the taking of this picture undid the patient work of hundreds of honorable camera men who had sought public confidence. There is a strong sense of honor, an undefined code which forbids shyster practices, even among this group of hard-boiled buccaneers. They feel keenly the loss of prestige which comes when one of their number goes beyond the pale. Bernarr Macfadden's now dead *Graphic,* with its composite pictures, is blamed by some editors with injuring the reputation of all news pictures. A picture that can't be believed naturally causes resentment.

The photographer, year in and year out, probably has many more chances to be crooked than the reporter or the editor. Jack Price estimates that he could have retired ten years ago, with a comfortable fortune, if he had not refused to accept bribes. It is said that Newport, Rhode Island, alone could supply a wealth of bribery and blackmail money—and perhaps it sometimes has. But most of the accredited picture men, whether at a society resort or at the racetrack, are honest. They have been known to refuse bribes and then destroy their plates anyhow when some good reason, in morals or sense, was given them as to why the printing of the picture would be needlessly damaging, contrary to the public good, or possibly useful in a shake-down scheme.

The men who snap the pictures have a long tradition. They have done astonishing work. There was William Warneke, still alive and active, who was assigned in August, 1910, by the old New York *Evening World* to take pictures of Mayor William J. Gaynor as he was about to sail for Europe on the *Kaiserina Augusta Victoria.* Warneke was late. The other camera men had got their posed pictures and departed. Suddenly a crank shot Gaynor, and Warneke, the only camera man on the scene, got the pictures.

Among the more pugnacious and alert photographers is Captain Edward Jackson, still taking pictures of crimes and trials and accidents, who made history with his famous photograph when he caught Lloyd George, Orlando, Clemenceau and Wilson, the "Big Four," in an unposed, smiling group at Versailles. Jackson is a bloodhound when he sets out for a picture.

The photographers even have their specialties, their weak spots and crotchets. J. Hal Steffen is unbeatable on sports events; Jack Frank can handle almost any type of assignment, from the high-jinks zoological park to a big fire, and William Zerbe can take a really gripping picture of a steak smothered with onions and mushrooms.

Often it has been suggested that reporters should carry cameras and take pictures while covering their assignments. The idea has some merit; and has been tried out with varying success on some of the papers in the chain owned by Frank E. Gannett. But there are many difficulties. Taking pictures seems to require a knack, or certainly a liking for photography. Most reporters, particularly the older ones, will have no part of it. Moreover, a busy reporter rarely could find time to take good pictures, and the mechanical difficulties of writing his story and delivering his plate at the same time would lead to no end of delay and confusion. However, there are certain types of assignments on which a reporter, who was a good photographer also, might turn out distinguished results. If a paper, among a staff of, say, thirty reporters, has four or five who are interested in photography, it might bring excellent results to furnish each of them with a good camera and then try to pick assignments for them on which pictures might be expected. The camera is being developed rapidly. A clear photograph, of good size for reproduction, may be taken today, without a flashlight, of, let us suppose, a group of merry gentlemen in a rather poorly lighted saloon. Not a year passes without an improvement in the business.

The chances for better illustration in newspapers are incalculable. The papers and the news services will spend even more money in the next few years than they spend today for newsy, striking pictures. And no matter whether the next great war has its center in the Balkans or in Siberia, the news photographer will be one of the heroes. It won't do him any good to sit with the generals and receive the official communiqués; he must be in a tree, or in a plane, up where things are happening. His work is important enough today—more important, indeed, than many newspapers seem to realize—but it is almost surely to be of vastly more importance tomorrow. It is a great game for the young man with an expert knowledge of photography, with good legs, a gift of gab and an insolent willingness to stick out his neck and take his chances.

# SPORTS—VALHALLA'S BULL-PEN

L ITERARY commentators and analysts, often with
little more evidence than the recollection that the
late Ring W. Lardner once wrote sports news for the
papers, occasionally take the highly debatable position
that the sports writers have produced the only genuinely
original American literature of the Twentieth Century—
"earthy," "salty," "indigenous to the United States," "full
of the lusty, gusty spirit of mockery." In the sports field,
say these historians and watchers for portents, may be
found the fresh phrase, the language of the common man
of tomorrow, and the best all-around writing that appears
in the American press.

A rash verdict. At its best, sports writing is all that its
admirers claim for it, but even when it is considered pretty
good, it may be unnecessarily bad. The art, one of the
finest and most abused in all newspaper work, deserves
study by everyone who is even remotely interested in
newspaper work or in sports. It is better than condescend-
ing appraisers believe it to be. The bulk of it is open to
serious question.

As a distinct branch of American letters, sports writing
has existed only since about that period which Mark Sullivan, the Bat Nelson of political writers, has called the
Turn of the Century. In its infancy it was a lonely
orphan. Then came an era of luxuriant verbiage, when
no spade could be called a spade. Later the art had its
period of disillusionment and debunking, a period which
still hangs on, sometimes as a healthy attitude and sometimes as mere exhibitionism. Today the art seems to be
maturing, and in the larger cities it shows signs of produc-

ing a department of the newspaper distinguished by intelligent reporting and writing—the ancient, simple test of newspaper excellence.

The sports page once was the poor relation. It was read principally in barber shops and barrooms to supplant the *Police Gazette*. Publishers and managing editors knew it was necessary, but they didn't like it. Now the sports pages are second only to the general news pages in importance; indeed, on some days they may be more important. The clientele is wider; it handles more sports and finds its readers among ping-pong players, duck shooters, hikers, fishermen, bowlers and fencers. It is genteel, sometimes too genteel; fortunately some sports writers retain enough of the old beer, beef and beans flavor to ward off anemia.

It is not now a skimpy sports page, but a sports section. The space daily devoted to sports has more than doubled in the last fifteen years. The Sunday sections may run to twelve pages. It is, rightly, a department to which newspapers devote brains and money. Even more attention should be paid to headline writing and editing.

The character of the writers has changed. With a few scholarly exceptions, sports writers used to be rather unlettered chroniclers (muggs) writing for an audience of their own kind. Now much of the writing is done by college men, aimed at readers who are college students or college graduates. The boys who thirty years ago aped the late Charley Dryden, who probably deserves to be called the real father of modern sports writing, have dropped out or learned better. Too many of them were bankrupt in imagination and had to resort to tricks when something more than monosyllables was demanded. After Dryden, such men as Lardner, W. O. McGeehan, Hughey Fullerton, Damon Runyon, Grantland Rice, to name only a few of the signposts, brought to the business a grown-up judgment, some sense of proportion, a gentlemanly taste and even some literary quality.

The best of the moderns have learned that it is possible
to take a point of view. They know that the qualities
which vitalize all writing—irony, restraint, accuracy, illuminating detail and humor (which doesn't have to be
slapstick)—are as possible, even necessary, in sports writing as in writing of a murder or a parade of Negro Elks.
That is to say, the more discerning understand that one
can be a reporter. They can ask pertinent questions.
They can learn not only the spotted history and legal
dodges of Organized Baseball but they can actually find
out about the idiosyncrasies of the third baseman.

Many have found news when their curiosity led them
to look into the set-up of the organizations that control
some of the sports—the Amateur Athletic Union, the
United States Golf Association, the United States Lawn
Tennis Association, the National Boxing Association, the
New York State Athletic Commission and others. News
is not always the playing field. It may be in the club-
house, in the hotel rooms, on the street and in the homes
of the leaders of sports.

Does this sound elementary? It should be elementary,
but some of the highest paid and worst sports writers decline to play the game as newspaper men. These gentlemen have an honorable tradition in sports writing; men of
education and character have spent their lives at it. The
better the reporter—in observation, fairness, clarity and
vigorous writing—the better the man, whether he is covering a high school track meet or conducting a column.
Why cover up ignorance or indolence with cheap gags?

When Charley Dryden died in 1932, he had been in retirement for so long that sports editors, so little do men
think of the pioneers of their own profession, were surprised when a paragraph came over the wires announcing
his passing. They thought he had been dead a long time.
Until Dryden began writing in San Francisco in 1890, reports of most sports events had been written with much of

the unearthly beautiful, pungent style of a decision by
the Supreme Court of the United States. Dryden picked
on striking features of a game or a player. He would comment on the size of a player's feet, or his whiskers, and
would spin it through his story as a sort of theme song.
Soon Dryden's stuff was read as much for his comical
treatment as for the news it contained.

When Dryden came to New York in 1898 he drove the
irascible Andrew Freedman, then owner of the New York
Giants, to a frothing frenzy. Freedman had many pecu-
liarities (he was the genius who insisted that Christy
Mathewson should be a first baseman instead of a pitcher),
and Dryden went to work on them. Freedman warned
Dryden, who wrote of his interview with the mogul, quoting Freedman as saying to him:

"Young man, you are standing on the brink of an ab-
scess."

Freedman barred Dryden from the Polo Grounds.
Then he couldn't understand how Dryden's stories continued to appear. Dryden's friends, of course, had been
giving him the news of the games. Dryden then wrote
of how he had sneaked into the park disguised as an old
woman; at once Freedman set special police to scrutinize
old women. Then Dryden wrote that he had perched
upon a telegraph pole to watch the game; Freedman put
the cops to watching the poles. Freedman finally sold the
Giants.

Dryden stimulated, if he did not actually originate, the
idea that sports were worth writing about, and that they
could be written differently from a market report. Poor
fellow, he has much to answer for. He created a young
and lively language for sports; writers without his good
sense got the idea that all sports should be written in a
bizarre patois, and that to use good English was a sissy
trick. He had no idea of founding a school of writing.

He merely planted a few seeds, and a lush lot of vegetation grew up, much of it rank and unpruned.

He was an apt coiner of nicknames which stuck. The late Charles Comiskey, owner of the Chicago White Sox, was always "the Old Roman." Frank Chance was the "Peerless Leader." He is credited with saying of Ed Walsh, the pitcher, that he was "the only man in the world who could strut sitting down," a description which has passed into the common language.

Soon, on every sports page in the country, sprouted lines intended to impart the fresh touch. After all, the subject matter of sports is pretty much the same. Almost every suicide, murder, shipwreck and train collision is cut on a different pattern, and the reporter does not have to search for outlandish substitutes for common terms. One baseball game, however, is pretty much the same as another. The few standard nouns and verbs which may be used in writing of baseball, football, boxing and rowing become tiresome.

A baseball became "the old apple," "the horsehide pellet," "the elusive spheroid." In football the ball became the "pigskin" or even the "oblate spheroid." Home runs were "circuit clouts," "four-ply wallops," "four-masters," and "four-baggers." Baseball parks were "ball yards" or "orchards." A base-hit was a "bingle." When a man struck out he "whiffed the ozone." A bat was "the ash," "the willow," "the war club" or "the bludgeon." A left-handed pitcher was "a port-side hurler" or a "southpaw," although for some reason right-handed pitchers never were "northpaws." A pitcher's throwing arm was his "salary wing." The manager was a "mentor," "wizard," "miracle man," "generalissimo," or "master mind."

Some of these words and phrases were pithy and effective. To say of a fast ball pitcher that he "threw buckshot for nine innings" gave an excellent idea of his speed. The trouble was that when one writer hit upon a good phrase the others took it up and used it until it became threadbare. Thus "the Ruppert Rifles," used to describe the New York Yankees, becomes as monotonous as the late Joe Vila's continual references to them as "McCarthy's Bombers." Babe Ruth, too often for entertainment, has been called the Behemoth of Bust, the Mammoth of Maul, the Sultan of Swat and the Colossus of Clout (sometimes spelled with a K to be kute).

It was Rice who called Red Grange the Galloping Ghost, and the Notre Dame backfield, one year, "the Four Horsemen." These labels stuck.

Jack Dempsey was called "the Manassa Mauler," because he came from Manassa, Colorado, although it is probable that few readers ever understood this. Georges Carpentier was once "the Orchid Man." Primo Carnera generally was called "the Man Mountain" until McGeehan began to refer to him as "the Tall Tower of Gorgonzola." Tom Heeney, the heavyweight from New Zealand, was "the Hard Rock from Down Under." Paulino Uzcudun was "the Basque Woodchopper," Harry Wills "the Brown Panther of New Orleans," and Jack Johnson "the Big Smoke." Johnny Dundee, an Italian, was called "the Scotch Wop." In other times John L. Sullivan was "the Boston Strong Boy," James J. Corbett was "Gentleman Jim," and Bob Fitzsimmons was "Ruby Robert." Battling Nelson was "the Durable Dane," and Ad Wolgast "the Cadillac Wildcat." Jimmy Wilde, the British flyweight, was "the Mighty Atom."

Most of these nicknames and phrases were rubbed smooth by constant usage. Sports writers became dippy trying to think of new ones, which were almost invariably worse, until the sports pages were so much maudlin balderdash, an esoteric jargon which did not even have the authentic ring of American slang. It was purely synthetic; no one but the writers could understand what it meant. This dada school of sports writing flourished until after the war, and it still blossoms on some papers, but it appears to be losing ground.   It is probable that the increasing good sense and taste of the newspaper reading public, which has raised the level of much general newspaper writing in the last ten or fifteen years, is responsible for the trend toward clarity and sanity.

After the war there was a rapid and rather astonishing increase in the public interest in types of sport which previously had been ignored by all but a few.   The papers had to cover more sports and cover them more thoroughly and expertly.   In the old days the devotees of the so-called gentler sports were scoffed at by the hard-boiled veterans accustomed to handling professional sports.   But now the land was overrun with golf players, tennis players, yachtsmen.   College sports expanded enormously, and attracted more attention, with or without special promotion.

It was no longer possible to ignore the amateurs.   Local golf and tennis tournaments had to be covered because the participants, their friends, families and fellow club members represented a considerable circulation bloc.   Always the main circulation standbys are baseball, boxing, racing and football, but much attention was demanded by chess, polo, hunting and fishing, billiards, ice-skating, lacrosse, rugby, horse shows, dog shows and cricket.   The scores of football matches in England are printed.   Some papers have hired women writers to cover women's colleges and interpret "the woman's angle," whatever that is, to women readers.

In their first enthusiasm for the gentle or amateur sports, many newspapers overdid it and played down professional sports in a fashion that would be hard to justify.   A third-rate golf tournament might receive a banner headline, with photographs, while a stirring baseball game between the Yankees and the Athletics might receive only an apologetic half-column.   The first three or four pages of a sports section might be filled with solid amateur matter; a horse race in which thousands were interested might be buried in the back. Gradually the measure of importance was adjusted a bit more sensibly.

Arthur S. Draper, now editor of the *Literary Digest,* and for many years assistant editor of the New York *Herald Tribune,* was one of the leading advocates of a fuller, more competent coverage of amateur sports, and a more prominent display for them. His ideas, like almost all sound suggestions, were misinterpreted and exaggerated, so that much genuinely important news of professional sports was either ignored or treated with passing contempt. The panorama presented by the better sports sections may be still somewhat out of focus, but it is assuming a more logical shape. Often, rather pathetically, the section is still behind its readers in intelligence.

The sports reading public today is remarkably well informed. It cannot be tickled by mere extravagance of writing. A lazy and incompetent writer finds it increasingly difficult to get by with a sloppy story, spun on a thread of artificial conceits. The demand is that he give his readers the facts, and give them straight. When crowds of 75,000 and more attend baseball and football games and boxing matches, while millions more are listening on the radio, the sports writer should realize that he has an immense, well-informed audience which does not like to be fooled or short-changed.

The sports writer today is supposed to be not only a fair writer but an informed reporter, educated in his game, acquainted with its background, personalities and politics, if any. He is a specialist. To name only a few, such men in New York as Stanley Woodward on football and rowing, Will Wedge, Edward T. Murphy and Frederick G. Lieb on baseball, Harry Cross on a half-dozen subjects, Hype Igoe on boxing, William J. Macbeth and Henry V. King on racing, Fred Hawthorne on tennis and William H. Taylor on yachting, may not be great writers, but they do know their materials. One of the last of the really great baseball reporters, who understood baseball better than most players knew it, and who wrote classic English even when explaining the most technical points of the game, was the late William B. Hanna, a grumpy journalist but a great one. He hated trees, but he knew sport.

In sports writing, and in the attitude of writers toward sports, there are two fairly definite schools, sometimes defined as the "Gee Whizz!" and the "Aw Nuts!" wings. Grantland Rice, perhaps the most popular and respected gentleman ever to write sports, came out of the South long before the war bearing an unusual equipment—he had a good education, he was a poet at heart, and he had a genuine, almost fanatical love for sport. His career probably has been the most successful of all sports writers, although he, like Dryden, set an example for many a young man, who, seeking to be a word-painter, loaded his popgun with red paint and fired at the rainbow.

Rice wrote much poetry, some of it good; much of his prose was poetry too. His leads sang of sunsets which displayed the colors of the victorious college football team, which was an advantage, because except on rainy days the crimson of Harvard or the blue of Yale may be found in the late afternoon sky. A football team in a desperate stand near the goal-line reminded Rice of the French at the Marne, the Spartans at Thermopylæ or Davy Crockett and his boys at the Alamo. A fighter like Jack Dempsey, a former hobo, might carry the hammer of Thor or the thunderbolts of Zeus in his right fist ("maulie" or "duke"). A half-back, entering the game belatedly to turn defeat into victory, would remind Rice of Phil Sheridan at Winchester. Walter Johnson, Washington pitcher, was the Big Train roaring through. There were ghosts there too, strange but lovable visitors from that Valhalla where all good sportsmen go, hovering about in the dun light, advising the gladiators and making themselves useful around the place. Sometimes the reader had to wade through half a column of this fetching literature and mythology before getting any very clear idea of who won, and how they won. It was magnificent and, may God bless us all, pretty terrible.

A school of Rice imitators, never as good as Rice at his best, and much worse than Rice at his worst, grew up. Among them is the young man who will begin his story of a mile race at a track meet like this:

"Father Time shouldered his scythe and his hour-glass yesterday and withdrew mournfully into the shadows, another divinity who had seen his strength crumble before the strength of inspired youth. His conqueror was a lithe-limbed twenty-one-year-old Mercury from the wheat-fields of Kansas, for whom time and space do not exist. Before a throng of speed-mad thousands, gathered in the ivy-bedecked Harvard Stadium to see a test of endurance which will echo down the ages as long as men tell tales of prowess . . ."

And so on. A little later the word-crazed youth will divulge who did what.

The delayed ("Fabian") lead afflicts many otherwise fairly sensible writers. They devote half a column to telling of the dramatic and possibly revolutionary importance of one play before they get down to the story of the game. Another difficulty, and a dangerous trend, may be found in the addiction of some writers to the meaningless lead, which they either fancy is epigrammatic or gripping, but which really is just so much sawdust. A decade ago Heywood Broun covered a World Series for the old New York *World*. In one game Babe Ruth was the outstanding performer, and Broun's first sentence in his story the next morning was "The Ruth is mighty and shall prevail." Broun thought it was pretty good; maybe it was, although an argument might be made for the other side.

The most persistent writer today to attempt something

similar to the Broun trick is Richards Vidmer, with his "The Ruth will out—but not for long," "If thrills were a dime a dozen, Harvard and Army played a million-dollar game here today," "The Yankees lost by a toe yesterday and now lead by a whisker," "The Baer went over the mountain—" This sort of thing, even when it is understandable and apt, soon becomes meaningless, even obnoxious. There are many offenders.

The Beatitudes were a collection of excellent gags, but editorials would be even worse than they are today if each started with one of these holy lines.

Sports writers are allowed more latitude, not only in their style of writing, but in the expression of opinion, than news writers. They can make or break a sports event by their attitude before the event. They can puff or deflate any sports figure. It is hard to sue them for libel; the man who sues usually finds that he never dreamed how ridiculous he really is. On the other hand, the boosts may bring thousands to see what any reasonable citizen might have foreseen would more than likely be a drab event. After reading for a few days, or even weeks, of a forthcoming clash between behemoths, titans, or snarling ape-men, the ordinary taxpayer gladly spends his cash for a ticket.

The best example of this sort of ballyhoo was the Dempsey-Carpentier fight in 1921, which was promoted by the late Tex Rickard. Virtually every observer of prize-fighting knew beforehand that, barring accident or the collapse of Dempsey by poison or gunfire, Carpentier had no chance. Yet it became "the Battle of the Century." Ninety thousand saw it. It was a pointless battle, as a contest.

The fight was only one of the examples of "over-emphasis" from which sports pages suffered in the 1920s and from which occasionally they still suffer. An ordinary college football game, of a pattern played for years before

a strictly college crowd, drew thousands of the general
public on the strength of the publicity. The sports writers, in their time, have been guilty of much anti-social
ballyhoo, and of bilking the public on some raw deals. By
and large, however, they are honest men, calling them as
they see them.

It was in that period of overblown sagas that mighty
pasteboard heroes were built up. A few were broken.
Babe Ruth became, for some utterly unfathomable reason,
one of nature's noblemen, with just enough of the child
about him to enhance his charm. His real eminence as a
ball player was not enough. Jack Dempsey, who "defended the title" against Billy Miske when Miske was a
known invalid, and who needed twelve rounds in which to
knock out the beer-soaked old truck horse, Bill Brennan,
was presented as a ruthless killer.

Even when some hero was drawn unsympathetically, as
when Bill Tilden was described as a spoiled boy, the publicity helped draw the crowds. It can be tremendously
telling, this handling of men and events on the sports
pages. Thousands were kept away from the Baer-Carnera
fight in 1934 because the sports writers said that both men
were palookas, and that Baer, in addition, was a giddy,
empty-headed, puffed-up wisecracker who might have
come from any corner drug store. It turned out to be an
exciting fight, though unscientific.

Sense of proportion, it may be, is what has been needed
most in sports, and that sense is difficult to define. The
debunking period in sports, which corresponded roughly to
the period in which Henry L. Mencken was getting in his
heavy licks in the debunking of life and letters, is almost
past—not that the writers have become soft, but the best
ones understand more clearly that, as long as sports are
worth writing about at all, they might as well be treated
in proportion to their importance to the sports loving
public. The debunkers cut away a lot of dead wood.

It was about twenty-five years ago that the late Ring W. Lardner went to work on the myth that sports characters were glamorous—kind to their families, courageous in all circumstances, possessing healthy minds in god-like bodies. He began his "You Know Me Al" stuff, which pictured the typical ballplayer, a stupid, stingy, gluttonous, noisy, cruel lout. It is said that when George Horace Lorimer, editor of the *Saturday Evening Post,* received the first Lardner story he refused it because he didn't believe a ballplayer could be so dumb. But Lardner went on, bitterly, though he liked sports. At the end of "Champion," his short story of the prizefighter Midge Kelly, he summed up the public attitude against which he and all other honest debunkers have had to fight—the whole story of hollow ballyhoo and false writing:

"Suppose you can prove it," the sports editor would have said. "It wouldn't get us anything but abuse to print it. The people don't want to see him knocked. He's champion."

McGeehan was another debunker, though at heart a sentimentalist. No amount of build-up could convince him that a yellow or inept fighter was a potential champion. Nor could he see any resemblance between a fourth-rate sports event and the second siege of Troy. He was among the first to belittle Carnera's farcical knockout tour of the United States. He emphasized the professional character of almost all sports; while other writers might speak of "fans" and "sports lovers," he called them "customers." He coined many nicknames. James J. Johnston, the fight promoter, was "the Boy Bandit." Wrestlers were "pachyderms" and Jack Curley, the impresario of wrestling, was their "mahout." Boxing was "the manly art of modified murder." Baseball was the "ivory industry" and the club owners were "ivory traders."

In his exposures of papier-mâché gods, and in his allusions to the intricate financial and political system controlling sports, McGeehan relied mostly upon a gentle sarcasm. Other debunkers, notably John R. Tunis, showed how the "gate" was the dominant influence in all sports, and that no amount of romantic flapdoodle could change that truth. It is still hard to make the sports writers, even some of the grizzled ones, admit that all is not beautiful and clean.

A recent trend, and a healthy one, is away from the sports cartoon. Burris Jenkins, Jr., sports cartoonist of the New York *Evening Journal,* which has an incomplete sports section from a technical standpoint but an excellent one as a circulation builder, is one of the few whose stuff is worth printing. The average sports cartoon is without humor or point. When the Giants win a National League pennant, that fact will not be more vivid to the reader by a drawing of a burly ballplayer striding over the remains of a bear (the Cubs). A favorite, moth-eaten motif before a big game is to draw the teams as their symbolic animals or reptiles, such as the Yale bulldog, the Princeton tiger or the Army mule, glaring and snorting, while a weak-chinned half-wit labeled "Gus H. Fan" stares at them goggle-eyed. Silly business.

Newspapers in many cities have excellent sports pages, though often filled with too much syndicate material, but the best ones are in New York. In general, a paper's sports pages seem to be in keeping with the rest of its character; the *Times's* are made up exactly like the news pages, with conservative headlines, plenty of facts, usually thorough, and very dull; the *Herald Tribune's* usually contain all the facts, written by experts, but they often are erratic with stories of unusual competence beside a childish essay; The *American's* are bright, well-illustrated, carrying a little of nearly all the main events, but they are incomplete; in the afternoon the *Sun's* pages are authoritative, sober, a bit ponderous and probably the most satisfying in the city; the *World-Telegram* has some good stuff, but, like the rest of the paper, it often is written with a futile straining for effect.

The sports columnist is a natural development. Sports lend themselves admirably to personal comment. From Rice's original "Sportlight" to the most modern of the younger Addisons and Swifts, the column has enhanced or disfigured the sports pages. The fault to be found with the worst ones is that they attempt to conceal their lack of knowledge behind a jerry-built structure of wisecracks; the best ones are likely to become tired or bored. There were days, in the last years, when even McGeehan, whose "Down the Line" was one of the soundest of all columns, was actually hard to read.

Perhaps the most scholarly columnist writing sports in New York is John Kieran of the *Times*. He is the most erudite of them all. He has a usually harmless tendency to burst into poetry, and his humor is not often high-pressure, but he knows his business. He has had to file off the "I" on his typewriter to conform to the impersonal style of his paper, but he loses little by that, even in interviews ("And what did Mr. Simmons have to say about the claim that he was all washed up? 'Nuts,' said Mr. Simmons.") The matter is thus disposed of.

The late Joe Vila of the *Sun* had a system all his own; there was no other column like it. Utterly without literary pretension, he was still, even without overtones, one of the best reporter-historians. His column was a long-range view of sport. He had a voluminous and practically infallible memory. He was a walking record book, and could write two columns about the long-buried past, with names, dates and figures, with hardly a glance at the files. While others on the *Sun* staff might be writing of Carnera, Vila, likely as not, would discuss Peter Maher or Peter Jackson, with recitals of the circumstances and statistics of all their fights. The Baltimore Orioles of the young

John McGraw were as young and fresh to him as the Giants of Bill Terry.

He was almost always factual, seldom bitter, although he had an abiding dislike for Wilbert Robinson, long manager of the Brooklyn National League team. Vila was an artist at handling the running story of an event, which is of especial value to an afternoon newspaper, which tries to print the play-by-play stories as soon as possible. Vila is said to have originated this idea, in 1889, when he covered the Harvard-Princeton football game, writing in longhand or, when the game was hot, dictating to a telegraph operator.

Vila's old column, which carries the slightly boastful heading, "Setting the Pace," was taken over at his death by Frank Graham, who has made it one of the best ever seen. Graham's stuff is pleasant, lucid and informative.

Another popular afternoon columnist is Bill Corum of the *Evening Journal,* who fits perfectly into that paper's somewhat showy but always eye-filling sports policy. Corum, a bouncing, laughing man about town, is interested principally in fights and horses, but he has an excellent groundwork in other sports. Like many another, he is sometimes careless with his details.

John Lardner, son of Ring, who does a syndicate column which is printed in New York in the *Post,* has the equipment to become one of the greatest. With a background of general news reporting, which many sports writers miss, and with a genuine interest in sports, coupled with a restrained style, he is attracting a following. He is young, but his outlook is sane, and he is better informed on technical matters than many sports writers twice his age.

Joe Williams, the sports editor and columnist of the *World-Telegram,* is an expert of sound experience, but his stuff is uneven. A few years ago his column contained some high-class foolery, and on some days he told a narra-

tive, or expressed an opinion, which was easy to read.
Now he has become somewhat more editorial, and battles
for reforms. His ideas, even when they make dull reading,
still show the workings of a mind that is alive and inquiring.

The liveliest columnist, who realizes that it is possible
to possess an education and still avoid a limping style, is
Paul Gallico of the morning tabloid, the *Daily News*. He
could be as lyrical as Rice or as literary as Kieran if he
wanted to, but he slugs along with a simple, pliant vocabulary which makes him the ideal man for his spot.
When he spits on his hands and cuts loose with invective,
he is positively alarming. He puts on a vaudeville act, but
it is in good taste.

Another tabloid columnist, Dan Parker of the *Mirror,*
is generally underrated. The peculiar circulation of the
paper, among odds and ends of curiously assorted strata
of humanity, has led him to invent low-brow jokes for
his readers, a practice known among sports writers and
others in New York as "gagging for the goose trade." But
there is nothing wrong with his ability, either as a sports
analyst or a writer. He would be at home, once he got his
bearings, on the most conservative paper. He knows the
rackets and has courage. He endeared himself to a few
collectors of curiosa when he defined "Gloober's Disease,"
at that time a relatively little known affliction, as "spots
on de vest."

The Calvin Coolidge of columnists is George Daley,
sports editor who a few times a week writes a résumé of
the doings of the athletes and the horses for the *Herald
Tribune*. Coolidge, it may be recalled, once wrote,
"When a great many people are unable to find work,
unemployment results." Daley, as one example, wrote,
"Twenty-five years is a long time. Thirty-five years
is a long, long time." His interviews also are known

for their personal touch, such as, " 'Well, George,' said
Mrs. Isabel Dodge Sloane, 'I don't think so.' " Although
he probably knows as much about racing as any writer, he
finds it hard to believe evil of anyone. When Arnold
Rothstein, all around crook and sure thing gambler, was
shot and killed, Daley, at that time sports editor of the now
dead morning *World,* wrote an encomium of the slain
master, picturing him as a much-maligned sportsman.

Damon Runyon, veteran general reporter, is consistently good in the New York *American,* even when he
sounds a little like Brisbane. He is one of the best of the
stylists, and he knows all the rats and all the heroes. He
is by nature so kind-hearted, or it may be that he has a
streak of the promoter in him, that he sometimes goes off
balance over a prizefighter like Floyd Johnson or "Napoleon" Jack Dorval. Or he will hang medals on Herbert
Bayard Swope, New York's new Racing Commissioner.
He can write poetry when he wants to, as in the famous
refrain, "Never a handy guy like Sande bootin' them
babies in—" and he has a keen sense of the comic.

One of the best minds to attempt the sports column in
recent years was Westbrook Pegler, who in 1933 was hired
by Roy Howard as a counter-irritant on the discussion of
general affairs to Heywood Broun on the *World-Telegram.*
His sports stuff was sometimes highly amusing, although
often, unfortunately, he wrote of matters of which he
knew little. This scheme of shocking the reader can be
effective, but if carried too far it comes to be regarded as
mere show-off.

Are sports writers today really tougher in their attitude,
more honestly realistic, than those of another generation?
It has been debated hotly. The truth probably is that the
attitude itself is old, as witness the early Lardner and the
early McGeehan, but that more of the modern writers are
tough. The tough attitude has merit, for there is a tragic

tendency in sports to lose all sense of proportion and to live completely within the boundaries of sports.

The sports department is an attractive place for any young man who feels an urge to write of sports and the people of that world. If he doesn't, he'd better stay out of it. There is considerable truth in the public belief, fostered partly by the motion pictures, that the sports writer, taking one week with another, has a pretty easy time of it—certainly easier than is the lot of the average reporter on general news. But the sloppy workman, the man who isn't interested, for example, in learning baseball as Bill Slocum and Sid Mercer know it, or as the late Hanna knew it, has no business in the sports department. Above all, if he has a contempt for his materials, he doesn't belong. He doesn't have to be a drum-beater to have a respect for his work. The sports writer can have a good life, and an honest one (there is much less taking of graft than there used to be, although some of the boys still are inclined to let baseball clubs do too many favors for them) but the best ones know that the test of good sports reporting is not substantially different from that of all other good reporting.

# MAESTROS WITH BRASSES AND WOOD-WINDS

PRESS agents, in their multifarious wigs and masks, sometimes seem almost as necessary to the modern newspaper as a posse of reporters. They are part of the news machine. The hand of the publicity man, often carefully disguised, may be found in perhaps one-third the news items in many issues of a New York newspaper. He pipes his alluring tunes for the benefit of the clergy, for magazine and book publishers, hotels, railroads, charities, foreign governments and ambitious individuals. Much of the news concerning the activities of the Right Rev. William T. Manning, Protestant Episcopal Bishop of the Diocese of New York, must come through Alden D. Groff; likewise, the late Larry Fay, who was slain by a bibulous doorman in a night club, for a time employed Milton Raison, now of Hollywood, to interpret his complex character to the public. Both the bishop and the racketeer had as much right to employ public relations counsel as to call in legal counsel. Indeed, the press agent often can aid a man in situations where a lawyer would be helpless and in the way.

Members of this strange profession range from the frightened, somewhat ratty Broadway hanger-on, who hopes to pick up a few dollars for whistling up any fly-by-night enterprise which comes along, to such elegant and philosophical practitioners as Ivy Lee and Edward L. Bernays, who represent large interests and movements directed at what is known as the Mass Mind, and who have brains.

On the lower and more plainspoken levels, the press agent refers to himself as a bill poster who has had his

nails manicured and put on a top hat. A few rowdy
mountebanks have remarked upon the genuinely startling
similarities between some aspects of their work and the
more time-worn calling of the pimp. Others are like the
agile and amiable Charles S. Washburn, the theatrical press
agent, who whispers that he is "just a comical confidence
man out to take the suckers." In the higher reaches,
where the air is clearer, the publicity man insists that he
cannot be described accurately as a press agent, as his function is merely to give advice to large industries on matters
of policy, and that he rarely has any actual contact with
the press. Sometimes such disclaimers of the label appear
to be so much quibbling, as if the simple, blunt term "press
agent" was somehow an epithet, connoting low practices
and even a hint of immorality. A hereditary predisposi-
tion to public relations work may be observed; for example, Louis Zeltner ("Wireless Louie") was press agent
for restaurants and New York's locality mayors, and many
of his sons, as soon as they were old enough to write "press
releases," took up the same sort of work.

Whatever these men and women may choose to call
themselves—public relations counsel, publicity advisers,
special assistants to the president, good will ambassa-
dors, molders of the mass mind, shepherds of herd reactions, mouthpieces, advocates at the court of public
opinion, front men or spacegrabbers—they seek approximately the same thing. They are paid for using their
ability and ingenuity to the end that the interests they represent, whether it be a transit corporation or a visiting
magician, appear before the public in a light which is
favorable and pleasant, or at least in a guise as friendly as
the circumstances will permit. Their numbers have increased enormously. Their methods have undergone many
subtle changes and refinements. Essentially, however, the
press agent seeks the same goal he always sought—free and

profitable advertising for his employers and the good will of the public. Often the press agent is socially-minded; the work he performs may be for the public good. He practices what may be a bastard art, but which doesn't always have to be.

New York, where even the simplest projects must be carried out with as much indirection, hocus-pocus and sculduggery as human ingenuity can devise, is the natural home of the press agent. The city undoubtedly has more press agents, if the disguises of all of them could be penetrated, than it has working newspaper men. These many-sided John the Baptists are of importance not only to newspaper work but to the whole public. Often they determine religions and styles, emotions and diet. The agent's prehensile finger, his wheedling or commanding voice, may be discovered somewhere in so much of the news—or what passes for news—that he is worth study with microscope, test tube and scalpel.

No matter how effective he may be, or how much money he makes, it is still difficult to accord the press agent a professional status. His enterprises are extraordinarily diverse, and one client may require a technique different from another. The gentleman in the frock coat, representing a steel combine, and the nervous, hungry young man seeking a social note for a troupe of imported freaks, may be after approximately the same result, but they must go about it differently. Thus, every spring when the circus comes to New York, the scholarly and beloved Dexter Fellows has only to visit his newspaper friends, throw back his plaid top coat, tilt his cigar, utter a few homely remarks, and the papers blossom with stories of the wonders of the circus. The circus is a commercial enterprise, but the press agents, from Tody Hamilton to Fellows, with the willing cooperation of most newspapers, have made it accepted as legitimate news.

In scores of other news fields, some trivial and some of

great public importance, the New York newspaper man encounters the press agent. The booster of the humane societies is Miss Eleanor Booth Simmons, who used to be a reporter, and a good one. Miss Suzette G. Stuart has among her clients some of the more ambitious and eloquent clergymen. A big flower show would seem strange without the ministrations of the firm of Worth Colwell and Ed F. Korbel. The aviation industry has, among others, the veteran Captain Harry Bruno. The latest activity of Capt. George H. Maines is to attempt to convince New York that Senator Huey P. Long of Louisiana has been maligned by sinister plotters. News of many philanthropic organizations is sent out by Harry M. Propper, once an exceptionally able reporter. Frank L. Hopkins, old *World* man, handles publicity for the Merchants Association. Julian S. Mason, a former editor, is engaged in trying to revive, with the Republican Builders, the lethargic remains of what once was known as the Grand Old Party. Albert Stevens Crockett sings of the undoubted charms of the Hotel Vanderbilt. Louis Resnick, formerly a St. Louis newspaper man, handles much welfare news. Holman Harvey seeks good will for Irving T. Bush and for Raymond Moley's magazine *Today*. Howard Benedict, great poker-player; Richard Maney, a master of forensics, and C. P. Greneker, head of the press department of the Shuberts, are among the hordes employed to publicize theatrical and other amusement enterprises.

There are others, battalions of them, who handle the publicity interests of social climbers, peep-shows, banks, barrooms, politicians, steamship lines, beer and about everything else. Some are so useful, and companionable, that all newspaper men welcome them and their Messages, big or little; others are such chiselers and bores that reporters and editors take fright at their approach. As persons, these bearers of strange tidings run the gamut from such men as Cameron Rogers, the forthright and brilliant

literary man who devotes his talents to the glory of the
Grace Steamship Line, down to the cheapest little liar and
fakir who ever tipped a newspaper on a blackmail suit
about to be started by a shyster lawyer.

Some press agents seem to possess vastly more bounce
and shrewdness than even the best newspaper man.
Stephen Jerome Hannagan, a highly personable Irishman
who now is with the New York office of Lord and Thomas,
advertising agents, has in his day handled such clients as
the Indianapolis Speedway, Miami Beach, Montauk Point,
Jack Dempsey, and, in another year, Dempsey's rival, Gene
Tunney. To Hannagan goes the credit for the change in
sentiment toward Samuel Insull after the utilities operator
had been brought back to Chicago after his flight to
Greece. Hannagan advised, it is said, that Insull pose for
photographs instead of dodging; that he allow his family
to talk and be photographed, and that he adopt a policy
of frankness. The idea was, of course, to make the public
say, "Well, after all, he is a tired old man, and a rather
nice old man, and what he did was no worse than what
many other rich men did. They all guessed wrong in the
boom. So what of it? Why persecute the poor fellow?"
Such tactics can be tremendously effective. And yet Mr.
Hannagan, during the short time he worked as a newspaper man, was hardly regarded as a promising journalist.
Indeed, he says he was almost a total loss. He was wise
when he took up the life of a press agent.

Many newspaper men, viewing the careers of such men
as Bernays, Lee, Hannagan and many others, are inclined
to be envious. The wives of newspaper men, often esti-
mable enough women, covet the fine feathers which the
publicity man, who is generally regarded as a sybarite, is
able to provide for his loved ones; the news hunters themselves, aware of the droves of fawning women, the pent-
houses, the lean-bellied automobiles, the cellars of rare old
Madeira and all that sort of thing which the more success-

ful publicists are supposed to have without limit, are likely to sicken of the plain though spiritually nourishing fare which is provided them by their Spartan publishers. Thus, often, even the man who really loves newspaper work will leave it when the tempter, that old triple-threat devil of Easy Work, Short Hours and Big Pay, shows him how soft life can be.

Moreover, publicity work in its more intelligent forms has an attraction for men and women of more than ordinary ability. It draws the alert, pushing youngster who has little genuine affection for the newspaper life, and who sees in journalism only a grubby existence at best; it draws also the experienced, capable editor whose increasing personal responsibilities harass him day and night, and who feels that, uncertain though publicity work may be, it is hardly less uncertain than what he is doing, and the gamble is worth taking.

Likewise, the army of press agents is made up in large part of men who would have been incompetent at anything, and who are incompetent as press agents. Some have only one attribute, a colossal gall, and some are devoid even of that, and wander on the outer fringes of the show, chevying harmless people. For the newspaper man who has lost his job for whatever cause—a bad break, the sudden discovery that after all he is illiterate, or the alarming inroads of booze on what once had been a passably clear mind—publicity work is the first and sometimes the only refuge. Such a man says to himself, in candid diagnosis, "All I can hope for is some lousy press agent job." Sometimes, even if he can no longer find work on any paper, his acquaintances and experience may be useful to interests that need publicity.

There is, of course, not necessarily much in common between the inborn talents which make a great press agent and those which make a great reporter. And if the calling, or racket, of public relations work is the last haven

of the washed-up misfit of journalism, it is just as truly
the green pastures for the youngster who is surcharged
with the boiling virus of the go-getter, who yearns to do
Big Things for Real Dough. Often a contemplative and
paternalistic city editor, after having observed such a mis-
cast stripling, will summon the problem child and say:

"Champ, you are a nice boy and all that, but as a reporter you are neither a Richard Harding Davis nor a
Jimmy Durkin. My old friend Joseph Doakes, who owns a
chain of hotels which are anything but cheap bedhouses,
wants a press agent. It will pay at the start three times
what you are paid here. Better take it."

And yet, despite this friendly advice, and despite the
sound understanding which exists between the established
sources of publicity and the newspapers, there remains a
gulf. To the newspaper editor it is always a little sad when
one of his best men leaves the paper to take a publicity job.
The feeling, indeed, is sometimes bitter, and the editor
knows that, even though the man may be starving next
year, he cannot come back to his old job on the paper. The
door often is closed to many fairly able men who have
found press agentry less profitable and attractive than they
had expected, and who seek to return to newspaper work.
"You thought you were smart; now suffer!" is the attitude.

Possibly there never can be a time when mutual confidence will exist between the paid ringmasters of the herd
mind and the men who handle the theoretically undefiled
facts which make up the news reports. The press agent is
a counsel for a special interest. His efforts have a single
purpose—to impress the boss with results, which may mean
that a news story is toned down, or that the boss receives
reams of flattering clippings. No matter whether the
press agent is working for a bogus mining promotion
scheme or for a group of high-minded ladies who feel that
they are fighting at Armageddon and just coming up for

the tenth round, his object is the same: he must do the best he can for them.

The newspaper man is somewhat different. More truly than most men, he has three bosses: his own ravelled and uncertain conscience, strangled between the eternal verities and the wisdom of opportunism; the occasionally inexplicable brainstorms of his publisher, who may be savant, merchant, or the reincarnation of Richard the Lion-Hearted, but who pays the freight; and that drowsy, dangerous dinosaur, the reading public, who really holds the power of life and death whether he expresses his judgment by a sullen refusal to buy the paper or by a barrage of slingshot signed "Constant Reader," "Mother of Six," "Outraged Taxpayer," "Just a Commuter" and "Veritas."

On the one hand we have the newspaper man, who is supposed to stick to the facts, and who for generations has been hoping that sometime he might achieve a sort of professional standing; on the other we have the paid publicity man who, though he may have all the charm in the world, is of necessity a propagandist. Complete understanding between the two is impossible.

Some of the publicity men have become so influential that young men, even before leaving college, view them with the same sort of respect that youngsters of a generation ago held for such paragons of managing editors as Carr V. Van Anda and Keats Speed. For years the larger, more profitable newspapers have looked to colleges, or to the smaller towns, to find young men to fill the inevitable vacancies which result from death, retirement, an excess of women and liquor, or the departures of flaming genius for Hollywood. One day a city editor received word that a certain senior at Princeton apparently had all the earmarks of a great newspaper man: he could write, he had made a high record in his studies, he came from an old but lusty family, he had an engaging personality, an inquiring mind and all that sort of thing. The city editor summoned the

White Hope, was impressed by him and decided to offer him a job. But first he said:

"If you come on the staff I should like to have it understood that you are coming with the intention of staying a long time—that is, that you are pretty sure at this moment that you want to do newspaper work. The idea is that you should have in mind remaining with the paper, provided, of course, that you like the work and develop as you should."

The young man was honest in his answer, which cost him his chance at the job. He said:

"I understand your feeling, but I may as well tell you that if I came on the staff it would be with the thought of remaining only a year or two. Then I'd want to take up public relations work. In fact, Ivy Lee told me he would give me a job in his organization if I'd first get some sound newspaper experience. That's where the money is."

No one can blame the up and coming graduate for laying out his plan of life, and yet, newspaper executives do not like the idea of spending much time and patience on beginners, only to find after a few years that the paper actually has been training, not newspaper men, but press agents who would leave at the first offer of more money. There are two possible solutions: the newspapers should feel fairly sure that their recruits have a genuine talent for journalism and have no idea of using their newspaper experience as a stepping stone to propaganda work; and the papers should raise the pay of fast-blooming young men so rapidly, on the basis of outstanding work, that the flesh-pots of press agentry would have less attraction.

This is not to contend that there is some defect in the character of the reporter or copyreader who, tired of a monotonous round of run of the mine drudgery and the correcting of comma blunders and errors in middle initials of prominent citizens, dreams of himself sitting in a soft leather chair, working telephones with the ostentatious

virtuosity of a Herbert Bayard Swope, barking dynamic
orders and smoothing out the public relations difficulties
of a veritable octopus of industry.    Young men and old
men feel that they should eat, though it is possible to draw
up a convincing brief for the opposite school of thought.
If the young publicist attaches himself to the right
interests, and studies the methods not only of Bernays and
Lee but of the lesser masters as well, he may go far.    In an
incredibly short time he can fancy himself, and with some
reason, as a Svengali hypnotizing the hinds, a Machiavelli
who pulls the strings which cause the herd to cavort at his
will or to lie down upon a new style of bed.    Is the hat
business stagnant, and do ten million ostriches waste their
plumes in the desert?    The able public relations expert in-
duces a few "group leaders," as they are known, to wear
ostrich plumes, and soon the trick is done.    There is a
feather in every hat, and the ostrich retains only his sad
memories of glory and his sun-burned bottom.

It has been the custom to hold up Ivy Lee as the greatest example of what a newspaper man may do when he en-
ters upon publicity work ("Lee, family physician to big
business," "Lee, who made the American people love the
Rockefellers," "Lee, who taught the big men of Wall
Street not to fear the newspapers" and so on), but it is
probable that Bernays is the more important as an American phenomenon.    He is more of a psychologist, or psy-
choanalyst, than Lee.    That Daniel Boone of the canebrakes
of the libido, Dr. Sigmund Freud, is his uncle.    Bernays has taken the sideshow barker and given him a philosophy and a new and awesome language: "conditioned
reflexes," "the creation of events and circumstances," "dramatic high-spotting," and "continuous interpretation."
He is no primitive drum-beater.    He has written books and
lectured at New York University on the methods and underlying psychological principles of his high art.    He is
devoid of swank and does not visit newspaper offices; and

yet, the more thoughtful newspaper editors, who have their own moments of worry about the mass mind and commercialism, regard Bernays as a possible menace, and warn their colleagues of his machinations.

There is a defense to the charge that the professional press agent is a conscienceless thimblerigger of helpless masses. It is, roughly, something like this: The mass, whether it knows it or not, is dominated by leaders of various groups. It is idle to argue that the mass mind, without manipulation by experts, would be free from all influences. Whatever a man does is the result of suggestion from some source. Once Irene Castle cut her hair, and her photograph was attractive. Barber shops, beauty parlors, hairnet manufacturers, the comb industry and the hat business were affected for better or worse. Business men are at the mercy of a million such whims. It is better for them to attempt some intelligent direction of these whims, so that they will know what to expect. Otherwise some morning they may find themselves ruined.

Thus the defense, which is persuasive even if incomplete. The record of Mr. Bernays is full of examples of showmanship which could not be ignored by the newspapers. There was, for example, Light's Golden Jubilee. The story of Edison's invention was retold. To Dearborn went Edison, Henry Ford, and even the President of the United States, as well as a great crowd of other important figures. It was not Mr. Ford's show, or Edison's; or even the President's. It was simply a publicity stunt pulled off by Bernays, representing powerful and rich interests, to exploit the uses of the electric light. Newspaper editors who understood this may have felt sad, but what could they do about it—with the President making a speech and all those important persons there?

Again, Mr. Bernays was employed by Procter and Gamble, makers of Ivory Soap. He popularized the nation-wide contests for the best examples of soap sculpture. It is really startling what anyone with a bent for sculpture can do with a little soap. For the first few years he gained enormous publicity, and then the publishers asked abruptly "What the hell?" and now the publicity is much less.

Bernays must receive credit, or blame, for an important shift in the methods used by the larger advertising agencies. The late J. Walter Thompson, who might with considerable reason be called the father of modern advertising, doubtless would be astounded if he could observe the modern system, even the methods employed by his own firm. For example, in the spring of 1934 the word "callipygian" was known only to cross-word puzzle time-wasters, Greek proofreaders and an occasional innocent citizen who had picked it up somewhere. Then Max Elser, an exceptionally urbane fashion-plate who has been a newspaper man, syndicate owner and press agent, visited the new offices and inquired, "Did you ever hear of the word 'callipygian'?" He received various answers. One editor, a notorious ham-fancier, gave the right answer, "Of course. It means 'having shapely buttocks.'" Mr. Elser was frank, a virtue which is rare among his colleagues. He bore a copy of an interview with Bryant Baker, the sculptor, along with photographs of Mr. Baker's famous statue of "The Pioneer Mother" and of various models whose rear façades (or, as the girls say at the Colony Club, "fannies") were anything but repellent. Mr. Elser argued, with some logic, that it was interesting stuff, even though it was all part of a publicity and advertising program, not for one make of corset, but for the entire corset industry. The idea was that the news story, with the fresh word "callipygian," should appear first, with the paid advertisements to follow. Mr. Elser had varying success with his story; the more anatomically-minded papers printed the story, a clarion call for more shapely buttocks, but the others could find no legitimate excuse for it.

A few years ago advertising agencies devoted their attention to straight advertising. They spent their money for a staff of business men who were supposed to be experts on the art and science of advertising, who studied the newspapers and magazines, allotted their appropriations, and bought space. Now they have added research workers (which may be a good thing), and great numbers of thinkers, behaviorists, trend-observers, experts with chart and graph, child trainers, students of sleep and what not. Less money is spent proportionately on pure advertising and more on the experts whose astounding conclusions will, it is hoped, get into the newspapers as free reading matter. Many a business has stopped advertising entirely and hired a press agent.

It has been observed by many soul-searchers that a prosperous newspaper can afford to be more ethical, more independent and courageous, than the starveling which must toady to the desires of advertisers. During the depression which started in 1929, even the Cæsar's wives among American journals have heard the insistent, seductive nickering of the advertising man, and some of them have behaved shamefully. To begin with, few of the persons employed in the advertising department of any newspaper have any clear conception of the essentially different character of news and advertising, nor can they understand that, once it is granted that a newspaper is in business to make money, why it is that prostitution may still be wrong and, in the end, may lead to bankruptcy. Many advertising solicitors for newspapers, knowing that their jobs are at stake if they do not get a certain account, have been known to invade the city room with the most outlandish requests for puffs for a clothing merchant, a wine dealer or a drug store proprietor. This pressure, in one form and another, is exerted constantly upon the news departments. If it isn't resisted the newspapers will become pathetic harlots, headed for ruin.

The outlook is far from hopeless.  The owners of the newspapers, through L. B. Palmer, manager of the American Association of Newspaper Publishers, have been sending out bulletins warning the news departments of impending schemes for free publicity.  Most of these plots already would be discernible to the men who handle the news, but not all of them.  Mr. Palmer's storm signals have had a salutary effect upon the mental integrity of some editors merely by making them more secure when they feel like dealing sharply with the more brazen attempts at free advertising.  The old "front office must," which often is nothing more than a commercial puff, remains always as a potential threat to the news columns, even on the most squeamish newspapers.

It is possible, if the publishers can hold their united front against the moochers of free reading matter, and can make their positions clear both to their advertising and news departments, that enormous numbers of the high-powered merchandisers and philosophers will be forced to take up some more useful work, or even to starve.

The press agent for the commercial enterprise is, of course, the one who causes most trouble.  Press agents in many other fields have become almost indispensable to newspapers.  Without them the New York papers would have to double their staffs to take care of material which is now handled by publicity men who have come to be welcomed and trusted.  For example, a large convention would require the services of several reporters from each paper if the thoughtful press agent had not arranged the speeches, reports and digests.

Newspapers are particularly friendly toward the press agents of charitable, civic and educational institutions and movements, although these agents often are ravenous in their demands for space and attention.  Moreover, many of them are unwilling to aid the press in getting at the facts when the facts might embarrass or injure the interests they represent. That is why, when a story is outside the routine, the wise reporter observes the fundamental rule of never going near the press agent. Moreover, these institutional press agents often turn out extremely dull material, perhaps because the jobs do not pay enough to attract more competent men.

The observation has been made by a few newspaper men, as well as press agents, that news is easier to get than it was, say, fifteen years ago. Sometimes it is. Rich families, powerful business men, respectable persons faced with serious trouble, frequently seem more willing than formerly to give a straight answer to a straight question. They don't all feel, as they once did, that the newspapers invariably yearn for the crucifixion of public characters.

The public relations counsel like to think they are responsible for this change—if, indeed, it is a real change. Let them withhold their wreaths of bay for a season. The bespatted molder of public opinion still insists that he must be present when a reporter asks a millionaire whether he likes prunes for breakfast; he must be consulted before his employer can even make an engagement with the gentlemen of the press; he must, to earn his pay and bamboozle his employer, intrude himself into the orderly handling of even the simplest news stories. In short, he is a nuisance, hindering everyone and doing no one any good.

Ivy Lee is generally disliked by New York newspaper men because it is impossible to obtain any fact from him, no matter what the circumstances, until he is good and ready to make it public. It is next to miraculous when a reporter is able to reach him on the telephone. He is supposed to protect the interests of the Rockefellers, among others. It is no secret that John D. Rockefeller, Sr., might reasonably be expected to die sometime. Newspapers have received little help from Mr. Lee, in spite of the various requests, for information and advice that would aid them in making the obituary of Mr. Rockefeller complete, accurate and fair.

Some years ago John K. Winkler, an alert reporter for Mr. Hearst's New York *American,* received a tip from a reliable source that Miss Abby Rockefeller, daughter of John D. Rockefeller, Jr., was to be married to David Milton, a young New York lawyer.  Mr. Rockefeller referred inquiries to Mr. Lee, and Mr. Lee asked Mr. Winkler to see him a little later in the afternoon.  When Winkler arrived at the Lee ateliers he found that reporters from the other papers had been summoned.  The story was true, but Winkler felt that he had been deprived, and rather unjustly, of an exclusive story.  Again, an editor on a New York newspaper learned upon what he believed to be good authority that Mr. Rockefeller, Jr., one of the original supporters of the prohibition law, had changed his mind about the wisdom of the noble experiment.  This editor found Mr. Lee as inaccessible as the Dalai Lama, and appealed to Mr. Rockefeller, who tossed the ball back to Mr. Lee.  Some days later Mr. Lee released a statement from Mr. Rockefeller which explained his change of position on the dry law—an exceedingly important pronouncement which did much to hasten the final rout of the prohibitionists.

Of course Mr. Lee and Mr. Rockefeller were within their rights.  The Lee system, indeed, may be preferable to any other.  The only point here is that Mr. Lee has not increased good will of newspaper men toward him and toward publicists like him.  More, such tactics, when they have not tended to dull the enterprise of newspapers, often tend to drive reporters to use methods of news-gathering which might be called somewhat underhanded.

There has been a clear improvement, certainly in New York, in the relations between the press and the clergy, the law and medicine, but these gains have not been made through the intercession of press agents.  They have come through the efforts of a few editors and a few leaders of these professions. The editors try to assign more intelligent reporters to the doings of these men; and on their side, the rector may be willing to discuss a situation frankly, the surgeon may say "I don't expect Mr. Doakes to live through the night," and the lawyer, instead of pouting or snarling, may sit down and calmly discuss the case.

The Great Man racket, which consists of the inflation and labeling of enormous stuffed shirts, is always with us. Some of the press agents engaged in this calling confess that it is the most soul-corroding way of making a living known to man. Bernays defends it on its higher levels on the ground that the public is entitled to know the sort of man, his background and personality, who is the brains of an industry which furnishes the public with its goods.

The game is played on many levels, some of them amusing. Some years ago a gusty, two-fisted mining promoter named Charles V. Bob, who, when pressed, would admit that he had once knocked Stanley Ketchel down, came to New York to begin a career which later resulted in a mess of financial difficulties and a trial in Federal Court. Bob hired F. Darius ("Freddy") Benham, formerly a *World* reporter, to handle his public relations. Under the tutelage of the astute and sometimes admiring Benham, Bob became an associate of Gene Tunney, an aviation enthusiast, a booster for the Rev. Dr. Christian Fichthorne Reisner's Broadway Temple promotion ballyhoo, and a backer of Admiral Richard Evelyn Byrd on his first venture to the South Polar regions. Indeed, there was, for a short time, a range known as "the Charles V. Bob Mountains," which do not today appear on the atlas. The crash of Bob came only a short time after Benham had left his employ; it is doubtful if even Benham could have saved him. But it was great sport while it lasted.

What should the newspapers do about the paid publicity man? Is there any way of working out a sensible attitude? Some of the schemes, even when planted by such a brilliant and jesting Broadway press agent as the late Harry L. Reichenbach, can be identified a mile off, and, even when they work, do little damage to a paper's integrity. They only make the editor feel a little foolish. Moreover, the city desk of every newspaper often is annoyed by forty or fifty press agent calls a day about trivial matters ("I mailed you a statement about an hour ago; I hope you get it all right."), and could hardly be blamed if he hated the whole tribe.

One suggestion, which might prove helpful, is that material which is put out by special interests should be identified in the newspaper. Often, to be sure, the propaganda nature of news stories is clear even to the most stupid reader, if there are any stupid readers, but others are far from obvious. It would do no harm for newspapers to point out that a light jubilee is a Bernays project; it might be proper, without waiting for a Congressional committee to drag it out, to print the fact that Carl Byoir and Carl Dickey were handling German propaganda. This identification would not necessarily imply any impropriety.

Such a system might be useful. But it wouldn't settle the whole problem. The paid publicity man, whether in spangles or in the whiskers of the professor, will be a part of American life for a long time. And the herd mind, whether it is to be whipped up for another war or made receptive to a soporific mattress, must continue to take its pummeling. For the herd is both sleeping monster and defenseless guinea pig.

# NEWSPAPER STYLE AND "DON'TS"

SOME of the sleaziest writing anywhere is in American newspapers. Some of the best is there also. Every able news writer knows the feeling of disgust which comes when a well-meaning friend says, "That piece of yours was good enough for a magazine." Nothing can be too competently written for a newspaper.

That word "journalese" as commonly applied to newspaper writing may be a sneering defense mechanism employed by windy professors, bubbly dilettantes and wheezy lads who fancy themselves social philosophers, and stylistic posturers who really have nothing to say. Good newspaper writing today must observe rules older than Moses. It must be clear, vigorous and informative. If, in addition, it turns out to be charming, that is so much velvet.

The late George Bellows, painter and lithographer, once told a group of women who weren't interested: "Art strives for form, and hopes for beauty." Newspaper writing at its best seeks to present facts tersely, logically, completely. The result may be satisfying, amusing or even beautiful. But first it must respect the ancient precepts.

Newspaper writing can be taught. Most newspaper men teach themselves. About all an editor can do is to lay down a few rules of style, a few "don'ts" and hope for the best. The wonder of the profession is that many newcomers, after floundering for months, turning out awkward gibberish which violates all the canons of taste and sense, will transform themselves overnight into writers of force and distinction. It is as if the dawn had broken instantly. Others never learn. A bad speller at the age of twelve, it seems, is a bad speller at sixty.  A sloppy, disorderly mind at twenty-five usually remains so through life.

The young man, or even the old man, who seeks to improve his writing, can find all the useful examples, all the advice, that he needs.  He might read Thomas Carlyle to observe how not to write, and to marvel at how ghastly can be the literary gyrations of a master of fustian. Macaulay is dull, but his sentences march straight ahead. Montaigne remains rich in arresting ideas.  Dickens was a money-grubber and a hack, but a genius in reporting. It is the custom these days to jeer at old Kipling, but who ever wrote a narrative with such economy, such calm, apparently effortless effect?  The literary works of Lafcadio Hearn are not popular any more, but his lectures on writing are eternally sound.  Anatole France will bear studying.  His dissertations on the use of words and phrases have the ring of the true gospel.  Ambrose Bierce gave some pungent advice on writing, often excellent, but he sounds like an embittered poseur.

Arthur Brisbane, in his youth a brilliant reporter, still writes easy, effective stuff, shot through with inaccuracies. It is smooth to read, even when he is telling us once more that a gorilla could lick any two heavyweight prizefighters—an estimate recently revised and enlarged to four prizefighters.  The late Brand Whitlock, a newspaper man in the best tradition, wrote lean and masculine prose. When William Randolph Hearst (this is not meant as a joke) chooses to express himself in a speech, an editorial or a polemic, he is enormously powerful, a phenomenon which lends credence to the belief, held by a few thoughtful observers, that Mr. Hearst is a better writer than any man who works for him.  Henry L. Mencken writes news and comment with superbly lucid impact.  He formed his own style, influenced by Huxley.

No practitioner of the high art of newspaper writing

should be ignorant of the works of the late Professor H. W. Fowler, particularly his Dictionary of Modern English Usage. Here, set forth with wise and witty scholarship by a great authority, may be found a treasure of observation and definition. The Professor was British but what he has to say is as true in St. Louis as at Oxford.

Read them? The trouble is that many newspaper men have to be bulldozed into reading their own newspaper. Even today many a lazy dolt will boast that he hasn't read a book since leaving school—if, indeed, he had been to school.

Almost all newspaper offices of any account have their "style sheets" or list of "don'ts" which are necessary to insure uniformity. Some of these ukases are designed for purely local purposes, or to conform to the whims of the publisher, but there is a large body of rules which have grown up through the years, some founded on ordinary tenets of correct usage and some the result of the gradual evolution of judgment on what is good newspaper practice and what is bad. Most of these commandments, even the arbitrary ones, have sensible reasons for being. And, no matter how often they are set forth, they will be violated not only by writers of news articles but by novelists, clubwomen and sophomores as well.

A "Don't" list, of course, may have an unfortunate effect. Any such list which spoils freshness, which makes a man fear the bold experiment, thereby loses whatever usefulness it might otherwise have had. If it has the effect of making a reporter shy away from the crisp bite and the sting either of an old verb or a vivid bit of slang from yesterday's street brawl, it has failed. Indeed, the first "Don't" perhaps should be: "Don't be afraid to try something that isn't in the book of rules." Some day, it may be, there will come a story which can be told best by breaking every rule in the Koran of the Fourth Estate.

The younger James Gordon Bennett, for so long the

owner of the New York *Herald*, was a stickler for rules of style. His "Don'ts" were rigid, but most of them were sensible. Mr. Bennett died in 1918, however, and for all these years has been unable to froth over the red rags waved by careless writers. Indeed, many of his particular abominations are in almost universal use today, for better or worse. For example:

Don't call a theatrical performance a "show."

Don't apply "schedule" to the movement of persons, as: "Ambassador Bacon was scheduled to leave Vienna."

Don't use "New Yorker."

Don't use "week-end" or "over Saturday."

Don't use "guest of honor" or "maid of honor."

Don't use "gang" or "gangster." (What would he have said of the 1934 "mobster"?)

Don't use "diplomat"; use "diplomatist."

Don't use "minister" except for diplomatists.

Don't use "plan" except in connection with drawn architectural or engineering plans. Do not use it as a verb. "Planned" and "planning" are taboo. (Mr. Bennett would have had trouble with "planned economy.")

Don't use "house guest," "house party" or "reception guest."

Don't use (hotel) "patron" or "guest." (This rule caused much argument, some reporters attempting to refer to persons registered at hotels as "inmates.")

The bulk of Mr. Bennett's distilled wisdom, however, is still in force. Along with the sage rulings of Charles A. Dana, Horace Greeley and scores of unsung editors and copyreaders, they form the backbone of what may be called the common law of newspaper practice. The hodgepodge code may be summarized, roughly and informally, with a few side excursions, as follows:

Observe the laws of good taste, something which is impossible of exact definition, but which most gentlemen know by instinct. If there is no gentleman handy, when a borderline case arises, the baffled reporter must draw on his own resources.

Be fair. This does not mean that it is sufficient for an article to be libel proof. Every effort should be made to get the other side of the story, to avoid distortion and injustice.

Rarely is there such a thing as too much of a good story. The readers, God help them, have been bored enough by pewee sagas. When the chance comes to give them a real story, let them have it, fully and ungrudgingly. They will read it.

The lead, or introduction, is the most important part of a news article. It should be clear, provocative, and so simple that anyone can understand it. If it has a sharp adjective or adverb, so much the better. Usually it should start with a name, a noun or an article, rarely with a participle, a preposition or a quotation. Some papers have a rule against starting a lead with "The," but there is little justification for such a " 'Hell!' said the Duchess" philosophy.

The lead should be a promise of great things to come, and the promise should be fulfilled. It should be as direct as, "President Roosevelt, speaking yesterday to 500 Gold Star Mothers in the Smithsonian Institution, accused Joseph Doakes, one-legged mestizo Montana prospector, of unlawfully hoarding farina." And go on from there. The "Gee whizz!" lead annoys judicious adults.

Most news accounts are improved by quotes. Speech should be quoted exactly as spoken; sometimes quotes can be remarkably effective, and it is fair. However, improvised quotes, with which a reporter seeks to put into quotation marks what he thought somebody meant to say, are inordinately dull—a lazy man's way of covering up his lack of specific information.

Because a story is important, it doesn't follow that it must be long. There is rarely an excuse for profligate phrases. Don't say the mayor went to Brooklyn "for the purpose of laying a cornerstone." He went there "to lay a cornerstone." Copyreaders and rewrite men must perform cruel incisions on such bloated masterpieces.

Sentences and paragraphs should be short. Few writers can evolve a long newspaper sentence that flows and conveys its sense clearly. It can be done more readily in books, which usually are printed in larger type; the small type of newspapers makes long flights difficult to read, and confusing.

Pick adjectives as you would pick a diamond or a mistress. Too many are dangerous. Because one adjective is as revealing as a lightning flash, don't think that ten will make the story ten times as good. There is a law of diminishing returns. Adjectivitis, a dread ailment, is as common among newspaper men as dipsomania—perhaps more so.

Young men often are over-impressed when they receive an assignment which is more important than the work they have been accustomed to handling. They rear up rococo Taj Mahals of verbal flubdub, wandering on and on amid synthetic vaporous splendors. Naturally they are disappointed when a rewrite man, hardened to the sight of such excesses, deflates the structure and puts the vital material in half the space.

Leave no reasonable questions unanswered. The reader is no more intelligent than the writer—sometimes, more's the pity, less so. If the writer doesn't know the answers, he should find out.

Go to the source on every assignment. Don't think that it can all be done with a typewriter. Use your legs, or go to the telephone (Mr. Bell's admirable gadget is a godsend to newspaper men), and inquire. The more prominent the source of information, the more ready, generally, he is to discuss the news. Most so-called big men are as approachable as any peasant.

Don't try to behave as reporters in "The Front Page"

or in the other cinema and stage versions of news-collect-
ing. Such monkey-shines do little good, and may do much
harm. Be polite, be a gentleman—but always within reason. Few things are more sickening than a servile reporter.
He doesn't have to be that way. If he has lickspittle
tendencies, other pastures will afford him a rosier future.

Get the details down to the last drop. Sometimes it is
useful in interviews to observe what kind of necktie, suit
or collar a man is wearing. If Al Smith, testifying before
a legislative committee, wears button shoes with heavy
soles, that's news. It discloses that Mr. Smith is an individualist. The same is true of the wig of Lucy Cotton
Thomas Magraw.

Don't be afraid to write facts on the mistaken assumption that "everybody knows that." An inert workman
shuffles along inevitably to the graveyard of mediocre men.
What you write, even though you may not be a fine
craftsman, will be fresh if the facts are there. But first,
there must be no ball of lead weighing down the pants
(or, as Mr. Bennett always insisted, trousers).

Most stories are improved by printing the time of occur-
rence. This doesn't mean that one should write that there
was a collision at 2:15½ P.M., yesterday, but it certainly
is laziness to give the time merely as "yesterday afternoon."

In large cities, particularly New York, it is wrong to
assume that readers know the address of every obscure
hotel. Nor do they know whether 1440 Broadway is at
Fourteenth Street or Fortieth Street. The readers are entitled to know without having to look it up for themselves.

Once the introduction is satisfactory, the rest of the
article should follow smoothly, with the thought of one
paragraph merging naturally into the other in the orderly
progress of the account. There should be no jerks, no
patchwork. A story can be so well-constructed that no

editor on earth can take one phrase out of it without doing an injury.

No matter if you have a degree from Oxford, and your ancestors spoke only to Cabots and their ilk, do not despise the homely and familiar—even the sweaty. A good story is one in which the average reader, whoever he is, can imagine himself, and say, subconsciously, "Why, that could have happened to me!" Here a paper has what Lord Northcliffe called a "talking point."

For many years newspapers had rules against using the names of automobiles, on the ground that such use would be free advertising. This ancient taboo is passing. It improves a news story to say that former Mayor Walker's Duesenberg was sold to a Negro night life addict, or that somebody's Ford fell from a cliff.

The writing of obituaries, particularly those of unusual persons, is among the most difficult forms of newspaper work. The research should be as thorough as time will permit, even if it entails visiting friends of the dead person and reading a biography or two. There is rarely any need to present a dead man either as a saint or a monster. It is possible, with all respect for the soul who may be on the threshold of hell, to be realistic, even salty, without being unfair or in atrocious taste. And, usually, the surviving relatives will appreciate such handling. The dead man's closest friend should be able to lay down the paper and say, "That was Abner to the life."

Don't insult a race, even a helpless race. Unless a crime story is so important or unusual that race, background, genealogy and even religion come naturally into the picture, it is rarely necessary to say that "Four Italians were arrested." Such sentences as "the proprietor said he had been robbed by two young Jews" are bad. The man may have been mistaken; it is barely possible they were White Russians, or even Basques. This rule, possibly, should not apply to Eskimo pickpockets.

The battle against whimsy, which is a Peter Pan or Winnie the Pooh variety of faking, must be fought over and over. It is next to impossible to write a sensible story, surely for grown-up readers, in which houses, dogs, old ferryboats, ghosts and elephants are represented as talking. No matter how charming the idea may seem at first, it is best not to attempt such kittenish flights. This injunction also applies to accounts of the high intelligence quotient of crows. Crows can count to three, but there they are stopped.

Dialect seldom has a legitimate place in a news story. A few reporters can handle the nuances of the spoken language of the Jew in the garment district or the Italian organ-grinder. But not many. Negro dialect, even to a Southerner, is more difficult. A botched dialect story is worse than no story at all.

Use of too many quotation marks to apologize for either a fresh or a trite phrase generally is a bad practice. Elegance may be admirable, but sometimes the best phrase—indeed, the only precise phrase—is slangy and reeks of the streets. If so, don't spoil it by Nice Nellie quotation marks. It is possible to avoid jazz without being stodgy; there never is any necessary conflict between vigor and taste. The language lives, breathes and changes its colors.

It is all very well to say that a man died of encephalitis lethargica, myocarditis or phlebitis, but it requires only a little extra trouble to explain to the possibly puzzled reader that they are sleeping sickness, etc. The cause of death, whenever possible, always should be printed.

Writing the news of deaths is hedged about on various papers by arbitrary rules. One of the most awkward, and most common, locutions is, "Mr. Doakes is survived by two sons, Egbert and Rene." Why not say simply, "Two sons, Egbert and Rene, survive," or "Surviving are two sons"? Likewise, it is illogical to say that "Mr. Doakes's wife sur-

vives him." A woman might survive an attack of small-
pox, but few husbands are notably virulent.

Moreover, when Mr. Doakes dies it is his wife, not his
widow, who survives. His body, not his "remains" is
buried, not "interred," in a coffin, not a "casket," which
in turn is covered with flowers, not "floral tributes," while
the clergyman (not "minister"), praises Mr. Doakes's good
deeds rather than "pays tribute." The "pay tribute" label
is not only overworked, but it is inexact in meaning and
smacks of man-worship.

In writing of churches, or reporting sermons, the de-
nomination and address of the church should be given unless, of course, as in New York, it is such a well known
place as St. Patrick's Cathedral or the Cathedral of St.
John the Divine. Introduce the clergyman by his full
title, as "The Rev. Dr. Christian Fichthorne Reisner."
Thereafter in the article refer to him as "Dr. Reisner."
Clergymen who are not doctors of divinity should, after
introduction, be referred to as "The Rev. Mr." Few
name handles are so maddening as the bucolic "Rev.
Jones." In reporting the sayings of the clergy, great care
should be used to quote them exactly. They are the most
touchy set of quibblers who ever plagued a well-intentioned editor. Some will even find fault with a steno-
graphic report, attested by a dozen albino notaries,
swearing on a Gutenberg Bible.

Study of the terminology of the Roman Catholic
Church is an arduous chore, but every reporter, whether
atheist or Primitive Baptist, should immerse himself in it.
Most newspapers realize that the abbreviation "Fr." for
Father is silly. In general, the abbreviation "Mgr." for
Monsignor is permitted. A priest should be introduced as
"The Rev. Francis P. Duffy." Much needless misunder-
standing is caused by the ignorance of reporters and editors
of Catholic titles and ritual. It is a large and difficult
field, but it can be mastered, certainly sufficiently for

purposes of ordinary news reporting.  Even today bizarre but authentic tales are told of young reporters who, interviewing a Roman Catholic Bishop on his birthday, inquire solicitously about his wife.

"Mr." should precede the names of most men who are in good repute, except in cases where it would be ridiculous or an obvious affectation as in "Mr. Gandhi," "Mr. Ruth," or "Mr. Lincoln."

No American is "Honorable."  "The Hon. Franklin D. Roosevelt" is as incorrect as "The Hon. Bath House John Coughlin."  It is strictly a British handle and has a precise meaning.  It is used by Americans who think, mistakenly, that it connotes respect or flatters American officeholders.

A Congressman may be either a member of the House of Representatives or a Senator.  It is always easy to give the exact title.

Charles Evans Hughes is Chief Justice of the United States, not "Chief Justice of the United States Supreme Court."

It is the American Ambassador to the Court of St. James's, not "U. S. Ambassador to the Court of St. James."

"President" is an awkward and rarely authorized name handle for anyone except the President of the United States or of some other republic.  Most style sheets insist upon "Dr. Nicholas Murray Butler, president of Columbia University," and thereafter simply "Dr. Butler." "Borough President Levy" is regarded as proper, but "Mr. Levy," wherever possible, is preferable.

What is a "clubman"?  There is no such identification although the man in question may be a member of many clubs.  Likewise, what is a "business man"?  Is he a delicatessen dealer or plumbing contractor?

There is no such thing as "the club section of the city." Clubs cause much trouble.  No man is a member of the

Colony Club in New York, but this fact is ignored several times a year by the best newspapers, usually in obituaries. The Union Club often is confused with the Union League Club. It is The Lambs and The Players, not "the Lambs Club" and "the Players Club."

That dirty but majestic stream, the Hudson River, flows down to the Atlantic, but it is not "the North River," although the piers are designated officially as North River piers. There are North Rivers elsewhere, but not in New York.

Most reporters, without thinking, will refer to a pier as being "at the foot of" West Eighteenth Street, as if a pier might possibly be situated at such a waterless point as Broadway and Forty-second Street.

Such passages as "at the corner of Fifth Avenue and Forty-second Street," occur frequently in the copy of reporters and rewrite men. There are four corners. Why not indicate which is meant, or, if the intent is to give only the general section, simply "at Fifth Avenue and Forty-second Street."

Two of Mr. Bennett's rules, "Don't say honeymoon, say 'wedding trip,'" and "Don't say a man spends time; he 'passes' time," still survive on many newspapers, where they do no harm.

Why say a lovesick young man in New York made "a long-distance telephone call" to San Francisco? It could hardly have been a short-distance call.

The word "blood," though sometimes necessary, usually may be avoided. It is assumed that when a man is shot, stabbed or slashed, he will bleed.

All ships are feminine, even battleships. Not even a child or an animal should be referred to as it.

Ships make so many knots, not so many "knots an hour." "Knots" means rate of speed, so many nautical miles an hour, and not distance. Many newspaper men of fifty years' experience still cannot understand the meaning of "knots."

"Suffered injuries" is better than "sustained injuries" or "received injuries." Moreover, it is doubtful if anyone ever "had his leg broken," an operation which implies a rather quixotic design on the part of the injured person.

Criminals are indicted "for" and convicted "of" crimes. It is incorrect to write, "following his conviction for grand larceny."

Rum is a definite kind of liquor, esteemed highly by many drinkers. "Rum" should not be used to describe liquor in general, which includes whisky, gin, benedictine and many other potable classifications. Of course, "rum-pot" and "Rum Row" are part of the language.

"Said" is an excellent word. It can become monotonous. There are plenty of apt synonyms for it, but it is better to use "said" over and over than to put too much faith in the somewhat pompous "state," "declare," "aver" or that ace of ugly words "asseverate."

A building usually is "situated," not "located," unless the Missing Persons Bureau has been searching for it and has found it.

A fire starts. It doesn't "break out."

A ship, unless it is on the beach, cannot burn "to the water's edge," though it may burn "to the waterline."

Do not say that Mrs. Joseph Doakes has filed suit for divorce "from her husband." Women don't sue their uncles for divorce.

Hesitate before converting nouns into the feminine form. Lioness, actress, huntress and many other forms are accepted everywhere. "Aviatrix," "poetess," and "authoress" have little or no justification. As well say "cookess."

One man is different from another, not "different than." This error, almost universal in conversation, protrudes like a mocking effigy of Noah Webster from the works of most sports writers. (Not "sporting writers.") The alert detective also may find the curious phrase in the works of one of the most careful of writers, Walter Lippmann.

Why call a Jew a "Hebrew," a Chinese a "Chinaman," or a Negro a "colored man"?

Style in society news is sometimes difficult, but understandable. A man marries a woman; a woman is married to a man. The man is a bridegroom, not a "groom." Married women in a wedding party are matrons of honor or attendants, not bridesmaids.

Unforeseen events, such as fires, accidents, crimes and collapse of buildings, "occur"; eclipses and ceremonies "take place."

The verb "claim" is a pitfall for the slipshod writer. "He claimed that he was entitled to the legacy" is wrong. "He claimed the legacy" is correct. Elementary? To be sure, but violated every day by men and women who should know better.

Probably the most persistent of all errors of style is what is known as the "was given" monstrosity. Thus, "Joseph Doakes was given a horse." Sensing that something is wrong, many reporters will change that sentence to "Joseph Doakes was presented with a horse." Both versions are unutterably bad. Friends gave the horse to Mr. Doakes. The horse was given to Mr. Doakes. Mr. Doakes received the horse. Much better. Likewise, upon the filing of the will of Mr. Doakes's grandfather, it is not disclosed that "Mr. Doakes was bequeathed a valuable clock." The clock was bequeathed to Mr. Doakes; or, Grandpa bequeathed the clock to him. Moreover, when Doakes gets into trouble and is sentenced by the court to thirty days at hard labor, it is not proper, or even sensible, to write that Mr. Doakes "was given" the sentence.

It is a mistake to assume that the foregoing is all primer stuff. Even the rules which have been accepted and imbedded in the canons of English usage for centuries are violated daily, not alone by the raw cub reporter but by writers of repute and by such a supposedly fool-proof work as the Encyclopedia Britannica. The broad rules, which shade off into rather unimportant little pedagogical aversions, are necessary.

The newspaper writer, possibly like any other writer, should not worry too much about the straitjackets. The language is growing and increasingly alive, and not even the rhetorical maltreatment of the unfortunate Joseph Doakes can kill it. Good writers always can make something with the most inadequate tools, as some sculptors doubtless could produce passable art with a meat-ax. But no law forces any man to mistreat the weapons of his trade.

NEWS PHOTOGRAPHERS STANDING ON STEPS OF COURT HOUSE AT LONG ISLAND CITY, DURING SNYDER-GRAY CASE

*Photo N. Y. Herald Tribune*
BEVERLY SMITH

WALTER DAVENPORT

ST. CLAIR McKELWAY

*Photo Editor & Publisher*
J. J. O'NEILL

*Photo Harper's Magazine*
ISHBEL ROSS

*Photo Editor & Publisher*
FRANK WARD O'MALLEY & FAMILY

*Photo N. Y. Herald Tribune*
BOB PECK

*Photo Wm. H. Zerbe*
W. O. McGEEHAN

ALVA JOHNSTON

THOREAU CRONYN

MARTIN GREEN

MEYER BERGER

# SERMON ON ETHICS

*There is a third large and important domain in which there rules neither Positive Law nor Absolute Freedom. In that domain there is no law which inexorably determines our course of action, and yet we feel that we are not free to choose as we would. This is the domain of Obedience to the Unenforceable, which I always think of as the Domain of Manners. . . . It covers all cases of right doing where there is no one to make you do it but yourself.*—LORD MOULTON

THERE are many codes of ethics for journalists. Some have been drawn up by associations of editors, others by individual newspapers. There has long been, in the curious business of journalism, a yearning for respectability, a pathetic hankering for righteousness. There have been solemn meetings at which pious tenets have been set forth as guiding principles for working newspaper men. Somewhat in the fashion of sentimental madams who obtain an inner glow from attending early Sunday mass, the editors feel better for a few hours after such sessions. Then they return to the job of getting out a newspaper, there to find what they knew all along—that it is a business of imponderables, of hairline decisions, where right and wrong seem inextricably mixed up with that even more nebulous thing called Good Taste.

Despite the well-meaning codes, some of which soar high toward Heaven, the truth remains that the commonest indictments against newspaper practices still retain much of their force. These indictments charge that the press will be unfair, that it will be swayed on occasion by advertisers, that its partisanship will prevent it from giving its readers a straight account of a political campaign, that it will persecute individuals, that it will print unprivileged but sensational matter if it is deemed safe, that it will sometimes assume the functions of the law in the conduct of criminal cases, that it does needless injury to the defenseless, and that in its wolfish eagerness for news it will lie, steal, and bribe.

It is probable that no paper in America has at all times been entirely innocent of all these sins, although to say this is not to indict the whole press as being unethical, for it is not. As a body, in the give and take of professional conduct the press has a sense of right and wrong which surely compares well with that of the medical profession, the clergy, and the law.

Most newspaper men, in their ethical relations, are guided only by their own instincts and common sense. They know right and wrong as a gentleman is supposed to know conduct. Their codes are under their hats, not in the rule books. There are two commandments: do not betray a confidence, and do not knife a comrade. And these two have their practical reason for being. The man who violates a confidence will lose his sources of news; the man who double-crosses a colleague will, on some bloody tomorrow, find himself naked and helpless.

Actually the conscience of the newspaper man bothers him little. He senses, without knowing why, that this is right and that is wrong, or in foul taste. Seldom is he called upon to do anything which really grates upon his sense of propriety. Even then he can rationalize the deed. Once a baffled young reporter, in a moment of soul-searching, said to a gray copyreader:

"This is a lousy business after all. I stole a picture today. I invaded privacy where I really had no right to. I used subterfuge to get a story. And the story itself will, I fear, embarrass several innocent persons, though it is safe."

Said the copyreader, who had lived through decades in which he had read the sagas of murder, rape, political corruption, elopements and what not:

"I wouldn't worry about that. Just don't get in bad with your friends, and don't get the paper in a libel suit. We do a lot of funny things, which might be hard to defend. A lot of nice people will get hurt, but remember by printing all this stuff we are helping evolution. Even printing the dirt helps the human race get ahead."

Indefensible in any code, of course, but not an uncommon attitude. It is based on the first order of any city editor: "Get the news!" The chicanery and deceit sometimes necessary to get the news, although condoned by none of the formal codes, may be defended on occasion on the grounds of public policy; that is, there may be a news story, the printing of which would be clearly for the public good, which is being suppressed. Exposure of such situations as the Teapot Dome scandal, the growth of the Ku-Klux, graft and corruption in public office, and many other bottled-up but tremendously important news stories, cannot be brought about by completely frank dealing on the part of reporters digging up such material. They are on the trail of tricky persons; they must, in turn, resort to tricks.

Does such investigation, which may usurp the functions ordinarily assigned to governmental agencies, mean that the press is overstepping its prerogatives? Quite the opposite. There have been abuses, some of them shameful, but the willingness of a newspaper to resort to unusual measures to expose a situation which is clearly a matter of public concern often is the measure of that paper's resourcefulness and courage.

The Bible of the American journalist, which he rarely reads, is the "Canons of Journalism," which was adopted in 1923 by the American Society of Newspaper Editors. It represents the first attempt of representative editors from all parts of the United States to reduce the inchoate practices of newspaperdom to a set of fundamental principles. It follows:

### Canons of Journalism

"The primary function of newspapers is to communicate to the human race what its members do, feel and think. Journalism, therefore, demands of its practitioners the widest range of intelligence, of knowledge, and of experience, as well as natural and trained powers of observation and reasoning. To its opportunities as a chronicle are indissolubly linked its obligations as teacher and interpreter.

"To the end of finding some means of codifying sound practice and just aspirations of American journalism these canons are set forth:

### I. *Responsibility*

"The right of a newspaper to attract and hold readers is restricted by nothing but considerations of public welfare. The use a newspaper makes of the share of public attention it gains serves to determine its sense of responsibility, which it shares with every member of its staff. A journalist who uses his power for any selfish or otherwise unworthy purpose is faithless to a high trust.

### II. *Freedom of the Press*

"Freedom of the press is to be guarded as a vital right of mankind. It is the unquestionable right to discuss whatever is not explicitly forbidden by law, including the wisdom of any restrictive statute.

### III. *Independence*

"Freedom from all obligations except that of fidelity to the public interest is vital.

"1. Promotion of any private interest contrary to the general welfare, for whatever reason, is not compatible with honest journalism. So-called news communications from private sources should not be published without public notice of their source or else substantiation of their claims to value as news, both in form and substance.

"2. Partisanship in editorial comment which knowingly departs from the truth, does violence to the best spirit of American journalism; in the news columns it is subversive of a fundamental principle of the profession.

IV. *Sincerity, Truthfulness, Accuracy*

"Good faith with the reader is the foundation of all journalism worthy of the name.

"1. By every consideration of good faith a newspaper is constrained to be truthful. It is not to be excused for lack of thoroughness or accuracy within its control or failure to obtain command of these essential qualities.

"2. Headlines should be fully warranted by the contents of the articles which they surmount.

V. *Impartiality*

"Sound practice makes clear distinction between news reports and expression of opinion. News reports should be free from opinion or bias of any kind.

"This rule does not apply to so-called special articles unmistakably devoted to advocacy or characterized by a signature authorizing the writer's own conclusions and interpretations.

VI. *Fair Play*

"A newspaper should not publish unofficial charges affecting reputation or moral character without opportunity given to the accused to be heard; right practice demands the giving of such opportunity in all cases of serious acccusation outside judicial proceedings.

"1. A newspaper should not invade private rights or feelings without sure warrant of public right as distinguished from public curiosity.

"2. It is the privilege, as it is the duty, of a newspaper to make prompt and complete correction of its own serious mistakes of fact or opinion, whatever their origin.

VII. *Decency*

"A newspaper cannot escape conviction of insincerity if while professing high moral purpose it supplies incentives to base conduct, such as are to be found in details of crime and vice, publication of which is not demonstrably for the general good. Lacking authority to enforce its canons, the journalism here represented can but express the hope that deliberate pandering to vicious instincts will encounter effective public disapproval or yield to the influence of a preponderant professional condemnation."

Obviously, the canons are excellent. They set forth possibly as clearly as the job could be done, the dream of the decent journalist. Yet there can be no enforcement. The only outward penalty for flagrant disregard of the canons is expulsion from the society. Among the violators was the late Frederick Gilmer Bonfils, publisher of the Denver *Post*. He violated canons of decency and good taste and made a fortune out of it. After bitter attacks on Albert Bacon Fall and the Teapot Dome lease, he suddenly ceased firing; later he admitted having received $250,000 from Harry F. Sinclair. The American Society of Newspaper Editors expelled Bonfils, but the Denver *Post* continued to prosper and Bonfils remained the friend, more or less, of the great.

There have been dozens of other high-minded codes. They make strange reading. As far back as 1910 the Kansas editors drew up a code, passages from which follow:

"We condemn as against truth the publication of fake interviews, made up of the assumed views of an individual, without his consent.

"We condemn as against justice the practice of reporters making detectives and spies of themselves in their endeavors to investigate the guilt or innocence of those under suspicion.

"However prominent the principals, offenses against private morality should never receive first page position, and their details should be eliminated as much as possible."

In Oregon, the editors once drew up a long code, eloquent and even spiritual, in which the following appears:

"The reputations of men and women are sacred in nature, and not to be torn down lightly. We therefore pronounce it appropriate to include in this code:

"We will not make privileged utterances a cloak for unjust attack, or spiteful venting, or carelessness in investigation, in the case of parties or persons.

"We will aim to protect, within reason, the rights of individuals mentioned in public documents, regardless of the effect on 'good stories' or upon editorial policy.

"We will deal with all persons alike, so far as humanly possible, not varying from the procedure of any part of this code, because of the wealth, influence, or personal situation of the persons concerned, except as hereinafter provided.

"It shall be one of our canons that mercy and kindliness are legitimate considerations in any phase of journalism; and if the public or social interest seems to be best conserved by suppression, we may suppress; but the motive in such must always be the public and social interest, and not the personal or commercial interest.

"We will rise above party and other partisanship in writing and publishing, supporting parties and issues only so far as we sincerely believe them to be in the public interest."

And so on. The Oregon journalists were as clean as so many penitents at the mourners' bench at a Methodist camp meeting. But there have been others. In 1921 the Missouri editors declared:

"In every line of journalistic endeavor we recognize and proclaim our obligations to the public, our duty to regard always the truth, to deal justly, and walk humbly, before the gospel of unselfish service."

The Greeleys of sirocco-blistered South Dakota in 1922 put themselves on record:

"News should be the uncolored report of all vital facts, accurately stated, insofar as possible to arrive at them. . . . Upon those who practice this profession rests the sacred duty of keeping these mighty means of communication with mankind pure at the source, undefiled of intent, and free of bias."

Certain newspapers have expressed their feelings in their own codes. The Brooklyn *Daily Eagle* says:

"When a person is charged with crime, or has done something immoral or discreditable, do not intrude the names of prominent relations, who are in no way involved. In writing obituaries, do not emphasize unfortunate incidents in the lives of well reputed persons."

The commandments of the Detroit *News,* written with a sob and a prayer, contain this:

"Time heals all things—but a woman's damaged reputation. Be careful and cautious, fair and decent, in dealing with a man's reputation, but be doubly so—and then some—when a woman's name is at stake. . . . Even if a woman slips, be generous; it may be a crisis in her life. Printing the story may drive her to despair; kindly treatment may leave her with hope. No story is worth ruining a woman's life, or a man's either.

"Keep the paper clean in language and thought. Profane or suggestive words are not necessary. When in doubt, think of a 13-year-old girl reading what you are writing."

There seems to be a popular feeling that the Hearst newspapers are not greatly concerned with these high matters. And yet the instructions to the Hearst papers contain this:

"Make a paper for the nicest kind of people—for the great middle class. Omit things that will offend nice people. Avoid coarseness and slang, and low tone. The most sensational news can be told if written properly. Talk as gentlemen should. Be reliable in all things, as well as entertaining and amiable.

"When a wrong picture is brought in by a reporter or a wrong picture is used (through lack of care or neglect); or when grossly inaccurate statements are made by a reporter, or copyreader, such copyreader or reporter will be asked to hand in his immediate resignation."

The Philadelphia *Public Ledger,* now unfortunately dead, had this plank:

"Uphold the authorities in maintaining public order, rectifying wrongs through the law. If the law is defective, better mend than break it."

The *Ledger* was a dry paper.

In the happier days when the late Warren Gamaliel Harding was publishing and editing the *Star* at Marion, Ohio, he nailed these admonitions on the wall:

"Treat all religious matters reverently.

"If it can be avoided, never bring ignominy on an innocent man or child, in telling of the misdeeds or misfortunes of a relative. Don't wait to be asked, but do it without the asking.

"I want this paper to be so conducted that it can go into any home without destroying the innocence of any child."

William Allen White, the canny old editor of the Emporia, Kansas, *Gazette,* once had a code for dealing with the news of intoxication. He decreed that when a citizen was arrested for drunkenness for the first time, nothing should be printed about it, out of respect for the sot's wife and children. However, if the lusher were arrested a second time, then the *Gazette* should set forth in print the facts, wife and kiddies notwithstanding. Here Mr. White fell back upon the common law, debatable at best, that every dog is entitled to one bite.

Perhaps the most succinct statement of the dreams of those who long to bring journalism into a state of perfect respectability is the following, from the code of the Wisconsin Press Association:

"We believe in the right of privacy of individuals in all matters not of public concern.

"We believe that a newspaper which goes into the home should publish nothing that cannot be read aloud in the family circle.

"We believe that news of crime, scandal and vice should be presented in such a manner as to deter readers from attempting to imitate the criminal and the vicious.

"We believe that editorials should present the truth as the writer sees it, uncolored by bias, prejudice or partisanship.

"We believe that advertisements should be as clean and wholesome as the news and editorials."

In all this groping for a coherent philosophy there is much that is ridiculous; mostly such attempts to codify journalistic practices seem like the musings of a shyster lawyer, with a trace of the old college spirit still left in him, who on his day off tells himself that after all there are such things as ethics, and that henceforth life must be a little cleaner. Not a bad thing, this eternal seeking for sanctification. There is, it may be, some hope for any reprobate who is capable of turning his head on his pillow and asking: "Why do I have to be so rotten?" But the next day comes the avalanche of reality. There are compromises. It was always so. The saving law is: We do the best we can—in the circumstances.

One of the oldest laws of the Fourth Estate is the one which forbids faking. There are few editors who deliberately would print a news item which they knew to be false. There are, to be sure, borderline cases, particularly in the field of whimsy—that playground of the pixies of journalism where animals are represented as talking, where trivial items are inflated, with conversation and wisecracks which ring hollow, and where the simple truth is mauled and twisted out of all semblance to reality. Newspapers are always confronted with the decision of where harmless embellishment ends and dangerous faking begins. Usually it is a matter of ordinary judgment by the city editor who passes the story.

There have been monumental fakes. The moon hoax of the old *Sun*, and the old *Herald's* story of the escape of all the animals in the Central Park Zoo, were tremendous sensations. The first got circulation, but both did harm. The outstanding modern fake was the story, printed in 1924, in the New York *Herald Tribune*, of a large floating night club, an old steamship riding outside the raiding limit, where pleasure-seekers went for their drinking and dancing. The man who perpetrated this hoax was fired, but he has been employed by many papers all over the country since then. Another man, who also has not lacked employment, was fired by a tabloid for writing a spurious story, accompanied by pictures, of the landing of liquor in New York harbor. Both these men were adjudged competent reporters; they merely went too far once too often.

It is true that, among the better papers, there is "general professional condemnation" of fakers. And yet it is strange that so many of the younger men, just coming into the business, appear to feel that a little faking here and there is a mark of distinction. One young man, who had written a good story, replete with direct quotation and description, was asked by the city desk how he could have obtained such detail, as most of the action had been completed before he had been assigned to the story.

"Well," said the young man, "I thought that since the main facts were correct it wouldn't do any harm to invent the conversation as I thought it must have taken place." The young man was soon disabused.

The codes constantly are in collision with actual practice. For example, in the fall of 1924 the Rev. Dr. Percy Stickney Grant, a New York clergyman, entered a hospital suffering from anemia. A story, not based upon any public record, was circulated concerning him and a housemaid

who had been in his employ. In addition there was the
innuendo that the clergyman's physical disorders had affected his mind. All the New York papers printed the
fact of his illness. A few managed to get across the leer
that somehow there was something wrong. The morning
*World* had this to say of the handling of the story:

"In the case of Dr. Grant only one conclusion is possible.
His privacy was ruthlessly invaded, and no conceivable reason
of public policy can justify the attack upon him. He is the
victim of as indefensible a journalistic practice as one can
imagine. . . . The fact that this practice was repudiated by
the conscientious metropolitan press is evidence of common
agreement as to the canons of good taste in this sort of thing."

The trouble is that there was no such "common agreement." The case of the helpless, dying Dr. Grant, was
used as a circulation builder by the sensational part of the
press, and even the more respectable papers were not above
doing a bit of genteel prying. The weekly organ of the
newspaper business, *Editor and Publisher*, asking what was
right and wrong, said this in an editorial:

"The answer is simple. The line between right and wrong
is, or should be, as clear to any editor as it is to any gentleman
in his place of business or his home. Backstairs personal gossip,
calculated to ruin the reputation of individuals, is not repeated,
until it becomes a matter of public concern through some action
by the public's responsible representatives."

Is it that simple? At least one reputable newspaper man
defended the printing of all the news, authorized or not,
in Dr. Grant's case on the ground that the cleric, by his
many activities over a long period of years, had made himself what is known as a "public figure." A "public figure,"
it seems, is a man who waives all immunity, and who must
expect not only invasion of privacy but calumny as well.

Another case: one Dot King, a beautiful young woman, was found dead, apparently murdered, in her apartment. The newspapers learned that one of her friends was John Kearsley Mitchell, a Philadelphia banker. Ferdinand Pecora, at that time chief Assistant District Attorney of New York County, was in charge of the investigation. Mitchell, before his name had been connected publicly with the slain woman, went to New York and conferred with Pecora. As he left the conference he told reporters that he would have nothing to say. Several reporters, led by a man of tremendous physique, once a member of the Chicago school of bone-crushers, chased Mitchell into the subway, cornered him and demanded "the low-down" on his relations with the dead woman. The banker finally got away, shaken, but still silent.

At that time there was an ambitious organization in New York known as the Newspaper Club, which is long since defunct because of the failure of newspaper men ever to form themselves into any cohesive group. The club had a committee on ethics, which held a meeting to discuss the offense, if it was an offense, in the hounding of Mitchell. One faction in the committee wanted to ask editors to take drastic action (euphemism for firing or suspension) against the over-zealous reporters. Another faction held that the reporters should be commended for their unusual zeal. The committee adjourned.

Like the red rockets and catherine-wheels that float before the eyes of a tossing dipsomaniac runs one thread through all the deliberations of the seekers after light— that is, let's not drag innocent persons into this. Here is one of the saddest, and most futile, of all the canons. There are millions of examples. Three will be enough.

Alfred E. Smith, blameless in his private life, had a nephew named Glynn who was always getting into serious scrapes. In headlines, and in news stories, this unruly fellow was always referred to as "Smith's nephew."

Vincent Richards, the tennis player, had a half-brother
who was a thief and a gunman, and who finally was killed.
The accounts of the doings of the scapegrace almost always mentioned the innocent athlete.  Indeed, the aberrations of the relatives might have been dismissed as fairly
unimportant had it not been for the prominence of the
names that could be dragged in.

An underworld character, Vivian Gordon, a beautiful
but shameless vixen, was found murdered at a time when
New York City was excited over an investigation of vice
conditions.  In searching into her background it was
found that she had a daughter, a schoolgirl living quietly
with her father, from whom Vivian Gordon had long been
separated, in a small town in New Jersey.  The newspapers
printed the fact of the existence of the daughter, who
read the news and promptly killed herself.

Of course, there is a defense for all this.  Names make
news.  It proves something, probably that even the best
families may produce an occasional black sheep.  Moreover, it was all true, wasn't it, and the identification was
natural?  News shouldn't be suppressed because of the
prominence of relatives, or some one would think there
was something queer.  And so on and on.  One may
rationalize such news forever, and sometimes it would
make sense.  But the point is that the dragging in of relatives in such cases, however much it may be defended as
a journalistic practice, still goes contrary to the highest
ethical canons.  In instances of this sort, perhaps more
than in any other, the sonorous declarations of the high
priests of journalism appear as so much hypocritical flum-
mery.  It may be that the canons, like the Ten Commandments, were drawn up in an atmosphere that was too rarefied.

Most newspaper men are suspicious of lawyers, and vice
versa.  The legal profession has produced many highly
articulate prosecutors, as well as defenders, of the press.

A lawyer talks better than a newspaper man, a circumstance which the journalist regards as just another evidence of the lawyer's spiritual kinship with the medicine
man.   Does the lawyer. laugh when he reads the canons
drawn up by the American Society of Newspaper Editors?
That laugh is nothing compared with the coarse guffaw,
with Bronx cheer overtones (the Bronx cheer is a noise
somewhat similar to that made by the ripping of an old
collar), which newspaper men emit when they read the
lovely canons of the American Bar Association.   The newspaper man has observed too many shysters, too many ambulance chasers, too many political confidence men, too
many blackmailers, so that, even when he peeps through a
keyhole, he still is able to thank God that he is not a lawyer.
    And yet the lawyers, in their criticisms of the press, are
not always beside the point.   Even the best of them may
be afflicted with the triple curse—ponderosity, prolixity,
and litigiosity—but they too are fumbling for truth.
    Henry W. Taft, former president of the New York Bar
Association, collected newspaper clippings to prove, among
other things, that newspapers often do great damage to
blameless persons; that they show little disposition to be
accurate or fair in reporting court news, and that often
an incorrect impression is left in the public mind because
of the tendency to print a column of accusation for each
paragraph of exoneration.   Mr. Taft's exhibit demonstrated that in many a criminal case there were, at first,
many columns.   Gradually the stories would become
shorter, until finally a stray paragraph might give the final
disposition—or, more likely, the end of the case might be
left a total secret.   Mr. Taft had a good case, but his proposal for a remedy was peculiar, as when he said:

"I believe it is a correct statement that no newspaper in New
York has in its employ for the purpose of reporting legal decisions a man who is a lawyer.   This is an anomalous and im-

possible situation. Supposing that the newspaper wanted to report upon music, literature, baseball, economics or finance, and employed a man who didn't know about these things."

Mr. Taft, who was on the right track, plopped into several obvious errors. There are, and have been, many New York court reporters who were lawyers—not good lawyers, perhaps, or they wouldn't be working for the pay of a court reporter. Again, it is possible for a reporter who never opened a law book in his life to write a fairer and clearer report of a legal proceeding than a graduate lawyer. There are many excellent music critics who can't play a piccolo; some of the best sports writers couldn't knock a baseball out of the infield. But they know how to handle their materials with journalistic expertness.

Another lawyer who has been critical of the press is Clarence Darrow, who, of all lawyers, is perhaps most loved by newspaper men. He said:

"In all cases that attract any attention the newspapers with their publicity and their eagerness to get special stories destroy the real right of trial by jury, and not only do the newspapers publish all the facts but they spend time and money working with detectives to hunt up every weird tale possible that may prejudice the jury and the court. . . . Trial by jury is rapidly being destroyed in America by the manner in which the newspapers handle all sensational cases. Of course, it could not happen in England, as far as I know, or in other European countries. It is a species of mob law more insidious and dangerous than the ordinary mob law."

The Committee on Integrity of the Press, an offshoot of the American Society of Newspaper Editors, reproached Mr. Darrow for his statement, reminding him that "all newspapers are not alike." He replied that the very existence of a "Committee on Integrity of the Press" was proof in itself that something was wrong. He said:

"I am quite certain that in England the papers are not permitted to make comment on the facts of a case and to express
opinions as to the guilt or innocence of the defendant or what
should be done with him. I have no doubt that the public is
entitled to be informed upon crimes as well as upon any social
activities, but in important cases, practically all the jurors come
into the box with a definite fixed opinion on every important
question connected with the case and most of the so-called intelligent jurors tell the court that their opinion cannot be
changed and that it would influence the verdict."

Mr. Darrow, who said all this ten years before his brush
with General Hugh S. Johnson during the trying times of
the New Deal, is a clever dissembler, a man who believes
everything and nothing. In the summer of 1934 he hoped
that Hitler would be murdered, yet he is strong for all
humanity. He points out that such comment as the
American press gives to criminal cases could not be given
in England, ignoring the fact that the English papers,
adhering always to the rules, are sometimes more sensational, perhaps even more prejudicial to the rights of the
defendant, than the American press ever could be. Moreover, if the American press is in contempt of court, or
guilty of libel, there is a remedy at law. One other consideration: England and America are different. In England the judges, despite their occasional deviations from the
normal, are respected, and regarded as uniformly honest
and upright; in America, the citizen respects a few judges,
wonders about others, and knows perfectly well that the
remainder are crooks or ignorant hacks.

If ever there was a country in which the full, honest
investigation and report of the judicial processes, in all
their strange manifestations, could be construed as a mandatory public service, that country is the United States.
The only real complaint is that the press doesn't do this
watching more thoroughly and more accurately. The private life and professional equipment of judges might be

more open to scrutiny, for the public good. Moreover, there is much bunk in the charge that juries are swayed by newspaper reports.

The editors in conclave always decry "partisanship." Here they have a sound and beautiful idea, one which some-time may be possible of accomplishment. The trouble is that most newspapers, even when they subscribe in theory to the idea of absolute fairness, lose their perspective, for-get all their high resolves, in the heat of the campaign. A Republican paper is supporting a Republican candidate on the editorial page. Very well. No one can quarrel with the expression of any opinion. But on the play of the news, and the writing of the news, the picture is diffi-cult. Even if the news articles are fair and complete, even if one candidate receives exactly the same space as his op-ponent, there may still be unfairness in make-up—the favored candidate, although he may have little news, will have the preferred position on the first page, while the other one will be buried. Newspaper editors insist that they are getting away from this sort of partisanship, but when the showdown comes, in those last days before the herd goes to the polls, the news values go awry. It is too bad. They don't have to do it.

In the end it must be that ethics remain uncodified, and unenforceable except by the boycott of the reader —and the reader wants the news. Akin to ethics is taste. And what is taste? Any soda-jerker can give his opinion. The dirtiest thinkers in any newspaper office are the ones who most often say, "Be sure it's in good taste." There is no Emily Post for newspaper practice. Do you want your daughter to read of a rape case? Do you want to open your paper at breakfast and read of a monkey-gland operation? Do you want to open a page and see the pic-ture of a dying gangster pillowing his head on the lap of his sweetheart?

How frank should newspapers be? In 1934 a respectable morning paper in its news stories printed the words, "syphilis, gonorrhea, abortion," all in one week, and there were no complaints from readers, although commendations came from the medical profession which had long been sick of the namby-pamby "social diseases" locution. It was in 1934 also that the New York *Daily News*, with commendable frankness, in reporting a hearing in Washington at which Senator Huey P. Long figured, forsook the old-time dashes and abbreviations and printed the complete epithet, "son of a bitch."

It may be that sometime a code of ethics and taste, applicable to all the press, can be put into effect, but the betting is against it. A newspaper is like a man; he is welcome or he is frowned upon. The newspaper, like the man, must pick its company. A filthy business? Sometimes, but not necessarily. It is as decent as the men who make it and the people who read it. If its codes are loose and contradictory, then so are all codes—subject always to the proviso that sometimes black is white "in the circumstances."

# THE NIGHTMARE OF LIBEL

HORACE GREELEY, a brave, tortured soul and probably the most absent-minded of all journalists, once said that no metropolitan newspaper was any good unless it had a batch of libel suits pending against it. This was not because Uncle Horace was fond of litigation, but he knew that libel suits might be the measure of a newspaper's alertness, the quality of its courage and even of its devotion to public welfare.

A paper which doesn't take chances is a dead paper. A too close attention to the absolute rules regarding libel, a too cautious combing of every article to avoid the slightest possibility of danger, might result in a product which is flat, insipid, devoid of all those adornments of narrative, epithet and description which make a great newspaper a living thing.

The best libel lawyers, on many occasions, when called upon to pass judgment upon an important but questionable news article before publication, may make one or two changes in text and then say: "Strictly speaking, it's libelous as hell, but I'd advise you to go ahead and print it. It's a good story. The public ought to know about it. The account is fair. It can be defended. Moreover, it is very doubtful if a suit will be brought." Relying upon such advice, and their experience in such cases, most newspapers take chances every day.

And yet the fear of libel is the bugaboo which causes editors to toss in their sleep when they remember some slip of which they had been guilty in their haste. And reporters turn pale when the city editor informs them: "Well, you got us into a fine libel suit this morning. It seems that the man you said was arrested for rape was not George Spelvin, but Joseph Doakes." The law of libel has a few general principles, and infinite variations depending upon the laws of the various states. It depends also somewhat upon the changing times; one period may allow much less freedom of expression than a period twenty years later, although the laws may remain the same.

It is curious, but few newspaper men pay much attention to the actual laws governing libelous publication. They know in a general way what may be printed and what may not be printed, but they come to know these things not so much by study as by experience, which gives them a sort of instinct. The veteran editor may read a news article at tremendous speed; suddenly he will pause, and his pencil will cut out an offending word or sentence which might have cost his paper enormous sums in defending a libel suit. It has proved to be impossible to avoid all libel suits; the ordinary news story passes through the hands of the reporter, the city editor and the copyreader who writes the headline, the night editor and the proof-reader—and sometimes a rewrite man and the managing editor. All of these ordinarily careful gentlemen, it may be, are afflicted with a blind spot at the same time. Why didn't any of them catch the libel? God knows.

Again, some individuals in newspaper work are cursed with a dangerous malady, a sort of low-grade infection akin to that of the unfortunate group of persons known as "typhoid carriers." That is to say, they may have the best intentions in the world, but they are a menace around the office; they seem to breed libel suits. No newspaper man is absolutely safe. Some of the best reporters who ever lived, who were not only careful by habit but learned in the law, have had a record of twenty years without even the threat of a serious libel suit, only to wake up some morning and find that they have perpetrated a paragraph

which even the rawest cub would recognize as libelous.
Why? It just happens.

A city editor may have become famous for his adroitness
in avoiding suits, for his unfailing weather eye which is
able to detect from afar the smallest hint of libel, and then,
after long years of building up this reputation, he may
plunge his paper into a half-dozen bad libel suits in one
week. Maybe it has something to do with the ductless
glands, or maybe it is the law of compensation catching up
with him.

There used to be a type of journalistic quack, always
extremely rare, who would reason thus: "Well, here I am,
just hired as a reporter on a great paper. I want to keep
that job, but I'm afraid I'll be fired. How to hold the job?
I'll get the paper into a swell libel suit. They may have
to keep me on the payroll for years. They'll need me as a
witness to defend it." There haven't been many of these
harpies, but the type is recognizable to any connoisseur of
confidence men. At the end, their fate is usually rather
dreadful; they wear a brand that they carry to the gutter
and then to the grave.

Almost every large city has at least one lawyer, or a
small group of lawyers, who read the newspapers carefully
with an eye out for chance to bring a libel suit. Some of
these gentlemen have been known to telephone a shamefully libeled person, who hadn't up to that moment realized that he had been mistreated in print, and inform him
that he had an unbeatable case against a newspaper. Let
one of these lawyers obtain a verdict or a substantial settlement, and he is avid for more. Usually, however, they
find themselves in a tough fight; newspapers, certainly in
recent years, have fought to the last ditch rather than sub-
mit to what they conceived to be a shake-down for easy
money. The publicity obtained by the lawyers who sue
newspapers for libel is very little, and lawyers, by and
large, are as fond of favorable publicity as any deprecating

bishop. There is general agreement among newspapers not to print extended news items concerning libel suits, unless the circumstances are of obvious public interest or unless some important principle is upheld or set aside by the verdict.

The attitude of the community toward its newspapers, and the general temper of the period, has an important bearing upon libel. For example, if the popular trend of thought is to "soak the rich," and a newspaper is known to be prosperous, there is danger ahead. A memorandum from a New York lawyer, retained by newspapers to defend many libel actions, follows:

"The current tendency of juries in this city in their verdicts in personal injury actions, such as negligence and libel, results, we believe, from a combination of factors, including a determination of jurors to make sure to make up for the decreased value of the dollar, a semi-socialistic prejudice of increasing strength in favor of individuals against corporations, and so far as libel suits are concerned, a spreading spirit of hostility to newspapers among judges and juries of the sort that existed a few decades ago, but that has been absent for fifteen or twenty years until recently.

"In short, the current public agitation against what is regarded, whether rightly or wrongly, as undue emphasis on crime news, as unfair sensationalism and as fantastic reports of judicial proceedings, is beginning to get in its inevitable effect. For at least part of this agitation the sensational papers, particularly the tabloids, are largely responsible. This is particularly true in respect of reports of legal proceedings where the tabloid tendency is to exploit the sensational, and through limitations of space to print the bane without the antidote."

This is a correct statement of the case. Wild sensationalism, obviously flagrant invasions of privacy, insistence upon presenting a wild story without even attempting to obtain the "other side," the merciless hounding of individuals, the brutal or dishonest methods of obtaining in-

formation—all these have had their effect upon the public
mind. Respectable, careful newspapers have sometimes
paid the penalty for the misdeeds of their bullying or
scapegrace colleagues.

Probably the three principal pitfalls of the newspaper
man under the laws of libel are to be found in cases of mistaken identity; in the abuse of privilege, which means the
dragging in of extraneous matter into a story which, if
confined to the record, might be printed safely; and in the
writing of headlines, in which exigencies of space, or the
misguided zeal of the copyreader, tends to cause overstatement or perhaps to impute guilt in a case where the
body of the story itself does not justify any such bald in-
ference. A primer definition of libel is this: "A newspaper publication is libelous of any person, if its obviously
natural effect is to make those who read it think worse of
that person." It does not matter what the publisher intended to say; the question is the effect on readers of what
the story actually said.

Every newspaper publication is libelous that imputes
unchastity to a woman or a crime to any person. It is
probable that seventy-five percent of all libel suits are
based upon stories imputing some form of criminality; the
rest are based upon stories relating in one form or another
to unchastity or breach of the currently sanctioned moral
code. Does such a report make the reader think worse of
the person about whom the charge is made?

Here is a confusing battleground. Opinions differ. For
example, in the Southern States it has been held libelous
to state that a man is of Negro blood when he is not. Of
course, in those States the reputation of the person would
be injured. There are, however, several decisions in Northern States that such a charge is not libelous, and when the
newspaper prints a correction any threatened trouble is
ended. That is because the courts in the North feel that
the imputation of Negro blood does not necessarily expose

a person to hatred, contempt and ridicule in the community.

In general, it is not libelous to publish of a person that he has done something which he has a legal right to do, even if the thing which he is said to have done was an unpopular thing or something of which the consensus of the community would not approve. But to say of a person that he has done something which, in fact, he has a legal right to do, may become libelous if the thing done—that is, the exercise of a perfectly legal right—is of a peculiarly contemptible sort. For example, to call a man a "profiteer" is not to charge him with any violation of the law (at least before the NRA was put into effect), but the term has been held libelous, especially in wartime, for it is regarded as a term of contempt. One case, quoted by libel lawyers, goes back into literature, as follows:

"For example, did Shakespeare libel Shylock in speaking of the latter's determination to have his pound of flesh? Shylock's right to the pound of flesh was expressed in the bond and no one questioned his right thereto. Portia herself could not question his right to the pound of flesh, she only urged limitations upon the method of taking it. It is a pretty close question whether Shylock was libeled. But if Shakespeare did not libel him he came close to doing so, for the exercise of such a legal right as Shylock had in the circumstances was likely to be violently disapproved by a very considerable segment of the community."

There are many small differences between the laws of New York State and the other States, but in New York there has been a larger amount of litigation and a more complete development of the law, so that, in general, a knowledge of New York practice covers virtually every point likely to be encountered in any State.

The burden of proof, in a libel action, always rests upon the publisher who is being sued; this does not mean that the publisher must prove "beyond a reasonable doubt" that he has a good defense to the action, but it does mean that from the beginning of the case to the end he has the burden of proving by a fair preponderance of the credible evidence that he has a defense.

Many libel suits are brought as gags upon a publisher, particularly in the heat of a political campaign. Or else, some candidate loses his temper, or hopes to make an opposition paper watch its step.

Political or semi-political suits, inspired by various motives, are common. When John F. Hylan was running for reelection as Mayor of New York, the *World* published articles on the early business activities of that amiable politician, including his relations with the promotion of an automobile company. Hylan sued, but as soon as he had been reelected he dropped the suit, exercising his legal right to quit on payment of costs.

A few cases have been known in which a man brought a libel action against a paper for a large amount, and then used the pending action, with the hope that he would collect, as a basis for obtaining a loan.

Hot-headed Mayors sometimes threaten suits against newspapers for "libeling the fair name of the city." This is so much nonsense. Municipal corporations, the government, the states, counties, cities and towns cannot, as such, be libeled. However, an article reflecting upon a municipal corporation may touch an individual officeholder who might be justified in suing.

Another common misconception is that a man who has been held up to "ridicule" may invariably sue and collect. If it is mere ridicule, creating a laugh at his expense, making him the subject of a practical joke, or using his conduct as an occasion for merriment, there is no libel. Ridicule of this sort, even when it causes great discomfiture, is safe under the law. To be libelous the publication must be more than a mere jest, more than a playful shaft of humor; it must carry some sting which will be demonstrably injurious to the reputation.

Almost universally, in spite of the old English maxim of "the greater the truth the greater the libel," the truth is an absolute defense to a civil action; likewise, almost universally truth as a defense to a criminal proceeding is qualified and will be defeated by proof of actual malice.

Second to truth, the great pillar of the press lies in the defense of privilege. Truth is a defense of natural right; privilege is given to publishers on account of considerations of public policy, and when privilege is established the plaintiff cannot recover damages, even though he may have been ruined, and even though the publication may have been permeated by the most malicious intent.

This absolute privilege of the defense may be defined as that privilege which exists in oral or written utterances which are pertinently made in the course of legislative, judicial or other public and official proceedings by participants therein. To newspaper writers this defense is relatively unimportant; what it means in practice is that a participant in a legislative, judicial or other official proceeding cannot be sued for libel for a statement pertinently made in the course of the proceeding, no matter what his purpose, motives or malice may have been in making the statement. Under the rule any blackguard in the Senate may rant and abuse anyone and be perfectly safe.

Is this wrong? At first thought it might seem so. But there is a defense. Harold L. Cross, one of the ablest of New York libel lawyers, and a good newspaper man in addition, has made the following philosophical observation on this point:

"What is the reason for this rule which seems at first blush to be susceptible of such injustice? The answer is that consideration of public policy, that it is better far that the reputation of an individual should occasionally be assailed than that citizens, through fear of libel suits, should be restrained from making pertinent charges as participants in legislative, judicial or other public and official proceedings. If a member of the Legislature, he might naturally refrain from making a statement which, in the light of sound public policy, should be made. The same situation obtains in respect of the plaintiff in a lawsuit. He might be restrained by fear of a libel suit from seeking an adjudication of a genuine legal controversy. Similarly a lawyer in the protection of a client might be lacking in the courage to say something he should say if he might be subjected to the expense and annoyance of a personal libel suit. Similarly judges might be lacking in courage in making judicial determinations; and so, for all these reasons, the law says that participants in legislative, judicial, and other public and official proceedings shall have an absolute privilege to make pertinent statements in the course thereof without any fear of being called to account therefor in a libel suit."

As distinguished from absolute privilege, there is qualified or statutory privilege, which is very important to newspapers. Under it newspapers print reports of trials, indictments, arrests and a vast amount of material which might be held dangerous. Of the defense of such privilege, Mr. Cross says:

"This defense also rests on public policy. Because of the rule, it will sometimes happen that a person's reputation is blasted by widely published imputations upon him of some crime or other disreputable action of which he is in fact innocent. He has no relief whatever against the original maker of that imputation if it was pertinently made for he will be confronted with the defense of absolute privilege. He will have no relief against the newspapers which fairly report the imputation for there he will be confronted with the defense of statutory privilege unless he proves actual malice. Nevertheless, it is better far, so the law declares, that the reputation of an individual should sometimes be unjustly blasted than that the public should be kept ignorant of certain transactions through fear on the part of newspapers that they be sued for libel. Indeed, it is not too much to say that the business of newspaper publication as at present conducted and even our modern institutions depend upon a just and liberal interpretation of statutory privilege."

The law of New York State on this point follows:

"A prosecution for libel cannot be maintained against a reporter, publisher or proprietor of a newspaper, for the publication therein, of a fair and true report of any judicial, legislative or other public and official proceeding, or of any statement, speech, argument or debate in the course of the same, without proving actual malice in making the report.

"This section does not apply to a libel contained in the headlines of the report, or in any other matter added by any other person concerned in the publication; or in the report of anything said or done at the time and place of the public and official proceeding, which was not a part thereof."

The point of the foregoing is that absolute privilege protects only the maker of the libelous statement—that is, the participant in the proceeding, and does not protect the published report of the proceeding. That report must be protected by qualified or statutory privilege. A newspaper cannot escape responsibility for defamation by pleading truth, by showing that it published the charge upon the most credible or highest authority; yet it is always a defense to plead that the statement was made by another in the course of official proceedings. Thus, a newspaper, ordinarily, may print the reasons given by the Mayor for the removal of his police commissioner, but if the Mayor goes to a meeting of brother Elks that evening and makes a speech in which he calls the ousted official a lying, thieving skunk, the newspaper had better think twice, or even three times, before printing the remarks.

The handling of crime stories is an exceedingly ticklish business. A legal arrest is a public and official proceeding.

A newspaper may print the fact of the arrest and the charge, relying upon its statutory privilege. However, there is no privilege to report the investigations of the detectives which led to the arrest, or the deductions or opinions of the police as to the guilt of the person who has been arrested. Everyone knows, however, that newspapers are filled with such unprivileged matter. Of news articles in this field, which is of paramount importance to newspaper men, Mr. Cross says:

"If you do report such matters, there are, or may be, two effects: first, such matters are not in themselves privileged and their presence in the stories may destroy the privilege that would otherwise protect the report of the arrest and the charge. Your only complete defense will be truth and generally that means proof of guilt of crime and that is serious, for libel suits are rarely brought unless and until the arrested person is found innocent. I have said this is the most important public and official proceeding. I did so for these reasons. First, because most libel suits are based on stories charging crime; second, because stories of arrests always involve charges of crime, though not necessarily guilt of crime; third, because many libel suits based on crime stories arise on reports of arrests; fourth, because if an arrest story is not privileged, the newspapers' only complete defense generally is to prove the guilt of a person who has been found innocent, and, fifth, because at this point arises a serious, and probably the most serious, conflict between the libel law on the one hand and the newspapers' natural desire on the other.

"A crime is committed. The police seek the criminal. Finally an arrest is made. The law says you are privileged to print the fact of the arrest and the charge and no more. That may be and generally is a bald and uninteresting narrative. What newspapers desire to print and the public desire to read is the circumstances which directed suspicion toward the accused, the discoveries made by detectives, their accounts of their activities. Therein lies the romance, the news value, the very vitals of the story. But the law says: 'No. That you shall not print under the protection of privilege. If you print that you must prove it true.' I say that that is wrong. Many will disagree with me. In a few states, notably some in the Far West, such matter is privileged if correctly reported and the guilt of the arrested person is not asserted by the newspaper itself. That I contend is sound. This privilege is given to newspapers, not as judges of guilt or innocence or as Lord High Executioners, but as chroniclers of events of public importance. Of course, they should not themselves declare the arrested person guilty but they should, I say, be allowed correctly to report what the public officials charged with the enforcement of the law did and said.'"

In most large cities, despite the law, newspapers every day take chances; they tell of the early upbringing of the prisoner, his childhood peculations, his peculiar behavior, the complicated machinery necessary to catch him, the opinion of the detectives on whether he is a mere punk or Public Enemy No. 1, 2 or 3, and all that sort of thing.

As it is, there are many libel suits. The reason there are not more is that the arrested person usually is either found guilty, or escapes conviction by such a narrow margin, that he doesn't want to try conclusions with the newspapers. Reporters and editors, moreover, have developed a sixth sense in such matters, and usually can detect probable guilt or innocence at great distances. When there is doubt, they usually play safe. Moreover, it is no pleasant business for a suspected criminal to sue a newspaper; counsel can throw many thorns in his path, and reporters, usually working with the police, often are able to disclose facts so damaging that the man is eager to drop the suit.

One such plaintiff sued the newspapers once because, owing to a mix-up of pictures at police headquarters, his photograph had been reproduced as that of a notorious criminal. With a loud wail, this man, who was an ex-convict, cried through his mouthpiece that he had been out of prison for many years, that his life since then had been exemplary, and that publication of the photograph had ruined him, undoing at one stroke all his striving for the clean life. A little investigation revealed that the man had not done a day's honest work since leaving prison years before, and that he had been supported by his wife, a capable woman who operated a chain of third-rate brothels. The fellow decided that he hadn't been injured after all.

Reports of court proceedings are extremely difficult. It is easy for a reporter, even a pretty good reporter, to forget the rules of statutory privilege. Lawyers hold that the number of libel suits against a newspaper bears a direct relationship to the numerical volume of that paper's court stories. Mere threats of suit, affidavits which have not been made part of the judicial record, and comment of lawyers outside the courtroom are dangerous in the extreme. Statements by private detectives always carry a red flag; even the well-meant statements of the prosecuting attorney may be the basis of a serious suit. In reporting one-sided or ex-parte proceedings, where much of the real facts are as yet undisclosed, it is a good general rule to interview the "other side" and to print it. This course has these advantages:

Often it makes a better story.

It appeals to the strong American sense of fair play.

It may create the defense that the publication of the story was authorized or consented to.

It will make your report fair when otherwise it might not have been.

It will often carry through to verdict an article that is not a true report or as to which there is doubt as to accuracy.

If everything else fails, it will tend to keep down the verdict.

One of the great foundations of the freedom of the press is what is known as the right of fair comment and criticism. Defense of this right is always a qualified defense, and is destroyed when the plaintiff can prove actual malice. As a practical matter, it is largely limited to editorials and to criticism of music, the theater, art, books and such things as invite public attention or call for public comment. Such criticism, to be libel-proof, should be an expression of opinion as distinguished from an assertion of fact. Moreover, in general, the criticism should be directed at the product and not at the person who produced it. To say that the performance of an actor was "ham," that it was an outrage upon the audience, is not libelous; to add that the actor himself is a wife-beater is libelous.

Enormous leeway has always been allowed in such criticism. Years ago an inept vaudeville act put on by the Cherry Sisters in Des Moines was criticized bitterly by a local paper, and the sisters sued. They lost. Heywood Broun, in the days when he was a critic of the drama, once called a man the world's worst actor. The man threatened suit, but nothing came of it, and when the man appeared in his next play Broun commented that he was "not up to his usual standard." The critical opinions of George Jean Nathan, some of which have gone far over the line into the field of personalities, never have resulted in libel suits.

Of all the professional men whose handiwork might be assumed to lend itself to fair critical comment, the architects, in New York at least, are the least able to stand adverse comment. A musician can shrug off a blistering comment on his recital; a sculptor may say, "Sorry he didn't like it, but what the hell?", but let a critic print his opinion that a certain building is a monstrosity, and the architect will get his lawyer and go into battle with all the legal weapons from Blackstone to Max D. Steuer. The courts, also, have been surprisingly generous to the offended architects. This situation, it is probable, will not last forever. The architects should learn to stand up under criticism without whining; if they don't, the law some day will be changed to cover their status.

Of course, barring a few suits brought by political feudists while the great madness of a campaign is upon them, there is extraordinary freedom in political comment. One reason for this freedom is that when a man runs for public office in the United States, or in any other democratic country, he expects to be called names, to bear the cross of unfair attack, and to take calumny as a part of the game. Morris L. Ernst, the brilliant New York lawyer who has appeared in many libel actions, sometimes for the plaintiff and sometimes for the defendant, points out in his book, "Hold Your Tongue," that once it was seditious libel to say that a king had "betrayed" his subjects, but "if that were all that was said about a President of the United States he would feel himself highly complimented." He adds:

> Public office in this country has become a dirty and nasty thing. Its attainment in most cases implies chicanery and deceit. A corrupt people have never had honest rulers. Those whom we put into high positions of trust are honored by many, but the knee is bent not so much to the men as to the office or the title.

Few libel suits receive much publicity. One of the most interesting and costly was the $1,000,000 action brought by Aaron Sapiro, a lawyer who had organized cooperative groups of farmers, against Henry Ford. In the early 1920s Ford's Dearborn *Independent* started attacking Jews, playing the theme that the Jews were plotting to rule the world and already, indeed, were calling the American Rockies "The Mountains of Zion." Sapiro brought his suit on the ground that he had been accused of acting as agent of a ring of international Jewish bankers whose object was to dominate American agriculture through his cooperative farm ownership scheme. The attacks on Jews were abandoned in 1922, long before the Sapiro suit reached court. The case came up in 1927. Senator James A. Reed of Missouri was Ford's chief counsel; he was supposed to have received a retainer of $100,000 and $1,000 in addition for every day he passed in court. The transcript of the trial covered 5,000 pages; a speech by Sapiro, which the Ford defense read into the record, was 25,000 words long.

Suddenly Ford disavowed all attacks on Sapiro and the Jews and the suit was discontinued. The terms of the settlement never were published but it was understood that Ford was to pay Sapiro a substantial sum for expenses of the trial. Ford and his paper authorized a statement:

"Such statements as may have reflected upon Mr. Sapiro's honor or integrity, impugned his motives or challenged the propriety of his personal or professional actions are withdrawn. Likewise the charge that there was a Jewish ring which sought to exploit the American farmer through cooperative associations is withdrawn.

"Mr. Ford did not participate personally in the publication of the articles and has no personal knowledge of what was said in them. He, of course, deprecates greatly that any facts that were published in a periodical so closely associated with his name in the minds of the public should be untrue."

Another libel suit against Ford also had been pending, brought by Herman Bernstein, Jewish editor, for $200,-000, and based upon the statement in the Dearborn *Independent* that Bernstein had furnished the alleged information which had been used as a basis for the attacks on Jews. Bernstein charged that he had been represented as "a sort of spy in the service of your mythical combination of international Jewish bankers, against whom you have been directing grotesque assaults." Soon after the Sapiro apology, Ford apologized to Bernstein; the money settlement, if any, never was made public.

Ford has had hard luck with the libel laws. Back in

June, 1916, the Chicago *Tribune* published an editorial
under the caption, "Ford Is An Anarchist." Ford sued
for $1,000,000. The case came to trial in 1919 before a
jury in Mount Clemens, Michigan. It was a bad time for
the flivver tycoon. Counsel for the *Tribune* asked:

"Who was Benedict Arnold?"
"He was a writer. I think he worked for me," replied Ford.
"What was the United States originally?"
"Land."
"What is anarchy?"
"Opposing the government—throwing bombs."
"What is a mobile army?"
"A large army mobilized—an army ready to be mobilized."
"What is an idealist?"
"One who makes profits for other people."

Ford also said that, in his opinion, history was bunk. In
all truth, some of his answers, which seemed so excruciat-
ingly funny at the time, appear in the light of retrospect
to contain a good deal of horse sense. The jury returned
a verdict of six cents for Ford, and the *Tribune* had to
pay the costs; the publicity was of enormous value to the
newspaper.

One of the bitter fruits of the murder of the Rev. Edward Wheeler Hall and Mrs. James Mills, choir singer,
near New Brunswick, New Jersey, in 1922, was a libel suit.
The murder case was a great sensation, but after long investigation it was dropped. In 1926, following eight
months of investigation by Herbert Mayer, a reporter
under the supervision of Philip Payne, at that time editor
of the New York tabloid, the *Mirror,* the case "broke"
again. The charges made by the *Mirror* were startling;
they resulted in the indictment of Mrs. Hall, widow of
the murdered philandering clergyman; her brothers, Willie
and Henry Stevens; and her cousin, Henry de la Bruyere
Carpender. After a trial of five weeks Mrs. Hall and her

brothers were acquitted and the indictment against Carpender was quashed.

Payne, who had been an unimportant New Jersey newspaper man before he came to New York and exhibited a
genius for tabloid sensation, had telegraphed to Timothy
N. Pfeiffer, Mrs. Hall's lawyer, when the case was re-
opened: "This is a challenge to you as Mrs. Hall's legal
representative to bring a criminal libel action against me
personally if the statements published in today's *Daily
Mirror,* accusing Mrs. Hall, are not correct. I stand fully
responsible for the charges against Mrs. Hall." The end of
Payne, a sad but defiant editor, came when he took off in
the airplane Old Glory in the summer of 1927, on a flight
toward Rome, and never was heard from again.

Mrs. Hall, Willie Stevens and Carpender filed suit
against William Randolph Hearst, his *Mirror* and *Evening
Journal* for libel, asking $3,000,000. There were six suits
in all, each for $500,000. The complaints against the
*Mirror* cited two editorials headed "Fate!" and "Can a
Rich Family Get Away With Murder in New Jersey?"
The complaint of Willie Stevens objected to a composite
picture showing him leaning over the bodies of Hall and
Mrs. Mills and placing a card at the slain rector's feet, with
a caption: "While the bodies were still warm, Willie
Stevens placed telltale card at foot of minister, so state
charges. *Mirror* staff artist has constructed the scene from
records of trial." Mrs. Hall's complaint contained ex-
cerpts from the tabloid charging that she paid "$2,000 a
week to get the 'dope' on any witness who might give
damaging evidence," demanding to know why Mrs. Hall
went to Italy, "the only country with which the United
States has no extradition treaty," within a week or two
after the first investigation had ended, and daring her
to "turn over to the authorities the records of her detectives."

Settlement of these libel suits was announced in 1928.

The amount was never made public.  William A. DeFord, Hearst lawyer, had suggested a settlement of $35,000; Pfeiffer, the Hall lawyer, is said to have insisted upon $100,000.

In any event, the conduct of the *Mirror* and Payne, which might have been defended as "vigorous, crusading journalism," if the evidence had stood up, brought general public condemnation upon such methods.  It gave tabloids a bad name from which they still suffer.  It gave the "reporter-detective" a black eye.  It disgusted the public with the sensational press generally, and even affected the esteem in which all the press was held.

The tabloids have surprisingly few suits brought against them.  Usually they are adept at staying within the law, and the people they pick fights with are not in a position to fight back.  A frequent question is: "Why isn't Walter Winchell sued oftener?"  The answer is that he and his editors are clever at avoiding printing matter which is actually libelous.  But they are not always in the clear.  A heavy verdict was returned against Winchell personally in 1934 because of a slurring squib he had written about the directors of a Long Island club.

Although the gossip column, the jottings of many a Pepys at the keyhole, the sly and often smart-alecky little epics about people and things and strange surmises, are not new as journalistic fixtures, they have reached a peculiar flowering since the war, and such products often are marked with a professional competence and sophistication which the older columns lacked.  The latitude of the gossip column has rarely been tested in all its ramifications. Sometimes it is news; again it is a form of criticism.  An especially interesting suit is one filed in May, 1934, by General Douglas MacArthur, Chief of Staff of the United States Army.  He sued the Washington *Times* and Drew Pearson and Robert S. Allen, authors of "The Daily Wash-

ington Merry-Go-Round," a syndicated feature, for
$1,750,000.

General MacArthur charged that he had been libeled on
seven counts, and he sought $250,000 on each count. The
first article, according to the papers in the suit, charged
the General with attempting to succeed himself as Chief
of Staff, although Army custom specifies that the job shall
rotate. The column said, according to the suit: "Mac-
Arthur, however, feels that he should be an exception to
this rule, and he has been pulling every conceivable wire
to this end. Wire-pulling is one of the General's greatest
arts."

The General said that this was meant to convey the impression that he had been guilty of conduct unbecoming
an officer, contrary to Army regulations and the rules and
ethics of his profession. In the same offending article,
according to the General's complaint, the assertion was
that while he was in the Philippines he "chafed because he
wasn't being promoted fast enough," and that his wife
(now Mrs. Lionel Atwill), cabled her stepfather, Edward
T. Stotesbury of Philadelphia, and that Stotesbury later
"hammered at the desk" of the late John W. Weeks, then
Secretary of War, and that MacArthur got his promotion.
The other counts alleged that the General, in articles by
Pearson and Allen, had been held up to ridicule and contempt in various forms.

The outcome of this suit may have a bearing on the
stories sent out by the Winchells of Washington, who are,
after all, no more than up-to-date models of the old muck-
rakers of the Lincoln Steffens school of journalism. On
the other hand, it is more likely that journalistic fashion,
more than any libel verdict or settlement or withdrawal of
suit, will determine the trends of the special column.

Out of all the complex problem of defamation, a problem which has produced manifold injustice and heart-
break, there comes this question: Is it better to shelter the

citizen, to raise about him all the dikes and barbed wire entanglements known to the law, so that he may be secure to lead his own life in his own way; or is it better to throw most of the silly libel laws into the discard, modify drastically those which remain, and leave the citizen the prey of all the journals, good and bad, which seek to invade his ancient rights of privacy and to discuss his personality and his business?

There is no complete answer. It must be that truth and liberty thrive on the constant unhampered expression of ideas. How can rotten government be exposed, or dirty business methods brought to light, without unfettered expression? If some innocent person gets hurt in the process, it is still for the public good. If all newspapers were high-minded, and purged of their long-haired crusaders, their sensational circulation builders, and their incompetent publishers with senseless grudges, complete freedom might be more easily defended as a beautiful ideal.

One thing is certain: the laws governing libel need a thorough overhauling to make them simpler, less contradictory and more nearly uniform in the various States. Such an overhauling, it is safe to assume, will not be brought about for many decades, if ever.

Pilate's question, "What is truth?" was old when he asked it, but it is still pertinent, and the men in journalism are still making guesses at it and trying to keep within the law. Possibly Pilate would have made a good editor. He had an inquiring mind.

# THE JOB AND THE SCHOOL OF JOURNALISM

WHEN the scheme of the school of journalism was fairly new and startling, publishers and editors were divided on the practicability of such an institution. Many wanted to be friendly, and even praised the idea. Others, like the frosty reactionaries of today, could not be convinced that the ins and outs of the complex profession, game or business of newspaper work could be taught successfully in the classroom.

"Marse" Henry Watterson, editor of the Louisville *Courier-Journal,* snorted: "There is but one school of journalism, and that is a well-conducted newspaper office. I don't believe a journalist can be made to order."

E. L. Godkin, who was editor of *The Nation,* said: "The art of journalism lies in the expression; the science of it may be said to include all sciences, inasmuch as what it now undertakes to do is to help the public at large to think correctly on every subject of human interest. When we say this we say enough to show the absurdity of establishing a special chair or opening a special class of journalism in colleges."

Frederic Hudson, who was managing editor of the New York *Herald,* when asked if he had heard of the proposed school of journalism at Washington and Lee, said:

"Only casually, in connection with General Lee's college, and I cannot see how it can be made very serviceable. Who are to be the teachers? The only place where one can learn to be a journalist is in a good newspaper office. General Lee would have made a great failure if he had attempted to found a course for journalists in his university. College training is good, but something more is needed for journalism."

R. R. Bowker, the scholarly old gentleman who was literary editor of the New York *Evening Mail,* said: "There are two kinds of education for the journalist: the practical training of the composing room and the Knock-About College, and the development that comes of a regular college course, or its equivalent."

Variations of this same skeptical attitude are still expressed in newspaper offices. On the other hand many graduates of schools of journalism now occupy responsible and well-paid positions in journalism, which may prove little. Since the Columbia School of Journalism was founded in 1912 through the beneficence of the late Joseph Pulitzer, 1350 students have received degrees. The school of journalism idea has spread all over America, until every year there are 6,000 students in, as a fair estimate, sixty American colleges and universities.

The Columbia school is perhaps the best-known and most important, with the highest standards. Competent newspaper men have been graduted from such schools as those at the University of Minnesota, where the young but thoughtful Ralph D. Casey teaches; at the University of Texas, under the guidance of the veteran W. D. Hornaday; at the University of Missouri, at Wisconsin, Northwestern and many others. They are doing the best they can, no doubt, but the question still remains whether the experiment is worth all the pain.

In addition to the universities, many high schools have started courses in journalism, usually under the direction of teachers who have only the vaguest notion of newspaper theory and practice. There is a good idea here to teach English and current affairs, but often it is botched. In New York, particularly, these high school students, with all the good intentions in the world, constantly harass the newspaper editors for interviews on such questions as, "What is news, anyway?"; "What are newspaper ethics?"; "How does one go about writing a news story?"; "What is the history of your newspaper?" and "Do advertisers tell you when you can print a story and when you can't?" These earnest young people have little background. They are guiltless of the remotest understanding of what the press is about. They should be learning English.

The college journalism graduate, however, may be intelligent, with a certain smooth technical equipment, academic but sound enough. He knows something—not enough, God knows, but something—of the history of the Fourth Estate, the hallowed and sinful. He can use a typewriter. He understands that he should read newspapers if he expects to be a newspaper man. He knows little of libel law, or any other law, but that is not an insurmountable handicap. He may know a foreign language. Often he can spell a little better than the average college graduate, which is giving him no heavy garland.

Suppose he is fortunate enough to get a job in a good newspaper office, which hasn't happened very often in the last three or four years? What does he find? He finds that there is a great deal that he doesn't know, but his professors could have warned him of that, and probably have. He finds that the instruction he received in the school of journalism fades further and further into complete forgetfulness; there is so much fresh material to give a new or different meaning to the academic precepts.

Again, he may realize that what he mistook for a deep yearning to do newspaper work was merely one of those romantic dreams which annoy all young men. The drudgery, the monotonous round of small assignments, the constant and sometimes brutal drilling in the fundamentals, may be too much for him. Or, as sometimes happens, he likes the work, understands that even with the routine there is some sort of glamour in the business, and soon he begins to show signs of unmistakable talent—eagerness, judgment and a sure touch in his writing. No two young men are quite alike; that is one reason why, in making generalizations, it is difficult to avoid unfairness.

But always disturbing questions arise: Would not the young man have entered journalism better equipped if, instead of devoting most of his college time to studying reporting, copyreading, make-up or what not, he had paid more attention to the more fundamental subjects— foreign languages, economics, law, English, the physical sciences, the history of literature, and all that encyclopedia of information which should comprise the daily tools of the high-class newspaper man?   Isn't it often true that journalism courses are regarded as easy, and that the student takes them, not because he really wants to be a newspaper man, but because he knows he can pass with a minimum of mental effort?   Do the schools of journalism really save the managing editors and city editors time and money in training beginners?   And what is the school of journalism supposed to be, a sort of trade school, where the minutiæ of the business is taught, or a seminary dedicated to the higher and more philosophical aspects of the noble profession?

These questions still agitate parents, newspaper editors, teachers of journalism and the students themselves.   They can be answered, sometimes incompletely, for much of the evidence lies in the field of opinion, which may be biased. A committee appointed by the American Society of Newspaper Editors to study schools of journalism made a report a few years ago, the following two paragraphs of which present the divergent views on what should be the purpose of the schools:

"Your committee finds that there are two schools of thought among editors, when consideration of departments of journalism is brought up.   One school wishes the departments of journalism to stop turning out budding columnists, would-be dramatic critics and book-reviewers, young men who wish to start as editorial writers. Instead it wishes them to graduate men who will be good police reporters and expert copy-readers. Such editors frankly want the departments of journalism to be trade schools. They want to be relieved of the torturous work of teaching copy-reading, office routine, and the elements of news gathering. They believe that given relief on this score they will be able to discover such columnists, critics, reviewers and executives as they need. A majority of your committee, while seeing the point of this attitude, feels that it is too utilitarian, unconsciously too selfish, to be acceptable in this American Society of Newspaper Editors.

"Now the second school of thought with regard to preparation for journalism, and the one with which your committee finds itself allied, wants the departments of journalism to equip the youth of today for the journalism of tomorrow with a broader background, a surer cultural foundation, a wider understanding of the history and problems of the sciences, the arts and the manifold relationships of men to society, than most of us have acquired. We want the departments of journalism to turn out men, some of them our own sons and the sons of our friends, capable of appraising the changed and strangely new world which will be theirs tomorrow. We want these boys— of course they will start at the bottom—capable of rising to the posts of great newspaper power, equipped to wield that power intelligently. In other words, we wish them, while they are collecting police news and reporting banquets, to carry the mental equipment which rightly directed will one day invest them with editorial control. Each graduate ought to have in the knapsack of his mind the baton of the editor and publisher."

Beautiful! Also windy, as so often is the case when the high editors cross themselves and think of holy matters.

The committee, after this high-minded statement of the case, went further and recommended that the society of editors "seriously consider urging that departments of journalism be graduate schools." Carl W. Ackerman, who at the time the report was made public had only recently been made dean of the school of journalism at Columbia,

described the graduate school suggestion as "revolutionary." It was.

Undergraduates had been accustomed to beginning journalism training in many colleges, sometimes as early as
their freshman year. The question, as Ackerman pointed
out, is an old one: At what point in the curriculum is it
advisable that professional training should begin? In other
words, should the student who thinks he wants to be a
newspaper man be forced to spend four years studying the
arts and sciences before he has the opportunity of studying the strictly professional and technical matter offered
by the school of journalism? The difficulty lies in attempting to divide the fundamental academic studies from
the purely journalistic courses.

If the student is forced to wait too long before studying
journalism, he will fidget and wonder why he cannot be
permitted to have some inkling of how his boning upon
international relations will help him in newspaper work.
If he goes too soon into the journalism school, the teacher,
whether doddering former managing editor or a book
critic who lectures on his nights off, will complain: "I
can't do anything with this sort of material. He simply
doesn't know enough."

In 1932, a year after the report of the committee of the
society of editors, Dean Ackerman recommended many
changes in the Columbia curriculum. The requirements
were tightened rather drastically. The changes, now in
effect, make the requirement of admission the completion
of three years of work in a college or university approved
by Columbia. In addition, the dean may require a written
or oral examination of all candidates for admission to the
school of journalism; the course is limited to two years,
ending in the degree of bachelor of science; and the point
system has been abolished. Appraisal of work is on one
basis only, passed or failed.

Dean Ackerman's new system allows for great flexibility in the handling of students.   It places Ackerman himself in a position of virtual complete control of the school, with as much power to fire or promote as any managing editor.   Even allowing for imperfections of judgment in some cases, such a strong central control with advancement based upon actual accomplishment and discernible capabilities, seems to many an improvement over the old routine "point system."   Most of the music in newspaper work is played by ear anyhow.   If Dean Ackerman should decide to bounce a man because he didn't like his pompadour, or his peculiar hang-dog look, or merely felt, from his casual contact with the man, that he would never make good newspaper material, then the dean would be doing nothing more than is done by executive editors who have to deal with these imponderables among human beings.

Of course the strict requirements at Columbia do not exist in most of the other schools of journalism.   In the cow and wheat country a young man may figure, and with good sense, that by taking the regular college studies, picking up a few courses in journalism along with it, he can go back to his home town and get a job on the paper there—which may be what he always had wanted.   Most schools of journalism over the country are not in a position to demand the high scholastic background which Columbia insists upon.   Endowments and appropriations are small, the folks back home are having a hard time meeting taxes, and it is best to get the whole costly, messy process of "education" over with quickly.   A small college, or a pinched university in the South or West cannot be expected to apply the rigid tests of admission required at Columbia; in the first place, many of them would have no students.   Time, as observant reporters have noted impatiently, is fleeting.

If the United States were the lush paradise that it showed promise of becoming in the few years before 1929, when the prophets talked of two cars in every garage, and every honest and well-meaning clodhopper and clerk confidently expected to be able to send a passel of sons and daughters through the best colleges of the land, then there might be room for many schools of journalism, equipped with libraries, taught by the best brains of journalism, and filled with the cream of the raw material as students.

That is to say, there would be more excuse for high-powered schools of journalism if the newspapers were hiring enough people to make the schools any more than a pleasant academic exercise. If newspapers were still expanding rapidly, and felt more secure about their future, the unemployment problem, among old and young, would be much less acute. The truth is that the newspapers in 1934, few excepted, are uncertain of their future, and with good reason. Advertising revenue for almost a year has been generally better, but the way ahead is muggy, complicated as much by real threats as by hobgoblins.

But the papers must always have staffs? Yes, indeed. Many of them, even the ones most firmly intrenched, have difficulty in keeping the staffs they had. Scores of fairly good newspaper men—certainly men who deserved a chance, or a trial if they were beginners, or who surely could fit acceptably into many spots on a newspaper— have been living in New York on next to nothing for the last three years. A few youngsters of exceptional promise have been added to the staffs of some papers, but not as many as in other years. Always it has been considered difficult to get a job on a newspaper in New York; now it is much harder than before.

Dean Ackerman's 1931 report said that "even in New York City, a graduating journalist thinks himself lucky if he gets a position with a salary of forty dollars a week." Today "lucky" seems a weasel word for such a near-miracle. The newspaper offices are besieged by men with fine records just out of college, or out two or three years and still jobless, who ask for "anything at all, a job as office boy, anything to get started in this business and to have something to do." Indeed, a few Phi Beta Kappas have been started as office boys at $12 a week. Out of their ranks have come a few reporters who promise great accomplishment.

It is heart-warming to think that every young man entering journalism, whether he has been graduated from a school of journalism or not, possesses that equipment and character which betokens the great man of tomorrow—"in the knapsack of his mind the baton of the editor and publisher." The trouble seems to be that although the eternal verities are still operating fitfully ("there's always room at the top") there is an oversupply of batons. Idle somewhere, or piddling with some small job and glad to get it, are young men with these rusty little Northcliffe-model batons—batons which, for all their excellence, have little chance ever to lead the parade now led by W. R. Hearst, Adolph S. Ochs, Ogden Reid, W. T. Dewart, Robert R. McCormick, Paul Patterson, Amon G. Carter, Harry Chandler, Frank Knox and the others. Perhaps three-fourths of the batons should be disabused.

Maybe it isn't as hopeless as that. The business isn't bankrupt. Even in the depression, a few young men have obtained a foothold and gone ahead. There will be others tomorrow. Now and then a clear opening is presented for a beginner, or a trained man, in the shifting grab-bag of newspaper jobs.

It is debatable whether the schools of journalism are justified in keeping up their plants and their faculties for the production of White Hopes at a time when so few jobs are open. Take the history of the graduates of the Columbia School of Journalism. Since its founding in 1912 there have been about 1,350 graduates. A survey made of about 1,220 graduates between 1912 and 1931, discloses no data on 513, the majority of whom were women. A detective might assume that some had married and didn't take time to answer a questionnaire. Of those sending in answers, 293 gave themselves "no occupation."

Seventy-six got jobs on New York and Brooklyn newspapers or news services, but not all held these jobs. Eighty more are known to have obtained jobs on papers throughout the country. Eleven graduates said they were doing some writing; two, Sarah Addington and Morrie Ryskind, have become well known. Twenty-seven were working on magazines, in jobs ranging from editor to receptionist. Twenty-six were teaching subjects ranging from journalism to physical training. There was at least one farmer, a pawnbroker, a monk, a rabbi and a Christian Science practitioner.

The classes of 1932 and 1933, which were not included in the survey, appear less fortunate. Of the seventy-one graduates in the class of 1932, twelve are known to have found employment on papers of varying size. One is a waiter in a sandwich shop, another a C. W. A. worker, two are file clerks, and many do nothing.

The class of 1933, which had fifty-six graduating members, has placed eight on papers. There are two in New York, Bruce Pinter of the *Herald Tribune* and Jack Haslett of the *World-Telegram*, and another graduate works for a paper in Esthonia. The class produced a C. W. A. worker, a liquor store owner, two printers, a dredger, some department store clerks, and many unemployed. Some even have reached the ultimate futility; they are doing press agent work for nothing. Where now are those brave batons?

The school, of course, has turned out some good men. Among them are George Sokolsky, who has written some books; Joseph Freeman, who became editor of *The New Masses;* Dr. Leon Fraser, president of the Bank for International Settlements; Hickman Powell, Robert Neville, and Lincoln K. Barnett, members of the staff of the *Herald Tribune;* Lester Markel, Sunday editor of the *Times;* Burnett Olcott McAnney, city editor of the *World-Telegram;* Ben Franklin, who became night city editor of the old *World* and is now night editor of the *Herald Tribune;* Joseph L. Jones, foreign editor of the United Press, H. R. Knickerbocker, and Dean Ackerman himself.

Even among the more successful graduates of the school founded by Pulitzer there is a division of opinion upon the efficacy of schools of journalism in general, as well as upon the system at Columbia. Likewise, many of the students of 1934 are in doubt. They are baffled by the same questions that assail college men elsewhere: Is this worth doing? Hadn't I better try to go to work? Am I really learning anything? I came here expecting that when I finished, my journalism schooling would be sure to get me a job on a paper, but where is there a chance? There can, it appears, be no completely satisfying answer to the student. He is not sure, and neither are the editors and publishers.

It may point the way to a few undetermined and honestly puzzled young men and women to summarize some of the salient aspects of newspaper work as it is practiced today, with particular reference to the problems of the beginner. In the first place, it undoubtedly is true, as "Marse Henry" said long ago, that a good newspaper office is the best school of all. But that isn't the whole story.

One of the shameful things about many a newspaper office, even a pretty good one, is the way it treats a cub. On the theory that "if he can't take it, to hell with him!" many newspaper editors and sub-editors will haze the newcomer, or ignore him, or refuse to give him a few simple suggestions which might make a good man of him. The punch-drunk neophyte may lose heart, though it must be said that there is some sense to the hard-boiled theory that if the youngster has a real heart he can stand up un-

der any amount of punishment and emerge better for it.
This swim-or-drown theory is good for the occasional inflated ego, but in most cases the patient, kindly advice of
an editor or an older reporter is most effective.

Even the graduates cum laude from schools of journalism must learn actual newspaper work largely by trial and
error. There are, for one thing, subtle differences in the
atmosphere and organization of various newspaper offices.
One office may be like another externally, but there is a
difference in tempo. Therefore a young man may feel
lost on one paper, and immediately find himself on another.

Again, there is in newspaper offices, as in the police department and in corporations large and small, the thing
known as "office politics." Usually it is abominable, or
silly, but in one form or another it nearly always exists.
Curiously, it has been observed that some graduates of
schools of journalism are adept in understanding these un-
dercurrents; indeed, they have been known to spend more
energy and brains on getting the drift of office gossip
("Was Doakes really slugged in a brothel?") than on covering their stories. It requires years for some of them to
learn that they are employed as newspaper men and not
as ward heelers.

The majority of men fresh from college who have been
hired by New York papers in the last half-dozen years
have never seen the inside of a school of journalism. At
the start they may have lacked some of the technical ease
of the journalism graduate. In other respects they seemed
superior to the specially-trained men. Hardly a day passes
in a metropolitan newspaper office that there is not a call
for a reporter who can speak German, or who has something more than a superficial knowledge of art, or who
can stand up to the new French Ambassador and talk his
own language and his own figures, or who possesses more

than a smattering of American naval history—the list is endless.

An example: one of the best New York reporters today is Joseph W. Alsop, Jr., of the *Herald Tribune*. He was graduated from Harvard in the class of 1932. He had an idea that he wanted to be a newspaper man. His educational equipment was as nearly perfect as could be asked, but he knew absolutely nothing of newspaper routine, and was somewhat flabbergasted by some of the canaille whom he met on his first few assignments. They weren't in anybody's curriculum. The rule books forgot them. For two or three months he floundered, lost weight, and then suddenly he found himself. He realized that, on almost every assignment, he could draw on his literary, artistic and scientific knowledge, as well as that marvelous granary of trivia which seems to be part of the stock in trade of so many young men today. To be sure, he might have been improved by a course in journalism, but it is doubtful, and he is not an isolated case.

Two of the best reporters to enter the New York field in recent years were Lamoyne Jones, from Columbia, and Thomas Sugrue, from Washington and Lee. Both rapidly distinguished themselves, although neither had taken a journalism course. Possibly they might have been helped by such a course, but even without it they were good almost from the first day.

A complaint, which has some justice behind it, has been made by observers of the work of school of journalism graduates on the score of ordinary writing ability. Virtually all of the graduates have a ready, workmanlike style, but something, somewhere, seems to have happened to them. Is it because so many of their teachers never were very great shakes as newspaper men, and were added to the teaching staff at an age when they should have been retired?

The prose of the young master may march straight and

sure across the page, resulting in that immaculate copy which is the delight of the city and copy desks. But examine it closely. It is lifeless and hollow like a row of pretty but empty Easter eggs. The young man is trying with undoubted craftsmanship to conceal his ignorance of the real fabric of his story. Moreover, he is inclined to shy away from the fresh phrase, the verb that slaps or dances, and to cringe from putting zest into a moving, human narrative. In learning "technique" he has put his mind in a strait-jacket. The malady is as painful as cramps, and fatalities have been reported. It is of course akin to hookworm, with traces of strangulation.

Another complaint against the schools is that, although they are operated theoretically for the public welfare, an old Pulitzer dream, and for the greater glory of journalism, many of the graduates either immediately or very soon after leaving college enter some field of publicity work. Now, there is no shortage of press agents. Every youth who can write a 300-word "press release" with names spelled fifty per cent right, may carry in his knapsack the baton of Ivy Lee or even Gabriel's louder bugle. Of course publicity, propaganda, and all that sort of thing, is part of the news system, but publishers sometimes, when they feel in the mood, ask whether a "school of journalism" does not resolve itself into too much of a training ground for press agents. Indeed, many schools offer courses in "publicity." Dean Ackerman himself, before he took charge of the school at Columbia, was employed as a public relations counsel by General Motors.

All this is not to say that the high ideal of Joseph Pulitzer, the intelligent and energetic work of Ackerman, and the patient efforts of men all over the country to teach journalism sensibly, have all come to so much moonshine. Far from it. It is merely to suggest that the schools are still on trial, that they have not solved the problem of bringing well-trained recruits into the newspaper business, and that, it may be, there are too many of these institutions.

There is always talk of "professional" newspaper men. No one knows what the term means. One definition of the real professional is that he should be able to do everything on a paper: reporting, rewrite, copyreading, headline writing, and make-up. Even under the New Deal there is a dearth of high-class men who are artists at headline writing and making up a paper. News men who understand type are rare. And yet, the courses in typography are the least popular in schools of journalism. The study of type requires drudgery. It is pleasanter to study the technique of covering a literary tea.

The newspaper business cannot have too much brains, or too much character. Judgment, courage and real talent, however, it must be, are part of the man, just as style is the man. The schools of journalism have not yet proved that they can supply more than a small part of the high-grade talent that should find a place, and which, strangely, does find a place.

What is a good newspaper man? There are plenty of names: Russell B. Porter, Ray Daniell and Bruce Rae of the New York *Times;* Tom Pettey, Allen Raymond and Joseph Driscoll of the *Herald Tribune;* Charles M. Bayer of the *American,* John O'Donnell and Martin Sommers of the *Daily News,* and such men as Ernest K. Lindley, Theodore C. Wallen, Arthur Krock and J. Fred Essary in Washington. And there is that hard-hitting all-around reporter, Paul Y. Anderson of the St. Louis *Post-Dispatch.* And scores of others. Most of them are distinguished by the qualities which are implied in the definition which Don Skene, the boxing writer, gives of a gentleman— "a stand-up guy who will fight."

# THE FREE PRESS UNDER THE REVOLUTION

*Congress shall make no laws respecting an establishment of religion or prohibiting the free exercise thereof; or abridging the freedom of the press; or the right of the people peaceably to assemble, and to petition the government for a redress of grievances.*

—Section I of the First Amendment to the Constitution of the United States.

SINCE the first lumbering movements of the extraordinarily complex and sometimes revolutionary recovery machine of the administration of Franklin D. Roosevelt, the American newspaper publishers have professed to see many new threats to the freedom of the press. Even those publishers who were, in general, extremely friendly to the President, and hopeful of the wisdom of his program, cried out mightily when the codification of industry touched their own business. They argued that the freedom of the press, guaranteed in the Constitution, might be curtailed or even destroyed. In some quarters this protest of the publishers was looked upon as insincere, an almost wholly sham argument set up to protect their own pocketbooks. Indeed, President Roosevelt himself, in a press conference at the White House, answering a question on the subject of freedom propounded by a reporter for the Chicago *Tribune*, whose publisher and editor, Colonel Robert R. McCormick, has been principal leader in the fight against the implied dangers in the New Deal, said:

"Tell Bertie McCormick that he's seeing things under the bed."

It is true that most publishers guard their pocketbooks jealously, even fiercely. It is true that they seek to make

profits.   It is true that they are alarmed at every law or
regulation which would tend to hamstring them.   It is
true, moreover, that not all publishers are high-minded.
At the same time it is true that the threats to the freedom
and integrity of the press, financial and intellectual, have
been recurrent through American history, and that in recent years these threats have become ominous.

The ordinary newspaper man, when he ponders the history of his business, remembers three heroes.   There was
Edmund Burke, who turned to the press gallery of Parlia-
ment and flattered its members by naming them the
Fourth Estate.   There was Thomas Jefferson, whose ghost
must be whimpering through the halls of Monticello as
it contemplates the regimentation under the New Deal,
who said he would prefer a land with newspapers but no
government to one with a government but no papers.   And
there was Voltaire, who said to Helvetius: "I wholly dis-
approve of what you say and will defend to the death your
right to say it."

Grand old men, but would their ideas fit the baffling
period of the 1930s?   Well, every period is more or less
baffling, with the human race standing at the crossroads,
disaster or glory just around the corner, and all that sort
of thing.   It may be that the period following the administration of Herbert Hoover as President is a shade more
baffling than any other since the war.   On the one hand,
the new administration has sought to strengthen itself
politically by all the tricks from the Roman bread-and-
circuses era down through the cold craftiness of such masters as Mark Hanna and Frank Hague and ending with the
sleight of hand of that amiable but cunning Elk, James A.
Farley.   On the other hand, the administration has put
into practice a sort of super-Rotarian evangelism: the New
Deal has more press agents than labored to whip up fury
in wartime; there is the sob in the throat, the catch in the
voice, the appeal to the better nature of mankind; there

is the cry for all shoulders to the wheel, we're all pals together, this is God's country, and so on.

During the first year of the Roosevelt administration,
the press showed a general disposition not only to be fair
but friendly to all administration efforts to bring some
order out of the national mess, even when the devices employed were a bit startling.   It was not until the summer
of 1934 that the questioning of the wisdom of the Roosevelt experiments began to grow insistent.   Bureaucracy
had increased amazingly.   Taxes were higher.   Strikes
were spreading.   Billions were being poured into strange
projects.   Not only the Republican bourbons but a few
of the elder statesmen among the Democrats, notably such
men as John W. Davis, Carter Glass and James A. Reed,
were skeptical and alarmed.   The attack upon the Roosevelt program showed signs of gathering bitterness and
volume.   Is Roosevelt a Napoleon with a good radio voice,
or merely a lucky politician walking a tight-rope?   In the
criticism that is sure to come, the American press will
need all its freedom.

How real has this issue been in the squabbles over the
newspaper code?   Is it altogether a false fear raised by the
publishers to keep down their costs, or has it some sense
and reality?   Is there, and has there been, any genuine
danger?   It is difficult and dangerous to question the motives of men and organizations.   Perhaps the record contains an answer.

The National Industrial Recovery Act gave the President the right to license certain industries.   He could
withhold the license if the industry in question refused to
conform to the act's provisions.   To refuse to grant a
license to a newspaper, the publishers argued, would force
the suspension of the newspaper, which in turn would be
contrary to the Constitutional guarantee of a free press.

The government contended that no act of Congress
could supersede a Constitutional provision, and that

neither the President nor any of his advisers would ever dare to apply the licensing provision to newspapers. The publishers, however, still insisted that the newspaper code must contain specific protection for freedom of the press. Otherwise, counsel advised them, it might conceivably be argued that they had waived their Constitutional rights when they acceded to the code.

General Hugh S. Johnson, the truculent phrase-maker, took violent exception to the request of the publishers. This request was embodied in article 7 of the newspaper code, and was drawn up by Elisha Hanson, the lawyer for the publishers. It read:

"Those submitting to this code recognize that pursuant to Section 10 of the act the President may, from time to time, cancel or modify any order approving this code, but in sub-mitting or subscribing to this code the publishers do not thereby consent to any modification thereof, except as each may sub-sequently agree, nor do they thereby waive any constitutional rights, or consent to the imposition of any requirements that might restrict or interfere with the constitutional guarantee of the freedom of the press."

The publishers here demanded two privileges, both of which General Johnson thought were contrary to the spirit of the act, as they would place the publishers in a favored class. That is, they refused to allow further modification of the code without their consent, and they insisted on repeating a protective clause which, for their particular benefit, had been inserted in the Constitution nearly 150 years before.

It is probable that no one ever will know, for sure, whether without the protective clause the publishers would have waived their constitutional rights, thereby in-viting danger to freedom of the press. Colonel McCor-mick, chairman of the committee on freedom of the press of the American Newspaper Publishers Association; How-

ard Davis, president of that association and business manager of the New York *Herald Tribune,* and nearly all the
larger publishers and more important editors, argued that
the threat was real.

In one of the few legal opinions on the subject, Colonel
McCormick's counsel, Kirkland, Fleming, Green and Martin, of Chicago, held that newspapers might lose their constitutional guarantee of freedom of publication if they
accepted the code without a specific Bill of Rights proviso.
They maintained the general proposition that one might
waive constitutional rights by not insisting upon them in
proper form and before the proper tribunal. In other
words, newspapers could "contract away the right of free
publication." This opinion added:

"If the newspapers, by entering into a code, admit that
N. R. A. is applicable to newspapers, they would undoubtedly,
without the proviso contended for, admit that the rest of the
code is applicable to and binding upon them.

"If the proviso is unnecessary to maintain the guarantee of
the freedom of the press, it is, at most, surplusage which cannot
in any way bind or fetter the government in its program. If
the proviso is necessary to prevent a waiver, the government
wishes to have in its hand a weapon which it could use to stifle
the press. The very fact that Johnson is so insistent upon the
elimination of the proviso would lead an unprejudiced observer
to feel that he wishes to put the press on exactly the same plane
as other industry (notwithstanding its special constitutional
guaranties) so that in the event of hostility or adverse criticism
emanating from the press he will be in a position effectively and
summarily to gag it . . .

"If the proviso is eliminated, the question will arise whether
the press cannot be licensed, and this question will have to be
determined by the courts, which, we believe, are apt to decide
close questions in favor of virtual dictatorships. If the proviso
is included, the courts cannot, without stultifying themselves,
hold that licensing of the press was ever contemplated in the
adoption of the code."

Arthur Garfield Hays, counsel to the Civil Liberties Union, expressed the opinion that while the proviso was not essential it was "wise." He held that the publishers' position was a purely technical one "because this administration is a damned sight freer than any which has preceded it." He held, moreover, that freedom of the press depended "not upon legislative enactments but upon the ability of the press to fight for its own right."

After the code containing the proviso had lain on the President's desk for five weeks, Mr. Roosevelt and General Johnson accepted it. To his approval, however, the President appended an executive order which aroused the newspaper publishers to a fresh fury. Some regarded it as an "insult" and hoped the President would apologize. In this order the President said:

"Insofar as Article 7 is not required by the act, it is pure surplusage. While it has no meaning, it is permitted to stand merely because it has been requested and because it could have no such legal effect as would bar its inclusion. A man does not consent to what he does not consent to. But if the President should find it necessary to modify this code, the circumstances that the modification was not consented to would not affect whatever obligations the non-consented would have under the National Recovery Act.

"Of course, also, nobody waives any constitutional rights by assenting to a code. The recitation of the freedom of the press clause in the code has no more place here than would the recitation of the whole Constitution or the Ten Commandments. The freedom guaranteed by the Constitution is freedom of expression, and that will be scrupulously respected; but it is not freedom to work children, or do business in a firetrap, or violate the laws against obscenity, libel and lewdness."

That sounds like the writing of General Johnson. Editors all over the country protested. William Randolph Hearst said of the publishers:

"In making this fight for the freedom of the press, they have made the fight for the freedom of the nation."

The *Herald Tribune*, in calling for an apology from the President, said:

"The order cannot hurt the press of the country, which has a long and courageous record of public service behind it, lasting far beyond the span of any one man's life, to say nothing of any one administration. If only an attack upon the newspaper industry were involved, it would be fitting to pass by the outburst in silence."

The practical effect of the President's order, in the eyes of the publishers, was to stultify the meaning of Article 7, which they had struggled so long to save. Mr. Hanson, the veteran legal adviser to the publishers, wrote to his clients:

"The code committee, representing the newspaper publishers, has insisted upon the acceptance of Article 7 without qualification. If the code is assented to, with the qualification and modification of the President, in my opinion Article 7 has no force and no meaning whatsoever, and the President is correct in his statement that it has no legal effect."

Again the publishers and General Johnson went into conference. The General was more conciliatory than usual. The publishers insisted upon "the full force and meaning of Article 7 without qualification," and the President eventually signed a modification of the executive order which read in part:

"My comment with respect to Article 7 of the code of fair practice for the daily newspaper publishing business applies also to Section 17 (b) of Article 1 of the code of fair competition for the graphic arts industries, but said Article 7 of the code of fair competition for the daily newspaper publishing business and said Section 17 of Article 1 of the code of fair competition of the graphic arts industries are nevertheless, respectively, approved as submitted, without modification, condition or qualification."

The publishers had won their battle, and the President, although he had not seen fit to "apologize," nevertheless had acceded fully to their demands. The newspaper code took effect March 12, 1934.

In all their discussion of the freedom of the press, the argument for freedom in the abstract was inextricably bound up with the argument that the publishing industry should have privileges not accorded other industries. For example, despite the editorial protest at the President's language, publishers for months afterward were demanding the right to work newsboys ("children"), and there was every indication that only state laws or a Federal Child Labor Amendment could stop them from having their papers delivered by boys.

Much foolish argument has been let loose on both sides. No doubt some of the publishers could have done better by their boys. On the other hand, the argument that in the larger cities the poor little newsboy is thrown into bad environment, possibly resulting in criminality, is hollow at bottom. The telegram from Warden Lewis E. Lawes of Sing Sing Prison, read at a hearing in Washington on the employment of newsboys, in which that gifted shepherd of the malefactors said that the majority of the inmates of his prison had once sold newspapers, proves nothing at all. If the lads had not been busy selling newspapers, they might have had more time to hang around the pool room and get an earlier start at crime.

If the Warden had said that the poorer, congested sections of large cities produce a large proportion of criminals, he would have been stating a demonstrable fact, but to blame it on the selling of newspapers is as ridiculous as would be an argument from the publishers that, because

Alfred E. Smith sold newspapers as a boy, every youngster should be urged to begin life in that fashion. Indeed, the latter argument may not be as foolish as it sounds off-hand; most great American statesmen and industrialists must have sold newspapers, split rails or followed the plow, or they are outside the tradition.

During the Roosevelt administration there have been a few specific instances of what Colonel McCormick and his colleagues called violations of press freedom. Down in Alabama an agent of the Department of Labor is reported to have threatened the editor of the Tallahassee *Tribune* for writing editorials which the agent thought violated the N. R. A. Miss Frances Perkins, Secretary of Labor, heard of the case and ordered the agent to desist. Apparently the agent was merely an overzealous little bureaucrat.

In another instance General Johnson banned from his press conferences one James True, the proprietor of one of the many private news services which abound in Washington. Mr. True's clients were business men, and he had written some things which the General said were untrue and malicious. Of course General Johnson had the right to hold press conferences or not hold them, and to invite everybody or nobody; on the other hand, if Mr. True's stories were lies, his clients probably would have found it out soon enough. It is probable that the True incident was simply a case of ruffled temper on the part of the General; the issue at stake was hardly large enough to constitute any grave threat to anyone's sacred freedom.

Although, in the past, the courts have been uniformly friendly to newspapers in sustaining their constitutional rights, the publishers know that there are many laws which do constitute a potential threat to the freedom of the press, and that, with the changing temper of the country, these laws might be invoked, or other laws might be passed. Some of these possibilities follow:

It is possible that the Federal Government might extend

its power to license radio stations to newspapers.   The fact
that many broadcasting stations are newspaper-owned
makes their owners doubly anxious.

It is possible that the government might buy control
and set up a monopoly of the communications industries.
Such monopolies abroad have often resulted in direct or
indirect censorship by means of delayed or garbled messages.

It is possible that the tendency of the government to
concentrate power in periods of emergency, and to assume
control of power, heating, lighting and building equipment, might deprive a newspaper of its ability to publish
at all.

It is possible that the government, by the fixing of prices
on raw materials essential to publishing, by exorbitant
taxes, by excessive restrictions on profits, by demands that
labor be paid more than is economically possible, might
drive many good papers out of business.

It is possible that a food and drug bill could be passed
which would eliminate or regulate millions of dollars'
worth of newspaper advertising of food, patent medicines
and cosmetics, which might mean the difference, to many
papers, between solvency and bankruptcy.

It will be seen that freedom of the press therefore brings
up curious considerations.   As Arthur Hays Sulzberger of
the New York *Times* said in 1934 in a speech at Columbia
University:

" 'Freedom of the press' involves other factors than mere
escape from news or editorial censorship.   Special taxes, as for
example an unwarranted duty on print paper, a violent increase
in postal rates, or a governmental limitation upon advertising
would be, I believe in spirit at least, in conflict with the First
Amendment to the Constitution."

It is entirely possible that the passage of a few laws up-
setting the economic balance of the press would drive out

of business half the smaller newspapers of the United States, and perhaps many of the larger ones. These threats to the life blood of newspapers are real. Witness the forcing through by Senator Huey Long in Louisiana of a law taxing the gross advertising revenue of the newspapers —patently as a counter-thrust at his enemies, which include virtually the entire press of that state.

In theory every newspaper is in danger. When William Marcy Tweed was in power in New York City, the *Times* was leading a savage attack upon Tweed and his infamous ring. Tammany announced that a flaw had been discovered in the title of the real estate occupied by the *Times* which would enable the city authorities to place a receiver in possession of the *Times* building. The ruse failed, and after another attempt to revive the old English law of contempt of government, which likewise failed, Tweed and his crowd were defeated. Publishers, even of the most courageous papers, dread the visit of a building inspector who can find some technical fault which cannot be corrected except by the expenditure of a staggering sum of money. There have been dozens of instances of attempted gagging of newspapers by such roundabout methods.

The labor unions, of course, constitute another potential threat. Under the Roosevelt administration the labor unions are kicking up their heels. In the past there have been strikes of printers, press men and mailing room employees which forced newspapers to suspend publication temporarily. Doubtless there will be more of this sort of thing.

Some observers profess to see a grave danger to freedom of the press in the growth of the Newspaper Guild, the organization of news and editorial workers. This organization is not really a "guild" but a young labor union; already it has employed labor union tactics, and its organization is built upon a framework similar to that of the unions. It has already resorted to the labor union device of picketing.

Most newspaper men have an instinctive sympathy for the under-dog. If they become more "class-conscious," and veer more and more toward unionism, its members may acquire a "labor versus capital" complex which will make it difficult for reporters to write news stories on labor troubles without displaying a conscious or unconscious bias. If they do become class-conscious, they will become propagandists and not newspaper men. If the Guild fulfills the hopes of its founders, however, there will be no such foolishness, but the original conservative and somewhat professional attitude of the Guild has been largely lost as it has headed straight for unionism. Led by Heywood Broun of the New York *World-Telegram*, the organization has grown so radical that many of the ideas of its founders have been forgotten.

The trouble appears to be that the chief voting strength in the Guild is in the hands, not of the older, more experienced and long-headed newspaper men, but of boiling youngsters, many of whom have been at work only a short time, who show signs of becoming as class-conscious as any garment worker. These young John Reeds are hot for trouble, and on many occasions they have voted down the pacific programs suggested by the conservatives.

The Guild may become extremely powerful, and dangerous to the free dissemination of unbiased news; it seems more probable, however, that their innate sense of honesty, and at least some trace of professional pride, will keep most of the members straight.

It would appear that the fight to preserve "the freedom of the press," although often bound up in pettifoggery and evasion, is nevertheless at bottom a real thing. General Johnson himself, in a speech at Waterloo, Iowa, on July 12, 1934, delivered himself of this observation on freedom: "For a long time I thought sincerely that the newspapers' insistence on writing into their code a clause saving their constitutional rights was pure surplusage. As a lawyer, I am very sure that constitutional rights cannot be signed away. But I now see more clearly why these gentlemen were apprehensive."

Of course they were apprehensive, and they will remain apprehensive. There is no let-up in the efforts to impose upon the press, to pollute its news columns, to sway its editorial judgment, to cripple its advertising. Likewise, it is probable that there will be no let-up in the aggressive tactics of the press to preserve what it conceives to be its rights. To say that some publishers are not highly admirable characters has nothing to do with the case; the freedom of the press, its independence and integrity, are real, and worth any man's fighting time.

# NEWS ON THE AIR

THE fight between the newspapers and the radio broadcasting companies has been going on ever since it was discovered that news events could be transmitted to the public through the air with a speed which makes the printing press look like some hopelessly archaic piece of junk.

The conflict is not yet ended, although in 1934 a truce was declared under which competition between the broadcasting companies and the press associations was regulated —more or less. The problem is so complicated, involving as it does the ancient feeling of the public that it should have the right to receive the news as quickly as possible, the enormous investments of the newspaper manufacturers as well as the broadcasting companies, the peculiar "property rights" which exist in the collection of news, and the threat of ruinous advertising raids, that it may be many years before the issues are settled to the satisfaction of all sides.

The secret that Marconi drew from the heavens has developed into an industry which is appalling and fascinating —sometimes monstrous, sometimes banal, and sometimes brilliantly effective. Radio beats the newspapers on many fronts. Over the air comes the engaging, persuasive voice of the President of the United States; here is something more striking than all the newspaper reports of a speech, for it comes to the citizen seated, at his radio, fresh and direct, undistorted by the medium of the press. A man in a balloon going up into the stratosphere broadcasts his story of the ascent, and it is more satisfying to listen to this account than to read of it the next morning. A visiting

European statesman, here on an important mission, broadcasts his statement, or is interviewed, from a steamship down the bay in New York; hours later the readers of newspapers may receive the same thing on the printed page, but the freshness is gone.

Every year the broadcasters become more enterprising, and they do their job better. If all the newspapers in the country were opposed to the policies of President Roosevelt, he would still have in the radio a weapon of such power that the opposition of the press would mean little—certainly less than it would have meant a few years ago. No wonder newspapers are puzzled over this strange new thing, and are wondering whether to attempt to control it, to own it outright or to put it under strict government monopoly.

Surely radio has come to be considered a form of newspaper work. Many veteran newspaper men, as well as a group of newcomers, have found fame and fat salaries by going on the air. The reporter on the air should have all the equipment of the ordinary reporter—accuracy, honesty, fairness, speed and technical knowledge—and in addition he must have a good speaking voice. The journalist of tomorrow may be advised not only to learn to write well, but to talk well.

The beginning of real radio broadcasting was in 1921, and the first event of importance to be broadcast was the fight in Jersey City in the summer of that year between Jack Dempsey and Georges Carpentier. At that time the receiving sets were of small volume, and many persons doubted whether the radio ever would become popular. Indeed, sales of sets were declining. Then Major J. Andrew White, who was editor of a radio magazine, had an idea. He suggested to David Sarnoff, president of the Radio Corporation of America, that the fight be broadcast. Tex Rickard, the promoter, fell in with the idea.

Sarnoff turned over $2,500 to White but told him to use only $1,500 of it.

White's idea was to have the radio report of the Battle of the Century received in halls and theaters throughout the Middle Atlantic States. Amateurs were to do the receiving in auditoriums and make the fight description audible to the crowds. There were very few loud-speakers at the time. One of the first difficulties was in the erection of towers for the transmitter, which would have cost $8,000. The Lackawanna Railroad came to the rescue and allowed the use of its towers; the transmitter itself, borrowed from the General Electric Company, had been built originally for a battleship. There were weeks of testing, with many difficulties to be straightened out.

The broadcast was an enormous success. More than 300,000 persons were said to have heard it. The demand for radio sets increased amazingly overnight. Sarnoff went into action then and ordered a permanent radio station built. In the fall of 1921 hundreds of thousands of new radio enthusiasts listened to the broadcasts of the World Series and to the returns of the election which swept Warren G. Harding into the White House over James M. Cox.

Major White deserves all his titles—"the dean of broadcasters" and "the godfather of radio broadcasting." He was not only the first broadcaster of any importance, but one of the best. His advice to broadcasters follows:

"An event should not be broadcast unless it is a star event, of interest to many thousands. Then when it is broadcast there is no need of gilding (he meant painting) the lily. Just describe what you see in natural tones. The broadcaster must have a quick eye and a quick mind. Most important of all he must be thoroughly familiar with all details of the event he is describing."

The Major, before broadcasting a hockey game in New York, went to Canada to familiarize himself with the sport. He broadcast horse races and political conventions, and then went into virtual retirement at the age of 40 to pursue his hobbies, polo, painting and loafing.

Probably not the best of the broadcasters, but one of the earliest to handle news events and comment, is Floyd Gibbons, who gained his reputation by averaging 217 breathless words a minute. The average of broadcasters is about 125 words a minute. In his newspaper days Gibbons covered every sort of assignment. He gained his reputation as a reporter when, as a member of the Chicago *Tribune* staff, he was sent to Mexico in 1914. Later he was in London for his newspaper. Since turning to the air he has done many types of broadcasting—the fighting in Manchuria, sports events, reminiscences of exciting assignments, conventions and descriptions of the wonders of science. Radio broadcasters, like politicians and novelists, are the victims of changing public taste. Gibbons' folksy manner, and his synthetic excitement, may repel some listeners, but he can still tell a good story.

Another veteran radio reporter, whose work has been criticized probably more than that of any other, is Graham McNamee. He was a struggling singer in 1922 when he passed the WEAF studios in New York, dropped in and got a job filling in as a barytone soloist. In August, 1923, when Harry Greb and Johnny Wilson fought for the middleweight championship, McNamee made his début as a sports announcer. That fall he took over the second game of the World Series because the customers had complained that the report of the first game had been mumbled. Then he started covering football games, and in 1924 he helped cover the National Democratic Convention at the old Madison Square Garden in New York.

McNamee was never a trained news reporter, and he is far from being an expert on many of the events which he broadcasts. The key to the criticism of McNamee may be found in his own theory of broadcasting, which he gives as follows:

"Enthusiasm is the secret of creating an illusion over the air. When the average man goes to a ball game or a fight he wants to get excited. He'll miss half the blows that are struck in the ring but not one that's struck in the crowd. The sight of a pop bottle hurtling through the air is worth the price of admission—all good Americans naturally hate the umpire. These are the things I try to get in a broadcast. I think they are what Mr. Average Man sees at the game."

Devotees of this school of broadcasting seem to think that the listeners-in want to hear a gasp of "Gee whizz! Folks, this certainly is exciting!" They may be right. However, the public is growing more expert, certainly in its knowledge of sports events. McNamee, in his tremendous excitement, either real or simulated, sometimes gets mixed up. His broadcasts of prizefights have been criticized by boxing writers and by the lovers of the technical side of pugilism. The team of Sam Taub and Angelo Pelange, who suffer from execrable diction, are not as exciting as McNamee, but their fight broadcasts are more accurate, from the point of view of the ringworm, than most of the others.

Students of radio broadcasting have often wondered why more trained newspaper men were not employed to broadcast news events. There are several answers. Most newspaper men are poor talkers. Moreover, many broadcasters, such as McNamee, for all their imperfections, have attracted a large following, and it would be dangerous and costly to try to train and build up a new man.

Heywood Broun, the columnist and labor leader, was never a great success on the radio, although to many his calm, casual, ingratiating voice seemed to be a vast relief from the staccato, fake tongue-swallowings of the members of the bogus-emotion school. Alexander Woollcott, another old reporter, probably could make a fortune on the radio if he were so inclined. His broadcasts have helped bring him an enormous popularity. Grantland Rice, who has a smooth Southern voice, has done a few sports broadcasts which were both expert and charming. If he wanted to, it is probable that Elmer Davis, once a great rewrite man on the New York *Times* and later a novelist and magazine writer, could become a radio idol. He is extraordinarily glib and urbane, and has an excellent voice. His broadcast of the great beer parade in New York in the summer of 1932 was one of the greatest exhibitions of wit, learning and extemporaneous news comment ever put on the air.

A newspaper man who has made a great success on the air is Edwin C. Hill, who for more than twenty years was a reporter on the staff of the New York *Sun*. When, in 1931, he was asked to visit a broadcasting company to test his voice, he wasn't quite sure what an "audition" was, and he was not particularly interested in nibbles from the radio industry. In three years he became one of the highest paid of all the air's reporters and commentators. Hill's success came partly because of his good voice and assured manner, but mostly from his knowledge of the personalities which figure in the news. His trick is to take two or three items of importance from the news of the day and then attempt to give "the story behind the story," to describe the men and women involved, and to enliven his narrative with many adjectives. He seeks always to touch the human emotions; sometimes he seems a bit preachy, but his formula is sound.

Hill is inclined to side with the newspapers in their attempts to prevent the radio stations from broadcasting so much "spot news." He does not believe there are enough stories of general interest in the papers every day for a broadcast of fifteen minutes or more, and that when a broadcaster tries to cover the news thoroughly in a broadcast the result is little more than a series of unrevealing, unsatisfying headlines.

One of the most astute of the broadcasters is Lowell Thomas, a smart business man who had been a world traveler and a college professor before he discovered that there was a fortune to be made at the microphone. He is at his best in giving a summary of a few news stories, with enlivening comments.

A curiosity of radio broadcasting lies in the circumstance that no Washington commentator has become outstandingly popular, although many have tried. There must be something in the climate, or the psychology, of the city of Washington which destroys freshness. It is a well-known tragedy of the newspaper business that many excellent reporters, when they go to Washington, almost immediately develop either laziness or ponderosity. They lose their bite. There is room for much improvement in Washington broadcasting.

None of those who have tried to portray the currents of Washington life and the personalities of the capital has been notably successful. Frederick William Wile, one of the pioneers, who, when Coolidge was inaugurated, March 4, 1925, spoke from the steps of the capitol through a battery of microphones about to be used for the inaugural address, is an experienced newspaper man and a competent analyst, but he has drawn only a moderately large following on the air. H. V. Kaltenborn, who used to be an editorial writer on the Brooklyn *Eagle,* has a good background on national and international affairs, and, though one of the soundest of them all, has never achieved wide popularity. His following, however, is extremely loyal. William Hard, particularly during the Hoover administration, was on the air often from Washington, but somehow he never caused the heart to leap. Not even the able David Lawrence has been consistently popular.

A radio speaker who may continue to grow in popularity is Boake Carter, whose prestige has increased rapidly since 1932, when he is said to have received 15,000 "fan letters" after a broadcast of the news of the kidnaping of the Lindbergh baby. Carter was educated in London and for a time was a traveling correspondent for the London *Daily Mail*. He joined the staff of the Philadelphia *Evening Bulletin* in 1924. His comments on the air are cryptic and sometimes extremely lively, and his many mannerisms of speech do not seem to weigh against him.

Radio is a marvelous outlet for the man who likes to talk; most newspaper men are rather silent by nature. A born talker is John B. Kennedy. Even in the old days when he was connected with the magazine of the Knights of Columbus he never suffered from reticence. He was with *Collier's* for years, as a staff writer, but by 1933 radio broadcasting was his chief interest. His stuff consists of semi-sermons, anecdotes, oblique comment on world affairs, sly bits of big-brotherly advice, and some of the most astounding puns ever let loose. His fame increases, and thousands love his unctuous voice.

The reporter or editor on a newspaper usually is inclined to be contemptuous of the radio news announcer or commentator. Part of this feeling may be attributed to jealousy; the competent $100 a week reporter dislikes the idea of a less competent reporter on the air receiving $500 or $1,000 a week, or more, for doing very little work. Again, the radio journalists have been guilty of some rather heinous offenses against accuracy in the news, although in all fairness it might be pointed out that the more responsible stations have tried to be as careful of the authenticity of their news as any conservative newspaper.

The demand seems to be for more expertness in the handling of news and comment on the air. In sports, for example, there are few men so well equipped as Don Wilson, sports announcer on the West Coast for the National Broadcasting Company. He has the ability to see, analyze and put into words a play almost as quickly as it takes place. Ted Husing of the Columbia Broadcasting Company is another radio sports reporter who has steadily increased in competence; he actually makes some attempt to learn the technical side of a sport and to tell his listeners exactly what is happening.

Although the covering of "spot" news can be done with telling effect in many instances, the radio in 1934 appears to be useful principally as a forum for comment and analysis—a rostrum from which the Walter Lippmanns of the ether may seek to explain to the befuddled citizenry just what everything is about. Since the depression this yearning of the public for an explanation of what is happening—if there is any explanation—has resulted in scores of prophets who are only too glad, for a modest fee, to leap to the microphone and do their level best to clarify matters.

The fact that there is a direct conflict of interests between the press and radio is admitted by both sides, although neither party is quite willing to call for a fight to the finish. Newspapers, by and large, have been extremely short-sighted in their failure to recognize the value of the radio. And now, with the radio industry grown to such amazing proportions, no one knows what to do about it. The situation is further complicated by the fact that many newspapers own radio stations. The Chicago *Tribune* controls WGN; William Randolph Hearst is well supplied with radio outlets. A few publishers regard all radio broadcasting as a direct threat to their pocketbooks; others believe some way may be found by which the radio will aid the newspapers.

The debate became serious in 1933 at the annual convention of the American Newspaper Publishers Association. The radio committee of the association prepared a campaign which recommended to all publishers that radio programs be dropped from the news columns and be carried only as advertising, just as the papers carry amusement advertisements. Before this campaign got under way the two largest broadcasting chains asked for a conference, and the outcome was the organization of the Press-Radio Bureau, which furnishes the broadcasting companies with reliable news digests gathered from the news services. At the 1933 convention Adolph S. Ochs presented one viewpoint when he said:

"It is important that news flashes be broadcast. It whets the appetite of the public to get hold of a newspaper that contains all the news. News of importance is bound to be broadcast no matter what we do here."

A divergent viewpoint was presented by Roy W. Howard, who said:

"The broadcasting of news bulletins is not important. The commentators are the important problem. They skim the cream off a day's news report and put it out over the air. I would be opposed to selling news to chains and also to individual stations. There has been great stupidity in the newspapers' handling of radio. Out in Denver I heard one of our own newspapers broadcast practically everything that was in the next day's paper. If news is to be given away before I can deliver it, I'm interested in that. I'm interested in protecting my rights."

The publishers recognized the fact that there could be no monopoly of news, but they were concerned in the protection of their "property rights" in the news which they gather, and in the prevention of its illegal use by others. They did not give much consideration to these rights until broadcasters developed the practice of using news in connection with commercial programs.

While the argument of 1933 was going on, the Columbia Broadcasting System, under the direction of Paul W. White, vice-president of the company, started an experiment in the collection of its own news. White hired Edward Angly, an acute and enterprising reporter, away from the New York *Herald Tribune,* and put him in charge of the actual gathering and writing of the news. Bureaus were established in Washington, Chicago, Los Angeles, Paris, London and Moscow. There were six men in Washington, and seven or eight men working with Angly in the New York office. Correspondents were lined up in many cities all over the country, and were paid by the word. It was a costly system, but for a time it showed signs of being successful. From seventeen to twenty-five news stories were broadcast every night in a fifteen-minute period. It was pithy, expert professional stuff. The Columbia news, except for one or two bobbles, was authentic.

Some day some such scheme may work. Columbia dropped its experiment when the Press-Radio Bureau began its operations, by agreement between the publishers and the radio chains. The new bureau, which collated the news gathered from the Associated Press, the United Press and the International News Service, was placed in charge of James W. Barrett, former city editor of the New York *American* and the New York *World.* The scheme called for two daily short factual broadcasts of the news, and in addition provided that the broadcasting stations should be supplied with brief reports on important events for immediate broadcast outside the regular periods. According to the agreement, such important events must be "transcendent," a word which is difficult to interpret. One chain felt that the Carnera-Loughran fight in Miami in the spring of 1934 was "transcendent," and, although the bureau disagreed, it was finally decided that news of the fight would be "flashed" for "practice." Mr. Barrett's interpretation of the controversial word is:

"News is of transcendent importance if, when it is received, it is of far greater importance than anything else in interest for the public at that time, and also transcends in importance the ordinary news content of the daily paper."

The attempted assassination of President Roosevelt, the bank holiday, the results of a national election are cited by Barrett as news of "transcendent" importance.

Within a few months after it went into effect, the agreement between the publishers and the broadcasters was being violated, not by the larger chains themselves but by many independent stations. Many of the better known news commentators have become dangerously near the line by broadcasting what might be interpreted as "spot" news. Moreover, several independent agencies for supplying news have sprung up. It is possible that, rather than have incompetent agencies furnish and receive pay for news, the publishers will arrange to give or sell to the radio more and better news than they allow in the skimpy reports of the Press-Radio Bureau.

Since the agreement does not prohibit "broadcasting on the spot," this type of radio reporting has enjoyed an enormous increase in popularity. The radio people contend that such broadcasting does not harm the newspapers; indeed, they argue that a man who has listened to a radio account of a baseball game or a track meet or a political convention is made more eager than ever to read his newspaper for fuller details.

Whatever may be the upshot, it is admitted on both sides that the present arrangement probably will be changed. It is, in many respects, unsatisfactory alike to the newspapers and the radio. The newspapers believe that the radio programs should be paid for as advertising. The radio heads say that they could not afford it, and that the radio advertisers, who already pay more than they should for an advertising medium which is of dubious value, would not stand for the extra expense.

A few predictions: Radio eventually will drive many newspapers out of business. Radio news will become more reliable. Newspapers, certainly the stronger ones which survive the struggle, will become better. Some day (it is scientifically possible now) some sort of television device will bring a complete newspaper to the customer over the wire. Whatever happens, the public can't lose. And the reporter can't lose. That gentleman, whether on the air or at his typewriter, will always have his work to do.

# A GALLERY OF ANGELS

THE ladies of the press, who are rarely called sob sisters any more, have done well by themselves, but they are not yet out of the twilight zone. It is still easy for a newspaper to get along without them. A serious national Back to the Kitchen movement would work fearful havoc. The blanket indictments against women in journalism, some outrageously prejudiced and others based on sad experience, may be summarized as follows:

They are slovenly in their habits of mind, and in workmanship. They won't look up names and facts. The observant editor feels that if they were housewives, the dishes would still be in the sink.

They are impolite, screaming for "service" from overworked telephone operators, the help in the library and the office boys. They regard the whole organization as something created for their own convenience and whims.

They insist that they want to be treated as newspaper "men," but when the showdown comes, they instantly become women again. Then they sulk at reproof, disdain well meant advice, and, if rebuked sharply for a heinous offense, either burst into tears or lament that a monster office political cabal has been formed against them.

They plead that there is no sex in business. The first thing anyone knows they have developed an embarrassing fixation for the tall, emaciated copyreader, the third from the left, who already has a wife and more children than he can support.

They depend, even the good ones, too much upon their male colleagues to help them over the tough places in their assignments. They accept these courtesies as a matter of course, and then, without thanking the man, double-cross him as often as possible.

They become hoydenish, and worse. They think it enhances their standing in the world to talk like poolroom habitués, and to sit on tables, desks and railings rather than on chairs.

They do not understand honor, and fair play, and the code of human and professional conduct as men understand it. The ancient tenets of the gentleman, undefined but instinctively felt by newspaper men, are beyond the range of the woman's understanding.

They are uniformly devoid of humor, although many think they can write amusingly. Even on the lower levels of journalistic wise-cracking, the women's efforts are feeble compared with the work of dozens of men. This has something to do not merely with the sense of the comic or the grotesque, but with the high urbanity which distinguishes the conversation in a gentleman's club from the banter at a hen-party.

They protest that they are reliable, that they have a genuine love for newspaper work, and that men and marriage are outside their scheme of life; more, that even if they did become married to some one, it could not possibly affect their value to the paper. Then they leave for the first flattering ape that comes along.

They are masters of dangerous office intrigue. They can't do their work and then let well enough alone. They must pry, and start gossip, and pass their time, which might otherwise be used in improving their minds or learning how to write sensible interviews and obituaries, in carrying low tales about their own sisters in the profession and even about some poor lecherous copyreader who bays at the moon.

They—but enough of this. To all of these grave charges the newspaper women can plead "Not Guilty! That is, not always guilty." Some are guilty on all counts; others

on none. The careless, sloppy, bad-mannered, incompetent
and unreliable girls have given a bad name to a branch of
the business in which many able, charming and forthright
women have served with distinction and even with brilliance.

Whatever part of the foregoing may be true is just as
true of men, as the women can point out at once. The
men in journalism cannot be blue-printed with much more
exactness than the women. The men exhibit startling
variations; the women range from the sleazy, conniving
little ignoramus to the straightforward, capable woman of
education and character—with a thousand gradations in
between. There are dishrags and queens.

Most complaints against women in journalism have
arisen because of their lack of versatility as general workmen: that is, many types of assignments, no matter how
persuasively ambitious disciples of the New Freedom may
argue, simply cannot be done as well by a woman as by a
man. There are few women who can handle an important, involved murder mystery competently. Few have
distinguished themselves on police news. Ship news is
covered by men, and women are used only on special interviews with particular individuals who may be arriving.

Such important but boresome subjects as politics, city
hall, transit, the legislature, municipal government and
financial news, are mostly handled by men. Some women
have done excellent work at trials, where the evidence is
spread upon the record and the scene is before their eyes.
Many have shown a gift for descriptive stories. But, generally, a newspaper finds that it needs only a few women,
if any, among a large staff of men reporters.

There has been much meaningless talk, among the sooth-
sayers of journalism, about hiring women to present "the
woman's viewpoint." To suppose that, because God in his
whimsy created her thus and so, a woman alone is
peculiarly fitted to write of women's sports, women's

clothes, women's clubs, women's flower shows, women's
political ambitions, and to interview women, is as ridiculous as to assume that a clergyman is the ideal man to cover
religious news.

News is news. The reason so many women have been
employed to write of women's activities is not because the
women were necessarily exceptionally well equipped for
the work, but because few newspaper men like to write
about women's clothes and such strange matters as beauty
hints and advice to the thwarted in love. Not that they
couldn't do it just as well, but they shrink from the razzing
of their colleagues. A man, however, can often write a
better food column than a woman, just as a good man cook
is better than a woman cook. And men make better
society editors—always with exceptions.

Except for a handful who are kept on general assignments, most women on a newspaper are shunted into
special departments, where they do not have to deal with
the rough and tumble world of policemen, firemen, am-
bulances, gunmen, lawyers and politicians in the back
room. Thus women tend to become secretaries, research
workers, women's page experts, book and magazine section editors, librarians, promotion managers, advertising
writers or salesmen and what not. The field there is wide,
and it is full of women who are doing capable work.

These specialists face a different world from that of the
woman reporter who approaches the city desk every day,
not knowing whether she is to be assigned to a fire, a story
of a lost dog, or an obituary of a woman of Newport.

Mrs. Franklin D. Roosevelt, who appears to be the leading apostle of the theory that women can do practically
everything except become fathers, has given a tremendous
impetus to the women reporters. She prefers to have
women cover the news of her incredibly active career.
Forty years ago in New York the lone woman reporter on
a morning paper would be sent home, with escort, at

dusk; if she had to cover a night assignment, such as a
Bradley Martin ball, a man reporter possessing evening
clothes would be assigned to accompany her. Today the
women reporters fly with Mrs. Roosevelt, day or night.
They eat picnic lunches with her on Puerto Rican hilltops.
Sometimes, in Washington, Mrs. Roosevelt gives the
women a chance to see the President informally, at tea,
lunch or at his fireside; in the old days they couldn't do
that.

And Mrs. Roosevelt's own conferences with the ladies
of the press are informal. They are held at 11 o'clock in
the morning once a week, when this remarkably active
woman is in Washington, on the second floor of the White
House in the sitting room at the west end of the building.
The reporters and feature writers (known affectionately
as "the girls") sit around on chairs and on the floor. Usually from twenty to forty of the women are present. The
only man about the place is Stephen T. Early, one of the
President's secretaries, who admits them to the conference
but has nothing further to do with it.

The President's wife, in her relations with the press,
resembles her husband: both are astute politicians, with a
born knowledge of how to make friends. There are little
sly confidences, which cannot be printed now, but which
are somehow exciting to know about. The women are
proud of these intimate glimpses of Mrs. Roosevelt and the
memory of what she tells them, just as the male reporters
treasure and protect the confidences of the President.
Sometimes, indeed, this feeling of protection is carried
pretty far. The best example is of the New York newspaper woman, who, alighting from an airplane flight
with Mrs. Roosevelt, asked: "Wouldn't you like to be able
to pilot a plane?"

"Yes, I would," said Mrs. Roosevelt. "I make no bones
about that."

The reporter included this simple, innocent passage in

her report of the day's doings. An hour after her story had been received in the office she sent an urgent message: "Please delete sentence, 'I make no bones about that.' Think it undignified as quotation coming from First Lady."

Thus, far from being catty, the women protect their heroine even from phrases which were good enough for Chaucer and Shakespeare, and when the First Lady doesn't ask for such protection.

It is a common complaint against women, as against men as well, that when assigned to cover the comings and goings of an important person, they forget that they are newspaper employees and gape admiringly at the most trivial performances. The sense of importance which comes from a feeling that one is "in the know" may make a staid and sober workman lose all sense of proportion. Such a woman may become as jittery as a Winchell stymied at a door without a keyhole.

And yet, despite their little foibles, the women have a sound tradition in newspaper work. This business of hiring women to write news and features has been going on a long time. One of the first was Nellie Bly, born Elizabeth Cochrane at Cochrane's Mills, Armstrong County, Pennsylvania, in 1867. She got her first newspaper experience on the *Commercial Gazette* of Pittsburgh, and Erasmus Wilson, editor, named her Nellie Bly. In 1887 she went to New York and joined the staff of the *World*. She attracted attention by feigning insanity and gaining admission to the asylum at Blackwell's Island, a spot which in later years was to be known, officially and euphemistically, as Welfare Island. Her exposure of conditions there made good reading, as have many exposures of that place since then. Then she performed her most famous feat. In 1889 she went around the world in seventy-two days to prove the plausibility of Jules Verne's imaginative romance, "Around the World in Eighty Days." In 1895 she married Robert L. Seaman, a Brooklyn manufacturer who was seventy-two years old and who died soon afterward. She tried to run his properties, then returned to newspaper work for a time, and died in 1922.

Another woman journalist is "Dorothy Dix," whose real name is Mrs. Elizabeth M. Gilman Meriwether. She had married at the age of twenty, lost her health and had been sent to the gulf coast of Mississippi, where she met Mrs. E. J. Nicholson, owner and editor of the New Orleans *Times-Picayune*. Mrs. Nicholson bought her first story for $3. The young woman got a job on the woman's page of the *Times-Picayune* and over the years made herself known as the old master of what is called among newspaper men "the love-lorn racket." She took the name, Dorothy Dix, from one of those Confederate saints, "an old colored mammy," and, working on the theory that the principal interest in life for women was men, started her climb to fame. Hearst brought her to New York; millions read her. The picture of her wise gray head, and the fine strong face, inspire confidence in the hearts of yearners for romance and the crossed in love, and when she comes out against infidelity, her word carries weight. Verily, the bishops had to yield control of the sex of America to Dorothy Dix. For more than 33 years she has been at it.

Also of the old school is Mrs. C. A. Bonfils, now seventy-one years old, a genuinely talented woman whose copy for years has been syndicated under her maiden name of Winifred Black. But the newspaper world knows her principally as "Annie Laurie" of the San Francisco *Examiner*. She is one of the leading citizens of that lovely city. She was the first reporter to gain admission to Galveston after the 1900 storm; she interviewed President Harrison when he visited California; she "fainted" in a downtown street and obtained an exposé of conditions in the emergency hospital in San Francisco; she interviewed Henry M. Stanley, the explorer, as well as Sir Henry Irving and Sarah Bernhardt; she covered Harry Thaw's trial; she haunted the dives of San Francisco to learn how the Salvation Army worked. Any little graduate of Vassar, who thinks she has big ideas for looking into social conditions and writing newspaper stories, might study Mrs. Bonfils, who knows how it is done.

Another beloved woman is Nellie Revell, who for thirty years was a writer on papers in Chicago, Denver, San Francisco and New York. She covered prizefights, murder trials and the Czar's coronation, but she used to boast that she never had written a line for a "woman's page" or a line of society news. She started in publicity work for a small circus, and later did publicity for Lily Langtry, Mrs. Pat Campbell, Al Jolson, Frank Tinney and Lillian Russell. In 1919 she fractured her spine. The accident cost her a $12,000 a year press agent job, and resulted in years of confinement. In 1934 she said, "I'd rather be a newspaper woman than in the White House," although one can be both these days. She sometimes fears the modern girls are getting soft, as editors are more considerate of them and their mistakes than when she was a youngster.

Despite the increased freedom for women, and even in an era when women are welcomed at hotel bars, in the chicane of ward politics, and in laying out the grandiose dreams of the United States of tomorrow, many sour and crusty reactionaries who do the hiring and firing for newspapers are still skittish. They won't hire women. Ask them why, and they blush and stammer. Or they turn their hard heads to the wall and drop a furtive, icy tear.

It is still true that most women get their start in newspaper work through some sort of pull: they went to school with the publisher's daughter; their mothers were neighbors of the chief editorial writer's mother; they knew the managing editor's sister when they were little girls together. All that sort of thing. This system, curiously, brings some good women into the business; it is too bad that it is still so difficult for a young woman, just out of

college, or with a few years' experience on a small paper,
who really feels that she has a capacity for newspaper
work, to get the slightest encouragement in the larger
cities.

Probably the best place for a young woman to ground
herself in the fundamentals of newspaper work is in a
suburban town, or in any of the smaller cities throughout
the country. There they get a chance to do a little of
everything. In New York, particularly, the editors on the
old conservative papers have plenty of men to handle the
general news. When they do hire a young woman, they
are inclined to make the work too easy for her. They try,
in their gallant but fumbling fashion, to make things pleasant—to pick assignments on which she will "look good."
In that way she may do good work, but she won't acquire
the general experience which makes great newspaper
women.

For the woman who wants to be thrown into the midst
of the low-down machinery of all sorts of news coverage
in New York, her best bet is one of the tabloids, or, if she
can get the chance, one of the Hearst papers or the Scripps-
Howard *World-Telegram*. Some of the tabloid women reporters not only are charming persons, but they write well
and possess amazing ingenuity. One of the best of the
earlier ones was Julia Harpman, on the staff of the tabloid
*News* in New York during its first years. She married
Westbrook Pegler, the roving reporter and columnist.

Another is Grace Robinson, still with the *News*. She
covered the Rhinelander annulment trial, the trial of
"Legs" Diamond and dozens of other important stories.
She is a reserved little person, described by her sisters in the
profession as "mouselike and sweet," but she is one of the
outstanding reporters of the country. She was assigned to
follow Greta Garbo to Sweden in October, 1932, but she
dropped Garbo when she ran into James J. Walker, who
was starting his rush back to New York in a futile attempt

to be present at the city convention which was expected to renominate him for Mayor.

In 1933 Miss Robinson was assigned to cover the murder trial of Dr. Sara Ruth Dean at Greenwood, Mississippi. She telephoned to find out about the weather, and what clothes to wear. All she wanted to know was whether she would need a coat. Littleton Upshur, editor of the *Commonwealth* at Greenwood, thought to have a little fun at the expense of the New York journalist. He wrote in his paper as advice to Miss Robinson:

"You will find other ladies in the courtroom, probably quite as well attired according to the best New York taste. Please don't come into the courtroom wearing riding breeches, or a Mother Hubbard. And unless you surpass most of the newspaper girls in pulchritude, don't appear in a bathing suit."

Mr. Upshur, instead of being hailed as a Greeley of the blacklands, found that he had put his foot in it and had reflected upon Southern hospitality. The civic clubs met Miss Robinson at the train, took her to lunch, and then Mayor Will Clements showed her the local wonders. A delegation called upon Upshur to protest; the editor, licked, said to Miss Robinson: "If I have offended you, I will gladly dress in sackcloth and ashes and stand in the snow to appease your feelings." "But there won't be any snow," said Miss Robinson. They shook hands and all was well. Miss Robinson wired the story back to her paper, but said only that "a woman reporter" had been involved.

*The News* also has the only woman reporter who also is a former parachute jumper. She is Miss Edna Ferguson, who is married and has two children. Because of her endless ruses and her effective disguises, she has become known as the Lon Chaney of the sob sisters. She dresses to suit her assignments. If she is to have to deal with bums, she may dress like a bum. When *The News* decided it was unpardonably snooty of the Morgan Library to refuse to allow the public to get inside, and when other *News* reporters had been turned away from the library, Miss Ferguson was called upon. She bought a new and very smart bonnet, acted snootier than any Morgan librarian, and walked past the guards. She rarely writes anything. She gets her stuff and telephones it to the office.

Inez Callaway (Nancy Randolph) also of *The News,* follows the society people. Often she has to gain entrance to functions at which tabloid reporters are not welcome. She is attractive, dresses well, and can be as high hat as any of the dowagers at the Colony Club. She has resource. In 1928, when Katherine, daughter of Governor Alfred E. Smith, was married to Francis J. Quillinan, it was found that the church accommodated only 2,500, which made it practically a private wedding. The police were paying no attention to newspaper identification cards. Miss Callaway noticed, however, that the police were ushering in several important-looking men, in spite of the tremendous crowd outside. She sidled up to one of these top-hatted notables and said:

"Oh, Judge, I've got lost from my parents and they have my invitation. Please take me in with you."

The man, who happened to be Justice John M. Tierney of Brooklyn, was surprised, for he could not quite place her, but he assumed she was the daughter of a Democratic friend. He took her in, escorted by the police, and she got a close-up view of the wedding.

For that sort of newspaper work, which has a good deal to be said in its favor, the tabloid women reporters, who know tricks that would make the ordinary man reporter dizzy, have proved their value over and over. Maybe it isn't always cricket, but it gets the facts.

The *World-Telegram* in New York has had exceptionally good results from women writers. The old *Telegram* for years had Jane Dixon, who was adept alike at covering a spot news story or writing a column of elixir for the emotionally downcast. When Warren G. Harding was elected President she covered the doings, sayings and life history of Mrs. Harding as thoroughly as the women of the New Deal cover Mrs. Roosevelt. Miss Dixon married Captain (later Major) Walter H. Wells. "Cappy," as the popular soldier was known, was, and is, proud of his wife's record as a newspaper woman.

In these days one of the mainstays of the *World-Telegram* is Helen Worden. She knows society, she can write, and she has what so many women lack—a genuine curiosity to know the revealing details of the people and the town. It is doubtful whether any man is better versed in the lore of New York, and in who is who, than Miss Worden. Gretta Palmer of the same paper also got around town and put much spirit into the "woman's pages." Evelyn Seeley, who had made an excellent reputation, left the paper when her husband, Kenneth Stewart, went to teach journalism in Stanford University. Another of the *World-Telegram* women is Geraldine Sartain, who, getting away from the gush and sweetish froth which overlays the masterpieces of many newspaper women, is able to write a detailed, realistic, and genuinely amusing story in what is known among the cackling old bucks up at the Century Club as "a masculine style." Miss Sartain in the summer of 1933 married a publicity and advertising man.

Years ago the New York *Times* had among its writers Mary Taft, in the period when women were pining for the ballot box. The *Times* decided that politics was politics, essentially sexless, whether indulged in by male or female, and took the news in its stride. Miss Taft married. Later Jane Grant was a reporter on the *Times,* and a good one, though she was seldom troubled by the rough night assignments. When the *Herald* was sold in 1920 Rachel McDowell went to the *Times,* where for all these years she has covered religious news. In the spring of 1933 the *Times,* having no woman reporter available for covering general assignments, employed Nancy Hale, formerly of *Vanity Fair*—one woman among solid phalanxes of men. On the *Times* Washington staff is Winifred Mallon, formerly of the bureau of the Chicago *Tribune*. She has a rare faculty for a woman reporter: she has a retentive memory, knows Washington history and can reel off names and dates to the consternation of her less gifted colleagues. She was on the funeral train of President McKinley, and is not married. The Sunday staff of the *Times* has Anne O'Hare McCormick, who is married to an Ohioan who travels extensively. She goes along and writes about whatever seems interesting—and most of it is.

For many years the New York *Herald Tribune* had only two women reporters, Ishbel Ross and Emma Bugbee. Miss Ross came as near as any woman ever came to being able to cover any assignment, and was referred to as the perfect woman newspaper man. She left the paper in the winter of 1932 to write novels. Miss Bugbee, whose assignments during her long career were principally those judged to contain news of particular interest to women, is an expert on the politics and personalities of women, whether in Washington or in the clubs. Since the ascendancy of Mrs. Franklin D. Roosevelt, most of Miss Bugbee's reporting talents have been devoted to the news arising from the deeds and ideas of the most interesting, and most debated, lady of the land. Miss Bugbee, in 1934, was the only general woman reporter on the paper. But that is not to say that it is a paper produced almost wholly by men. Far from it.

Helen Rogers Reid, wife of Ogden Reid, the editor, is active as advertising director. Janet Owen covers sports which are supposed to be of particular interest to women and to women's colleges. Elsa Lang, able and hard-working, handles promotion work. Irita Van Doren is editor of the Sunday book section, and is assisted ably by Isabel Paterson and Belle Rosenbaum. Mrs. William Brown

Meloney, who in the old days was Marie Mattingly, remembered as a good reporter, is editor of the Sunday
magazine section.

There are so many others in the business. Elenore Kel-
logg, once worked for the Socialist *Call*, with the old
*World*, the *Herald Tribune*, and in 1933 joined the Associated Press staff in New York. Julia McCarthy, candid,
competent and experienced, in 1934 was writing some of
the best stories in *The News* in New York. Maxine Davis
writes free lance stuff, women's news from Washington,
and magazine articles about newspaper women with facil-
ity and profit. Marjorie Shuler has traveled in far places
for the *Christian Science Monitor*. Irene Kuhn, once a
tabloid reporter and a good one, went to Hollywood, and
later joined with the *World-Telegram*. Martha Coman,
for years with the old *Herald*, for several seasons handled
publicity for Smith College. Dorothy Ducas, probably
the best newspaper woman ever to be graduated from the
Columbia School of Journalism, has done most of her work
for Hearst and the magazines. Helen Rowland, through
years of ups and downs, has written her feminine wisecracks for the syndicates. Alice Hughes, excellent reporter, probably is the best of all on women's clothing and
get-up and merchandise. Lorena Hickok, who began more
than twenty years ago in Battle Creek, Michigan, at $7 a
week, and who later distinguished herself on the Minneapo-
lis *Tribune*, later was a hard worker for the Associated
Press in New York. Dorothy Thompson, wife of Sinclair
Lewis, has a remarkably clear mind and writes with vigor.
But that's enough. The women pervade the whole business
of getting out newspapers.

What is their status? The best answer probably comes
from one of their own distinguished colleagues, Genevieve
Forbes Herrick, who recently left the Chicago *Tribune*
after fifteen years. She started on the paper as assistant
exchange editor, a scissors and paste job. Later she went

to Ireland, returned as an Irish hired girl, and wrote a series
for her paper about conditions on Ellis Island. The Loeb-
Leopold Case, Al Capone, Queen Marie of Roumania—
she had something to do with all these. In a lecture in
1933 before the Chicago Woman's Club, she sounded almost mannish when she said that women were responsible
for the "woman's angle in journalism"—that they were at
fault in letting themselves and their stories become en-
meshed in silk and chiffon and the accursed filmy adjectives. She said:

"Somewhere between the sugar and the acid lies the truth
about women in journalism . . . How fast and how far the
coming women in journalism go depends first of all upon themselves, their equipment and their sincerity. Also upon the editors who give them their assignments . . . Typewriters are
sexless. Let her strive to write all her news better than as many
men as she can. Let her write the way the world says a man
writes; not the way a man says a woman writes."

Women in journalism have had to overcome an appalling
lot of prejudice. Of course, they have been to blame for
much of it. And yet, it is still true that they are not
always treated with a complete fairness. It is a common
thing for a weasel in a stuffed shirt to telephone a city
desk and complain about the manners, or the questions, or
the clothing, or the general demeanor of a man reporter
who had been sent out on a story; such complaints usually
are laughed off, and go hard with the stuffed shirt. But
when the case is somewhat parallel—that is, when the
bloated corset telephones to complain of the woman reporter, the reaction of the desk very likely is the ancient
groan: "Oh, hell! Another damn fool woman reporter
has got us in a jam."

Courageous and natural women for decades have fought
to have themselves recognized as people. A telling blow
was struck ten or more years ago by Clara Ogden, now

Clara Ogden Davis, wife of Burton Davis, the novelist and civic worker of Westport, Connecticut. She was a reporter on the *Chronicle* at Houston, Texas, of which the late C. B. Gillespie was editor. One morning Miss Ogden was sitting at her typewriter when a covey of strange females came into the city room and looked bewildered. She asked them what they wanted and if she could help.

They told her they were a committee from the Women's Christian Temperance Union, and that they had heard there was a woman reporter on the *Chronicle* who had been giving "wild parties," as the old saying had it, in her home in a respectable section of the city. At these parties, said the ladies, gin was drunk, and women smoked cigarettes, and there was the sound of whoopee through the night. They said, moreover, that they were looking for Mr. Gillespie, to demand that the girl reporter either be fired or forced to stop the dreadful orgies.

Miss Ogden, who realized that the she-vigilantes were talking about her, reared back in her chair, put her feet on the desk, lit a cigarette, thought a moment and then remarked:

"Well, I'll be God damned!"

The ladies fled, too shocked to wait for the missing editor.

Of course, this attitude of the puritanical matrons and spinsters is only a small and almost negligible part of the accumulation of evidence, prejudice and primitive fright which combine to make many otherwise bold newspaper editors shy away from women. There are so many of them seeking a chance—more than the traffic will bear. They are often too persistent, so pathetically eager are they to try anything. Even the ones who are fairly expert sometimes are guilty of all the weaknesses of which the callous male has accused the women. Actually, most men are highly agreeable to the idea of having women in the business; in practice, however, the editor with the power to hire shudders and fidgets and, out of some primordial impulse born in a Pliocene jungle, hums in his subconscious: "Woman, go 'way from my door." Ten minutes after she's gone he'll be singing it out loud, thankful that he has grown men, and not women, to cover the news. Wrong? Probably, but women have to face it.

The best women in the business are never resented by men. These paragons—level-headed, sure in their instincts and judgments, unfailing in their loyalty, warm in their sympathies—are among the glories of the greatest profession. Surely there will be more of them.

# TWELVE OF NEW YORK

## *Beverly Smith*

BEVERLY SMITH was born in Baltimore, August 9,
1898. He passed his boyhood in Maryland and
Virginia, and was educated in the public schools of
Baltimore, at the Johns Hopkins, the Harvard Law School
and at Oxford. He practiced corporation law in New
York for three and one-half years, and in August, 1926,
joined the staff of the New York *Herald Tribune* as a reporter. The first night he turned in a story, the night city
editor said: "You are literate and you know how to spell.
You will go far." At first he was so slow that he would
write his stories in longhand, then come bustling into the
office and copy them on the typewriter; it would take him
three hours to copy 1,000 words. Soon he became one of
the best reporters in New York. He had an especial talent
for writing about people. He says: "It is my settled belief
that there is nobody in the world who hasn't a story in him
somewhere. If you are willing to talk to him long enough,
and take enough punishment, and be bored until your
whole body jerks convulsively, he will eventually and surprisingly produce some weird belief, some fantastic experience, some moment of glory or tragedy." In 1932
Mr. Smith left daily newspaper work to join the staff of
the *American Magazine*. The news story which follows
was printed in the *Herald Tribune*:

Manualla and Ausseini, the two tribesmen whom Martin
Johnson brought back from darkest Africa and stationed at
the Central Park Zoo as trained nurses to his chimpanzees,
gorillas and cheetahs, have gone Harlem.

In their first day at the zoo, two weeks ago, Manualla and
Ausseini were still true children of the jungle. They wore
their red fez-like head-dress; they put on borrowed overcoats
to guard against the Arctic cold of New York's July Fourth;
they tasted ice cream, then flung it on the ground and fled
from it as from the demon Boreas.

John Kelly, genial proprietor of the Arsenal Restaurant in
the zoo, led them to the ice box so that they might select their
favorite foods. The door was opened, and Ausseini, who was
standing nearby, felt the breath of cool air. He vaulted over
the counter and did not slack his sprint until he was back kneel-
ing on his Mahometan prayer rug in the elephant cage which
he makes his living room.

In the evening, that first day, Mr. Kelly casually turned on
his radio. The two young Africans looked around with a wild
surmise, started for the door, were wooed by the jazz rhythm,
came back timidly, and went into a dance.

"War dance, peace dance or love dance—I don't know which
it was," says Mr. Kelly. "But they sure warmed up."

That was two weeks ago. And in two weeks, you can take
it from Mr. Kelly, "there has been such a change that I'm telling
you I didn't believe such a change could happen to anybody.
Look at them now. Would you ever think those Amoses and
Andys was just out of the African equator?"

A glance confirmed his words. Manualla and Ausseini,
perched nonchalantly on their white porcelain stools, were consuming strawberry sundaes, (or strawberry ice cream, with
whipped cream, grated pecan nuts, marshmallow and maraschino
cherries) with all the leisurely aplomb of a pair of University
of Virginia students in Pence and Sterling's in Charlottesville.

Ausseini was dressed conservatively in fawn gray felt hat,
brim à la Jimmy Walker; lavender pleated shirt, light blue coat,
Oxford bags, and tan shoes.

Manualla sported a Panama, even more Walkeresque in its
curves than Ausseini's fedora. His shirt, open at the neck in
sports fashion, was secured by an orange and pink cravat at
the base of the V. His coat was of the hue where blue shades
into purple. But his distinguishing garments were a pair of
plus fours, predominantly gray in color, with a plaid design,

and futuristic golf stockings that the richest golfer in New York—to paraphrase O. Henry—would have hesitated to wear. His yellow Oxfords put a tasteful finish to the ensemble.

"You notice the color of those sundaes?" said Mr. Kelly. "Pink. That's their favorite color. Cake with pink icing, cherry soda in bottles, pink lemonades. Pink is their favorite color. I believe they would drink red ink if you put some water in it. But I've had a lot of trouble with their food. When they first came, they'd eat anything set before them. You wouldn't believe how fussy they got in two weeks.

"First place, Manualla is missionary Catholic—won't eat any meat on Fridays. Ausseini, he's a Mahometan—won't eat any pork anytime. Manualla, he wolfs our hot franks. Ausseini, he stands by watering at the mouth, but he's real religious. Hasn't laid a lip on a frankfurter yet.

"When they wanted lamb—that was something they could agree on—they used to just come up to the counter and say 'Baa—aa—aa-h.' That meant lamb—sheep. Now they say 'Lamb,' big as life. And not half as easy to understand.

"They've gone in for American breakfast foods, this last week. They can't seem to get enough of them. Everything is paid for by Mr. Johnson, so they eat their heads off. And the hours have changed. They used to come in here bright and early at 6 A.M. Gradually they got later—7 o'clock, 8 o'clock, 9 o'clock, 10 o'clock."

"But why," Mr. Kelly was asked, "have they become so leisurely in their habits?"

"The delegations from Harlem," said Mr. Kelly. "Why, the last ten days they not only have been pestered by delegations, but they have been up in Harlem all hours of the night. That's something I would rather not talk about. You better ask the police and the attendants about that phase. I will just say this: There have been more Negroes in Central Park Zoo the last week than in all history."

Following Mr. Kelly's advice, a questionnaire survey was made of attendants, keepers and Lieutenant Burnell, of the Arsenal station. The Harlem delegations, it seems, representing dozens of Harlem societies, clubs, lodges, literary societies and guilds, have come down to the Central Park Zoo and made the place in front of the gorillas' cage, where Manualla and Ausseini pass their leisure, their forum.

"Second day after they arrived," said an attendant at the lion house, "a big delegation marched in here. He said the title of his speech was the Slaves of 1931. He quoted Lincoln and read the emancipation proclamation. Said Amos and Andy was the thin edge of the wedge for the revival of slavery to cure the economic depression. He quoted poetry. A great big fellow, he was. You could hear him all over the Zoo.

"The next bunch, they come the next day. The speaker says they were gonna call on the Mann act, whatever that is. He says that Amos and Andy have got to sleep in the elephant cage. 'Suppose that elephant rolls over in the night,' he says. 'What is going to happen to our brethren?' He also says Mr. Johnson won't even allow his slaves to talk to American people from Harlem. Now that's bunk. The fact is, these two black boys can't speak to anybody anyway. They can't even talk to me."

Mr. Johnson, when this situation was brought to his attention, solved it diplomatically. He met the delegations, escorted them to the comfortable room on the East Side where the Africans sleep, took them to Kelly's restaurant and let them watch Manualla and Ausseini consume strawberry sundaes, and gave details as to hours and pay. This was all right for one delegation, but it had to be done with all. Each day brought a new group of protestants.

Then new trouble developed. Harlem societies began inviting the jungle children to come up to Harlem, attend paid meetings, relate their lion hunting experiences through the offices of a Swahili interpreter—who came to this country thirty years ago as the servant of a British army officer. The African boys often returned home in the dawn hours.

The boys came to their work of feeding the gorillas later and later each day. The chimpanzee began to lose weight. At last Mr. Johnson felt he must take a hand. He arrived at the Zoo Saturday night just as a Harlem grand exalted turnverein was leading the boys northward. He protested. The lodge officials were indignant. More slavery. Mr. Johnson led his two charges into the authoritative atmosphere of the Arsenal police station.

"Manualla," he said in Swahili, "you have been having too many late nights in Harlem. You have been neglecting Congo, Goggy and Snowball, our gorillas. You have been strolling in to breakfast at 10 A.M. You have got to stop this stuff, or I will revoke your immigration bonds and send you back to Africa."

Apparently the threat had its effect. Last night an imposing delegation from Harlem arrived at the lion house. They bore as presents a dozen shirts, spotted like the cheetah and tinted like the peacock's tail. All this wealth of sophistication and color, they conveyed to Manualla by the sign language, would be his if he would come to Harlem and sit on the platform.

Manualla's eyes glistened and blinked. His pierced ears seemed to quiver with eagerness. Then he held up a powerful black hand and uttered one of the two English words he knows.

"No," said Manualla.

## Walter Davenport

Walter Davenport was born on January 7, 1889, on a farm in Talbot County, Maryland. He went to the University of Pennsylvania for two years and then got a job as a reporter on the Philadelphia *Public Ledger* at $9 a week. In 1913 he came to New York and went to work on the *American*. In the war he became a Captain. In 1919 he went to work for the New York *Sun*. In 1922 he joined the magazine *Liberty*, writing stuff which he says he should have been arrested for. In 1924 he joined *Collier's*, and since then has been an assistant editor and a special reporter for that magazine. While working for the daily papers he covered everything—politics, Charles Ponzi in Boston, Marcus Garvey in Harlem, the first stories of smuggled liquor sources after prohibition went into effect, and the time when Calvin Coolidge during the Boston police strike immortalized himself by remarking, "Have faith in Massachusetts." The story reproduced here was printed in the New York *Herald* (after its purchase by Frank Munsey and its merger with the morning *Sun*) and was one of Davenport's many excellent articles dealing with the illicit liquor traffic.

If you harbored the desire to create an uproar in, say Northampton, Mass., on a drowsy Sunday afternoon in August, it would be reasonable to presume that you would achieve a measure of success were you to drink a pint of moonshine whiskey and then, divesting yourself of all garments save your underwear, present yourself at even-song in Jonathan Edwards' Congregational Church.

Without wasting time and space comparing Northampton and Nassau, let it be understood that though the two towns be as widely separated as the poles in most of their respective virtues, they are united in the possession of singularly similar brands of fierce and inelastic respectability.

Nassau isn't dignified; she's prim. She has her scandals and her mental bankrupts but she manages to cloak them with a blanket of respectability that would pass inspection anywhere in New England or the suburbs of Philadelphia.

Even thus informed it will not be possible for any one not attending the Bootleggers' Ball in the Lucerne Gardens to gather how Nassau suffered and still suffers. It seems proper for the writer to explain that his experiences have not been so limited as to cause him to wonder at the commonplace. He has attended social affairs in Webster Hall and St. Mark's Place. Practically everything that could happen indoors came to pass on those occasions. Gentlemen even took to shooting.

But for full blown, shirts off entertainment he has never seen the true like of the Bootleggers' Ball that was held in the Lucerne Gardens here in Nassau, Sunday, July 31. To be entirely accurate, the affair started Saturday afternoon. Saturday night was quite an evening as nights go. But being a large affair it moved slowly and didn't really strike its stride until Sunday evening. It came to a close when the crews of the three fishing schooners, each laden with 2,000 cases of booze, departed for somewhere off the North Atlantic coast of the United States. It took twelve strong men to carry and drag those crews to their ships. What became of the schooners is a mighty mystery. They moved out into the open Atlantic at 3 A.M.

Saturday night was mild. There were several excellent fights, but they were all private affairs and quickly quelled. Mac, Pop, Ranger and Tampa, bosses of the party, remained sober, or at any rate sufficiently sober to maintain command. The ladies preserved their calm serenity throughout the evening despite occasional clouds that darkened momentarily the social horizon.

"Ladies, ladies, what the hell's eatin' you?" cried Tampa once when a storm impended. Tampa's huge face registered pained surprise that any one of the ladies should so far forget herself as to threaten to knock a rival loose from her cootie coops. "Please to remember, ladies, where you all are."

"Well," snapped the woman who had essayed to do the knocking, "where does she get off to get highbrow with me? Who's she, anyway? Her husband's nothing but a little liquor dealer. Mine's a honest to God bootlegger."

The offending wife of the plain publican had been spirited oft to her room. The threatened squabble was sidetracked. Tampa and Mac threw the orchestra out. It was midnight. It had been a mild night. As a matter of fact the crowd had not gathered. The Saturday night affair was but an incident in the assembling of the Nassau Harbor crowd. The boys from Gun Cay and Grand Bahama had not reported. They were due Sunday morning.

But early Sunday morning the boys from the out island reported. At 1 o'clock in the afternoon Gabriel Thompson and his four piece band—a cornet, a trombone, a double B flat tuba and a violin—mounted the stage and the dance was on. The setting was one to impress the stranger. An eight foot masonry wall encloses the gardens. Additional privacy is had by a line of royal palms rising above the coping of the wall and interfering with the view of the shocked but curious Nassauvians residing solemnly on the rising ground to the south.

There is a wide, rough dance floor. Over in one corner on a

plain pine bench Gabriel and his tense musicians hold forth frightfully. Lengthwise of the dance floor and two steps up is the stage where tables and chairs have been set. The drinking and general conversation is carried on there. The scene is set and there seems to be no reason why the dance should not begin. Dickie is fearfully drunk already; in fact Dickie is generally drunk. So Dickie is hurled out and admonished to remain out. To make certain that Dickie remains outside a guard is placed on the garden gate and Dickie's credit is revoked at the bar.

It is a thoroughly democratic affair. The man credited with being an unfrocked clergyman is dancing with the pretty wife of the young lawyer from Baltimore. There is a man in his shirt sleeves and a bad humor, who, The New York *Herald* reporter is assured, will go on trial for murder next month in Florida if the American officials can land him on United States soil. He is credited with killing a policeman. Tampa has decided to squire the prettiest young woman in the place—a rather winsome girl, woefully thin and tired looking. She has a story too; something like Madame Butterfly's.

There's a big, flat footed man in a violent silk shirt and pongee trousers. He looks like a policeman and the boys are rather hostile at first. But later on he rips a hundred dollar bill from an enormous roll and buys champagne. He says he wants to buy a fast schooner and ship a couple of thousand cases of stuff to Washington. He is introduced as a retired railroad man, but there seems to be something wrong. At first it's the Big Four system and later it is the New York Central Lines. He talks familiarly about two United States Senators—pals of his he says.

Publicly he bemoans the death of his wife five weeks ago. A little later on he rejoices in the fact that his wife trusts him implicitly and is the finest, prettiest, healthiest and wealthiest little woman in the middle West. Ten minutes later he is casually telling of his recent purchase of a seaplane and a Rolls Royce motor car. Anyway he's entertaining.

Pop has taken the limelight and announces that, despite the fact he is 62 years old, he can lick any man in the place if necessary. Pop is a whale of a man. He says that he and Billy

Muldoon used to wrestle each other around the country and that he'd like to take on Bill now.

"I could throw him any time I wanted to," announces Pop.

Pop insists that it was he and not Mervin Brobst who kidnapped Charles Vincente in Bimini last year.

"I used to work for the Government, too," says Pop. "But, get me right, I ain't got nothing to do with bootleggin' even now."

The Greeks arrive—Ekonome, Papopikopolis, Jack Greek, Marko and Mike. They're bootleggers and want the world to know it. Mike's rather erratic.

"Is there any Jews here?" he demands, taking the centre of the dance floor. "If they is Jews here let'em get out. In business I mix with them. In society, nothin' doin'!"

The challenge went unaccepted. A halt was called for supper. Gabriel and his band were paid off and told to remain as far away from Lucerne Gardens as possible. Obviously Gabriel's feelings were injured, so the Greek boys took up a subscription for the ebony musicians.

Supper was largely liquid. By the time another orchestra had been commandeered the dance resumed; the crowd was ripe for almost anything. Under the cover of darkness the younger Conchs—native white Nassauvians—stole into the gardens, looking clean and pharmaceutical in their starched white linens, rigidly cut and uncompromising of line.

A number of negroes, patting juba, had clambered to the top of the garden wall. Now and then, overcome by the jazz, they sang, and later they got out into the road and did a bit of home dancing themselves—the original Shimmi-sha-wabbl.

One of the town mysteries appeared. He is a tall, rather nice looking young man who arrived in Nassau some months ago with a modicum of baggage and two cocktail shakers. He may be seen nightly walking from oasis to oasis with his trusty cocktail shakers beneath his arm, inventing drinks. Folks follow him around observing his experiments. He has evolved some marvellous beverages, but concerning himself he maintains a baffling silence. He arrived at the ball with his shakers and at once gathered the ladies around him while he prepared what he announced as the Coast to Coast Flip.

Over and over again the orchestra played "Rosie" and "Margie," "The Love Nest" and "Oh By Jingo"—all new in Nassau. The silk shirted railroad man and a gaunt youth who said he used to play third base on a Federal League team became involved in an argument over their dancing. A young woman who looked rather the worse for wear appeared from somewhere or other denouncing all bootleggers.

"My Heavings, Nancy," she cried to a friend, "I never thought Greeks was so rough!"

Dickie, drunker than ever, had evaded the guard at the gate and was dancing with a pal from Bethell's bar. Both Dickie and his pal had removed their shoes. All the men had thrown off their coats and Ekonome, Marks, Mike, Ranger, Tampa and one or two more had removed their outer shirts. A quartet of college boys who were spending the summer bootlegging from Grand Bahama had joined the party and were teaching the ladies to toddle. A group of tall Britishers—adventurers who had come out of England looking for excitement and cash—came in, fetching a table of their own and a case of their own favorite rum.

A man, who was generally hailed as a former Internal Revenue Collector in the States, appeared with a lady on each arm. The ladies were singing. They reached the dancing platform, only to be grabbed by the captain and mate of a schooner that had arrived during the afternoon. It was fearfully hot and the mosquitoes, taking their cue from the mad Americans, had gone berserk. But despite the heat the dancing was all but continuous. The gentleman would wrap both arms tightly around the neck of his partner. The lady would reciprocate. A wrestling match ensued. Now and then they tossed each other off the platform.

There appeared about this time two lads who had lost their sense of proportion. Obviously they were poor judges of relative abilities. One declared himself a native of Eleventh avenue, New York city, and the other didn't have to announce his nativity. He was as fine a specimen of the Cockney as London develops. He was rather bigger and heavier than the usual Cockney, but the boy from Eleventh avenue was really big. He was almost a giant. He was good natured enough, but his English pal was nasty.

"Me and me pal 'ere," announced the Cockney, " 'ave decided to tyke the best two gels in the garden and walk out a bit on the beach."

He looked over the crowd on the refreshment platform and singled out an able bodied woman, who, instinctively apparently, had taken a firm grasp upon the neck of a beer bottle. The Cockney bowed to her.

"Aow abaht it, my dear?" he demanded, advancing toward the lady. "I'll treat you fair, y'know."

The lady flourished the bottle.

"Have I got to kill this louse, m'self," she asked, "or is there a man in the mob?"

It would be impossible to tell just who hit the two sailors first. At least ten champions of the insulted lady arrived upon the body of the Cockney at the same time. The boy from Eleventh avenue, having taken no part in the proceedings up to this time, began hitting out in splendid order and was getting away with a couple of huskies when some one took a flying headlock on him and at the same time broke a bottle on the top of his head.

They had taken the ambitious Londoner over to the wall, propped him up against it and hit him with everything except the piano. Several chairs were broken and everybody expected the shooting to start at once. But there was no shooting. Somebody had called in the Commandant of Police, and as that military figure entered the gardens, strong men threw the unconscious Cockney over the eight foot wall. The police hustled the two sailors off to the waterfront. They revived the Cockney, patched up the American and saw to it that they were taken out to the booze schooner of which they formed half the crew.

And finally the former Vice-President of Costa Rica arrived. It was not possible to verify the announcement that he was a former Vice-President of Costa Rica. They said he was. He looked like it. He acted like it. He arrived all alone. In each hand he clutched a half filled bottle. He wore a wide straw sombrero, and protruding from each hip pocket was the pearl grip of a large revolver.

"Me, I best engineer in de harbor. Me, da drunker I gat da faster I run da yacht to Savannah. Me, I drink more rum and marry more women and kill more hoosband dan any man in da worl'. Me, dat's me."

He paused to drink from both bottles. The second drink staggered him like a punch on the chin might. He shook his head as though to clear it and resumed his defi.

"Me, I make ten t'ousand dollar in a month bootleggin'. I tell da world, W'ad da hell do I care? You sing heem—you; ever'body, sing."

And they sang:

"Hail, hail, the gang's all here—"

He had plenty of friends present. His friends took him in hand and calmed him until he consented to sit down. He insisted that a lady occupy his lap, however. The woman who had armed herself with the beer bottle against the Cockney invasion was chosen for the job.

"He's all right. He's a good fellow," explained Mike. "He used to be boss of Costa Rica. Vice-President or something like that. Then he went to Mexico and started something it took the whole army to finish. He didn't drink a drop until about nine years ago when his wife deserted him and he's been hittin' it up pretty hard ever since. Nice fellow, too, and good engineer, get out at 3 o'clock this morning with 2,200 cases and he'll be in the engine room steady as a judge. Them Central American babies is like that."

The party didn't stop. It died out by degrees. Now and then somebody would yield up the ghost and slide under the table or collapse under the garden wall. That left the party smaller. Presently the orchestra lost control and had to be piled up under the royal poinciana tree. Eventually there were none remaining except the tall nice looking young man with the cocktail shakers. He was still mixing cocktails and still seeking a new combination.

It was three in the morning. Out of Nassau's harbor glided three heavily laden schooners. Along the shore the gangs of negro stevedores were stretching out on loose sisal. They had just loaded the three schooners. There would be nothing to do for ten hours more. The noise of the Bootleggers' Ball having subsided, the drone of the black men along the water front could be heard:

> "*Ole rum he go in de schooner at night,*
> *Boss man he campin' down,*
> *Mammy's boy he countin' gold.*
> *All right.*
> *All right.*"

## St. Clair McKelway

St. Clair McKelway was born in Charlotte, North Carolina, on February 13, 1905. His father was Dr. A. J. McKelway, a Presbyterian clergyman, and his grand-uncle, for whom he was named, was St. Clair McKelway, once editor of the Brooklyn *Eagle*. McKelway finished one year at high school in Washington, loafed a while and then went to work for $15 a week as a mail clerk on the Washington *Times*. He wanted to do editorial work, and got a job on the Washington *Herald* at $30 a week. He remained there until 1925, went to the Philadelphia *News*, and then in 1926 he met Frank Sullivan while covering a beauty contest at Atlantic City and was persuaded to join the staff of the New York *World*. In 1928 he went to the *Herald Tribune*, and a year later started on a trip around the world. He stopped for three years in Bangkok, Siam, where he was editor of the *Daily Mail*. He rejoined the staff of the *Herald Tribune* in 1933, did brilliant work for six months (the story reproduced here is an example of one of his crime stories) and then joined the staff of the *New Yorker* as a special writer.

Joseph Leahey, better known as "Spot," a West Side gangster and desperado whose long career of racketeering has been characterized by assaults and killings of studied cruelty, was stabbed in the throat just after dawn yesterday as he climbed to a second floor speakeasy at Broadway and 105th Street. He was left to die in an untidy heap at the bottom of the stairs.  Since his right arm was shattered by an adversary's bullet four years ago Spot had tried to teach himself to shoot with his left hand, but had given it up as too awkward and had adopted a short, sharp knife as his favorite weapon.  It may have been this, his own knife, police say, that his murderers used to slit his jugular vein.

Last night, after a day of investigation under the direction of John J. Sullivan, Assistant Chief Inspector, detectives were no nearer a solution of the murder than when the agitated speakeasy proprietor, Bobby Gleason, informed them at 6:30 A.M. that he had found Leahey's body when he left his place at 6:15. Leahey, they had discovered, was actively disliked by almost everybody who knew him, including those with whom he sometimes passed whole nights of drinking in the clubs and low resorts of the district.  Besides these gentry, any one of whom might have become infuriated by one of Leahey's customary brutalities of word or action, there were countless sworn enemies both in and out of the sphere of racketeering.

Leahey was recognized as a master of terrorism, an artist in mayhem with a knife or a broken beer bottle, and for years a valued gorilla on the outside staff of one of the bigger beer barons.  He was generally reputed to be on the payroll of Arthur Flegenheimer, better known as "Dutch" Schultz.  His tendencies were too sadistic and his methods generally too boisterous for him ever to reach the upper fringe of racketeering, where the big money lay.  But throughout his career he appears to have been treated with a certain deference by the courts and in the upper Broadway district, where he finally met his death, he occupied a position of dominance.

The most recent murder of which "Spot" was accused was the particularly brutal killing of his wife on May 17, 1931.  He was identified as her murderer by her brother, but when he gave himself up in Jersey City a month later, where he had figured in beer wars, he was discharged.

A short, rather plump man of thirty-seven, who dressed quietly but expensively, Leahey was evidently completing his Saturday outing in his accustomed manner when he started to climb the steps of the two-story loft building at 2744 Broadway early yesterday.

The speakeasy of Bobby Gleason, former middleweight boxer, is known as the Tonawanda Social Club. Its second floor entrance is of the look-see type now becoming rare hereabouts. It never closes. When Gleason retires for the day a little after dawn, a bartender known as Pete presides, and two assistants, Frank Howe and Ernest Hansen, alternate their services. There is a small bar and many booths with tables. There are usually three or four patrons there until 8 A.M. or later and Leahey, probably well loaded, evidently expected to join them for a last rye-with-water chaser, which was his usual choice of drinks.

Gleason and his employees say "Spot" never reached the bar. All the detectives could learn on this score was that Gleason notified the West 100th Street police station at 6:30 and that Leahey was lying at the bottom of the steps, breathing stertorously, when Patrolman William Nally arrived. He was dead by the time an ambulance from the Knickerbocker Hospital got there.

He had been stabbed neatly on the right side of his throat with a sharp knife. In his pockets was no weapon, not even the knife he had always carried since he gave up trying to be a southpaw gunman. There was only some change, less than a dollar, and the key to his hotel room. The absence of spending money is not significant, because Leahey never bought drinks.

Leahey's residence, somewhat to the surprise of people of the district who knew him as the toughest of gorillas, was discovered to be Manhattan Towers, the rather austere apartment hotel at Broadway and Seventy-sixth Street, on the ground floor of which is inserted the Manhattan Congregational Church. He commuted from there, it appeared, to his night haunts thirty blocks northward.

At the Broadway Towers, where Leahey was registered as James S. Boyer, he had managed to keep his rowdy manner under subjection. He used his $50 a month room only for sleeping, according to attendants, and always came in alone.

In his room detectives found only his wardrobe, consisting of several expensive suits, many white shirts and a few blue ones, all with collars attached, and other clothing.

Leahey's appearance was peculiarly suited to such a dual rôle. His countenance, puffy and faintly pink, was bland; he could maintain an immobility of expression even while enacting feats of cruelty. Speakeasy bartenders, who considered him one of the messiest men who ever stood at a bar, will never forget the terrifying quiet way in which he would say "Oh, yeah?"— drawing out the syllables while he reached for a bottle and broke off the neck in a rhythmical motion that would end as the jagged edge was ground into the face of some luckless bar-fly who had insulted him.

An incident typical of Leahey's career occurred on the afternoon of November 27, 1921, when he was perhaps at the height of his career as a strong-arm man. He was driving his automobile, with two cronies, along Forty-seventh Street near Sixth Avenue, when Vincent Trapani, of 311 Pleasant Avenue, a law-abiding citizen, stalled his own car immediately in front. Leahey blew his horn furiously but citizen Trapani could not get his car started. Leahey and his friends then dismounted and pulled Trapani out of his car. When police arrived the two friends were holding the luckless man and Leahey was beating him over the head, back and shins with a tire iron. When they let him go in order to run from the police, Trapani dropped senseless to the street, but later recovered from his injuries. Leahey got five years for this—the only sizable prison sentence that resulted from a score of arrests and arraignments during his career on charges ranging from disorderly conduct to homicide.

It was in a pistol battle over beer in West New York, N. J., on August 13, 1929, that "Spot" suffered the bullet wound that made his right arm useless. A policeman was killed in the battle, and two men were arrested, a third, John Sheehan, reputed to have been head of the Hudson County liquor ring, escaping. After Leahey got out of the hospital, where for weeks he had been expected to die from three bullet wounds in the stomach, he found that his right arm, the bone of which had been shattered by a fourth bullet, was stiff and useless. For months, according to his acquaintances in the upper Broadway district, he practiced firing a pistol with his left hand. He used the cellar of one of his vassal speakeasys as a shooting gallery. In the end, however, he gave up the idea.

Mrs. Leahey, the former Frances Paulson, was found dead in her apartment at 954 Columbus Avenue on the morning of May 17, 1931. Her head had been beaten in with some blunt instrument and a sharp knife had inflicted numerous mutilations on her body. Her brother, Arthur Paulson, had admitted Leahey to the apartment forty minutes earlier. Paulson had gone out for that length of time and had discovered the body on his return. "Spot" was gone.

Leahey was a boy of the old West Side, having grown up in Hell's Kitchen and received his early training with the remnants of the Hudson Dusters.

His record:

*Pistol charge*—June 13, 1915; sentence suspended by Judge Mulqueen, General Sessions.

*Pistol charge*—August 16, 1915; indeterminate sentence to New York reformatory, Judge Mulqueen, General Sessions.

*Petty larceny*—July 10, 1915; sentence suspended by Judge Rosalsky, General Sessions.

*Assault and robbery*—May 20, 1916, dismissed by grand jury.

*Burglary*—May 12, 1917; dismissed by grand jury.

*Criminal assault on woman*—February 28, 1918; acquitted, Judge Crain, General Sessions.

*Disorderly conduct*—May 18, 1918; sentenced to three months in workhouse, Magistrate Healy.

*Grand larceny*—July 24, 1919; discharged, Magistrate Nolan.

*Burglary*—July 26, 1919; acquitted, Judge Nott, General Sessions.

*Robbery*—December 22, 1919; dismissed and turned over to the United States military authorities as draft dodger.

*Robbery*—November 4, 1920; discharged, Magistrate Frothingham.

*Homicide*—November 14, 1920; discharged, Magistrate Frothingham.

*Pistol charge*—November 21, 1921; acquitted, Judge Rosalsky, General Sessions.

*Assault and robbery*—January 20, 1921; discharged, Magistrate Nolan.

*Felonious assault*—January 6, 1922; sentenced to five years in penitentiary, Judge Rosalsky, General Sessions.

*Escaped prison*—July 25, 1927.

*Re-arrested*—November 7, 1927, returned to prison.

*Pistol charge*—June 29, 1929, discharged, Magistrate Bushel.

*Homicide*—June 13, 1931, discharged, Magistrate Eggers, Jersey City.

*Consorting with known criminals*—March 8, 1933, discharged, Magistrate Aurelio.

Leahey used several last names—Doyle, Boyle, Boyer, etc., but was faithful to his first name, Joseph, or to first names beginning with the same letter—John, James, Jerry, etc. A brother, Francis Leahey, was shot and killed on New Year's Eve in 1924 in a poolroom at 88 Columbus Avenue. Joseph was at Dannemora at the time and was permitted to attend the funeral of his brother, handcuffed to prison guards. Another brother, Bernard, is now in West Side Jail awaiting trial on a charge of felonious assault.

## *Joseph Jefferson O'Neill*

Joseph Jefferson O'Neill was born a little more than fifty years ago in Philadelphia, where he attended Central High School. His first newspaper job was on the old Philadelphia *Press,* which was absorbed by the *Ledger.* By 1910 he was in New York on the *World,* where he soon became known as a brilliant reporter and a good writer. He covered the murder of Herman Rosenthal, and followed Billy Sunday on a tour in which the evangelist spent a great deal of futile time and effort in trying to reform O'Neill's drinking habits. O'Neill would always hit the sawdust trail when Sunday called upon him, and he was known to sing "Brighten the Corner Where You Are" from the press box. He left the *World* and went to work for Will Hays, the motion picture czar, and then he went to do publicity for a film company. Later he was employed by a Los Angeles newspaper. The story reproduced here was written while Lord Northcliffe was on his last visit to New York. Northcliffe liked it so well that he cabled it abroad to be reprinted in his own newspapers.

A seven hour reception.

A visitor about every three minutes.

A discussion of a different subject with each visitor.

A ready, informative answer to every question of any caller.

A sincere "Glad to see you!" An intense interest devoted entirely to you. A hearty good-by which conveys "Delighted you had a chance to drop in!"

That's Lord Northcliffe, the famous British publisher, on one of his days "at home." He had one yesterday at the Hotel Gotham, saw several hundred persons with various things on their minds, and wound up his day at 6:30, apparently as full of good humor and physical vitality as he had been when callers started streaming in at 10:30 in the morning.

An astonishing person, Northcliffe, to one who encounters him for the first time. Not because he is so delightfully friendly —particularly to the men and women of his own craft—nor because he is so unaffectedly democratic—he puts on no more lugs than a Tammany district leader—but rather because of the remarkable agility and versatility of his mind.

It works "snap-snap!" and he is never at a loss either for a direct reply to any query put to him, or for an incisive query to put to the other person. The questioner may jump from peace in Ireland to immigration in Palestine (as indeed, some did), or from "what really constitutes news?" to "what do you think of Prohibition?"—and the mind of a man who used to be plain Alfred Harmsworth flits from topic to topic instantly.

The reporter for *The World* who writes these lines saw Lord Northcliffe for the first time yesterday and spent most of the afternoon with him while he received callers, with the purpose

of trying to picture just what sort of a man he is and how he
handles callers—for his system is not merely a handshake and
"How do you do?" He gives something to each visitor or receives something.

Yesterday's reception was supposed to be for newspaper workers, but the master journalist did not refuse to see any one who
came along, and so his day was a busy one.

One of the early callers was a young woman reporter of no
great experience, who did not know exactly what she wanted
but finally asked:

"What kind of a story can I get, Lord Northcliffe, that will
interest readers of a syndicate service all over the world—
particularly women readers?"

"Tell your chief to find out what's to be done with the
2,000,000 superfluous women we now have in England," was
the ready reply. "We have that many more women than men.
That should interest everybody. I'd like to have such a story
myself."

A man from a trade journal that deals with the affairs of
newspapers was next in line. The host promptly reeled off for
him the list of papers he owns, their circulations, their editors'
names, their varying forms of production, and then whirled
into a series of questions of his own about American circulations,
production costs and so on.

"Why, that man knows more about the production side of
a paper than I do!" exclaimed the caller, who was an expert.
"Yet they call him an editor."

An evening newspaperman came along with a written query
to this effect:

"Will the people of the world tolerate much longer the con-
tinuance of trouble between England and Ireland?"

"They won't have to," said Lord Northcliffe. "That matter
will be settled. There may be some difficulties; there may be
some delays, but there will be peace and contentment, surely,
before long."

The publisher all this time was sitting comfortably in an
armchair, taking an occasional puff at an eight-inch cigar. He
wore gray flannel clothes, a soft white collar fastened with a

gold barpin and a reddish polka-dot scarf. He is of medium height—perhaps 5 feet 8—with dark brown hair that is still abundant enough, and keen, rather small, bluish gray eyes that he fixes directly upon his caller. He leans forward slightly, as though making an extra effort to catch every word offered. His slightly ruddy face is rather heavily jowled so that it appears almost square in outline. His voice is low and pleasant, rather more Irish accented than English. His talk is quite free from the "right-o" and "what-ho" and the like of many Britishers.

A man came along, previously unknown to Lord Northcliffe, who wanted to enter into a dicker for the sale of 150,000 acres of forest land in Newfoundland, the trees of which might be converted into woodpulp for newsprint paper.

"How much? What quality? How far from the seaboard? What cost to transport to England? What rail facilities? What advantage would it be to me?"

All these things the publisher wanted to know right off. It became obvious at once that he knew more about Newfoundland's woodpulp resources and their values than his interviewer did, which was quite natural because of his pulp interests on the big island. The deal was not consummated.

Lord Northcliffe turned to brief discussions of diplomacy when former Ambassador James W. Gerard, and former Chargé d'Affaires Nelson O'Shaughnessy, who was stationed at Mexico City, dropped in. He turned to the newest development in wireless telephony when a later caller was Colonel John J. Carty, the electrical wizard of the Bell Company. Precious stones were the basis of his conversation with Dr. Kunz, who is one of the chief figures of the Tiffany concern. And in every case he knew just what he was talking about.

Visitors of this type didn't take up much of his time. They chatted a couple of minutes only. But those who forgot themselves got a gentle reminder that their time was up. This was given by Lord Northcliffe half rising from his seat with output hand and a genial smile. It seemed to be almost a pleasure to be thus dismissed.

Four leading Zionists came in to thank him for the interest

his papers had taken in the settlement of Palestine. He was not any too sure it ought to be more settled at present than it is.

"I know Palestine," he volunteered. "It's rather a poor country. There's a lot of unemployment there now. The danger is you may get too many people down there to fit the conditions.

"I'm greatly interested in Jews. How many have you here in America? Three and a half millions? We've only 245,000 in England, you know. There's no discrimination against them there. They're not taken into clubs and so on here in America, I'm told. We don't ask a man if he's a Jew—only if he's a gentleman. You know there's a saying though that 'every country gets the kind of Jew it deserves.' Glad to have seen you gentlemen; I'll do what I can for you in my paper."

"Well, well! This is interesting!" (as thirty girls from the Pulitzer School of Journalism entered). "Glad to see you, my dears!" And the publisher shook hands with each of them, congratulated them on their choice of a profession and slipped in a few words of advice about getting the truth and printing it interestingly.

Scores of reporters and editors, merely for the purpose of meeting the master face to face and shaking hands, dropped in and out. Then a delegation from the Advertising Club called, and then another delegation from the Association of Foreign Correspondents. To these men Lord Northcliffe made his only speech of the day, and it was brief and pithy.

World peace, he declared, is being hastened by the freer communication of news from one country to another. Nations' suspicions of each other have been based largely upon ignorance. They didn't know each other; therefore they distrusted and even disliked each other. There should be even more inter-communication than there is now. There are not nearly enough cables between America and Europe. The cable rates are too high. The proposed Anglo-American press conference in 1922 or 1923 should take up these matters.

Lord Northcliffe commented upon the improving character of news dispatches sent from here to England. In the old days, American news consisted of "great fires, cyclones, lynchings, banquets to horses, and later came along the divorce scandals.

But now," he said, "dispatches tell of the really important happenings.

"President Harding's great proposal for a disarmament conference is fine and important news. I hope it proceeds as swiftly and successfully as the American people think it will. But the American people are not so used to political conferences as we are. This one may wander all over America and then Europe. I hope, however, that it will be successful and speedy."

Prohibition news makes interesting reading for Europe, Lord Northcliffe said. He came over with the idea that "you Americans, under dry laws, are working twenty-three hours a day and putting 99 percent of your earnings in the bank." But he hasn't found any Prohibition yet in New York. He frankly said he hadn't thirsted for any beverage of his desire.

News of international sports and the sports themselves tend splendidly toward better feelings between the nations. And all nations want more American news, "for we now see the Americans as they really are, one of the leading peoples of the earth."

Lord Northcliffe took time out during his busy afternoon, to motor over to the Fox film studios and pose for a few feet of action on the celluloid strip. He thought the place was marvelous. He thinks the movies are wonderful things—also that they shouldn't be too much censored.

In addition to his long hours of receiving, the distinguished publisher spent considerable time keeping in touch with his affairs on the other side, dictating letters and cablegrams and running his business across the sea leagues. He starts dictating before he gets out of bed in the morning, and his snappy little secretary—an ex-army chap—has to be on the job with sharpened pencil and oiled type-machine at 7 A.M. The secretary, a valet and a chauffeur accompany Lord Northcliffe wherever he goes and all three are constantly ready for a quick move of some sort or other.

Yet they say the English are slow-moving?

The eminent visitor will be here until tomorrow, at least, then will visit Washington briefly, then up to Vancouver, across to Honolulu, over to New Zealand and Australia, and then to Japan, India, and home.

## *Ishbel Ross*

Ishbel Ross was born in Sutherlandshire, Scotland, and was graduated from Tain Royal Academy, Ross-Shire. She began newspaper work in 1917 on the staff of the Toronto *Daily News* in Canada. She was the first newspaper woman in Canada to fly. Bert Acosta took her on a stunt trip. She did publicity for the Canadian Food Board in Ottawa, and in 1919 came to New York to the staff of the *Tribune*. She remained with the property (later the *Herald Tribune*) until 1933, when she decided to devote all her time to writing fiction. She is the author of three novels. During her thirteen years as a reporter in New York she covered such assignments as the Stillman divorce case, the Hall-Mills murder, the sale of the *World*, the Lindbergh kidnaping, the death of Starr Faithfull, the visits of the Prince of Wales and the King of Siam, the murder of Vannie Higgins, the death of Mrs. Minnie Maddern Fiske, the annual Easter parade on Fifth Avenue—in short, everything. She was known as a quiet, efficient, courageous and always dependable reporter. There is general agreement among newspaper men who worked with her that she was the best newspaper woman who ever worked in New York. She met Bruce Rae, then a reporter on the *Times*, while they were covering the Stillman divorce case, and soon afterward they were married. Her husband later became night city editor of the *Times*. The story reproduced here is not one of her most important, but is merely an example of her clear and compact work.

Funeral services for Miss Ella V. von E. Wendel, the last of the Wendel line, were held yesterday afternoon in the vast, dim house of mystery at Fifth Avenue and Thirty-ninth Street, her small dog Tobey prone before her coffin.

Nineteen persons attended the obsequies of the frugal spinster who lived consistently in the Victorian tradition and left a fortune of approximately $100,000,000. This number included the two officiating, her counsel and her servants.

The coffin lay under a blanket of calla lilies at the end of the hall, facing the carved oak staircase that echoed for years to the decorous footsteps of six prim ladies in rusty black. The old grandfather clock with wooden works stood in a corner and heavy curtains shut out the light of day.

The gas brackets hung in their accustomed places, but the gas-lit era of the Wendel family had ended at last. Electric lights, subdued and few in number, illumined the reception hall, a recent installation approved by Miss Ella after decades of resistance to the encroachments of modern science.

The ceiling and far corners of the hall were lost in shadow, but beams of light rested on Miss Ella, calm and faintly smiling in her eternal sleep. To one side were the windows where her father, the second John Gottlieb Wendel, used to watch the flow of carriages and the Sunday promenade in Fifth Avenue.

A carved walnut table stood in the center of the hall and old paintings in gilt frames hung on the somber brown walls; Miss Ella had rarely lingered on the ground floor of the house, whose blank and shuttered windows failed to catch the faintest reflection of the skyscrapers growing around it.

The small group around the coffin seemed lost in the dim, high-ceilinged hall. Before the services began Tobey refused to leave his mistress. Disconsolately he sniffed at the flowers and turned mournful eyes on the servants who tried to comfort him. Miss Wendel had lavished all the love of a starved heart on the small white poodle, last of a line of Tobeys that have played in a strip of garden shut off from Fifth Avenue by a tall fence.

When the Rev. Dr. Nathan A. Seagle, rector of St. Stephen's Episcopal Church, at 122 West Sixty-ninth Street, went into the dining room to put on his vestments Tobey trotted in at his heels and jumped up and down—"as if he were pleading to serve as an acolyte"—the rector later declared.

He followed Dr. Seagle back to the coffin, then lay quietly on the floor through the service, his eyes fixed on the clergyman. Dr. Seagle was assisted by Dr. Ezra S. Tipple, honorary president of Drew Theological Seminary, Madison, N. J., an

old friend of the Wendel family. In her will Mrs. Rebecca
A. D. Wendel Swope indicated that she hoped Miss Ella would
bequeath the house in Fifth Avenue to the seminary.

Dr. Seagle read the burial of the dead, choosing Psalm xc and
reading the lesson from the fifteenth chapter of First Corin-
thians. There was no music and no singing, but Dr. Seagle
recited the hymn:

> *"Just as I am, without one plea,*
> *But that Thy blood was shed for me,*
> *And that Thou bid'st me come to Thee,*
> *O! Lamb of God, I come, I come."*

The Wendels were Methodists and Dr. Tipple departed from
the Episcopal ritual to the extent of delivering an informal
prayer in which he alluded to "the gentleness, the kindliness
and human affection" of the last Miss Wendel.

The Apostles' Creed and the Lord's Prayer were repeated by
the assembled group and then Dr. Seagle pronounced the bene-
diction.

"Unto God's gracious mercy and protection we commit you.
The Lord bless you and keep you. The Lord make his face to
shine upon you, and be gracious unto you. The Lord lift up
His countenance upon you, and give you peace, both now and
ever more. Amen."

The group broke up. Tobey saw the coffin containing his
mistress being lifted up and borne through the long hall toward
the front door. He trotted after it and stood on guard until
the thick oak doors were closed. Out on Fifth Avenue a crowd
watched the house and moved forward with a single impulse
when the coffin was carried out to the hearse.

It was the first time that casual spectators had ever seen the
front door of the Wendel mansion opened wide. The shades
on the front windows were half way up and the glass was thick
with dust. Shutters were closed on the south side of the house.
The wreaths were few in number, for Miss Wendel's intimates
could be counted on the fingers of one hand. Calla lilies on
the coffin, three wreaths of irises and roses—that was all.

The crowd stood back and watched the last of the Wendels

borne from the house in which the family had seemed to the outside world to have been entombed for years. A 1910 model motor car containing a woman of ninety-two followed the cortège to Trinity Cemetery at 155th Street and Broadway.

Those who attended the services both at the house and the grave, in addition to the two clergymen, were Charles G. Koss, senior counsel for the Wendel family, and his daughter, Miss Isabel G. Koss; George F. Warren jr., junior partner of the firm; Mr. and Mrs. John B. Maddock, Mrs. Benjamin West Clinedinst, old family friends; Mrs. Tipple, Mr. and Mrs. William L. Dyas, Mr. and Mrs. Frank Bloom and Mr. and Mrs. Stanley Shirk.

Mr. Shirk is the nearest living relative of the family, although no blood connection. He is the nephew of the late Professor Luther Swope, Miss Ella's brother-in-law. Mr. Bloom is superintendent of the Wendel estate at Irvington-on-Hudson. Two woman servants and a man servant also went to the cemetery.

The committal service was read on a bleak knoll with a March wind whipping over the small group of mourners. At least 100 spectators had found their way into the cemetery and surrounded the family vault on the hill. A plain gray stone, rectangular in shape, marks the burial place of Miss Wendel, along with her six sisters, her brother, her father and mother, and her grandfather and grandmother. The inscription is simply:

1841

WENDEL VAULT

John Gottlieb Wendel, the fur merchant who founded the family fortune, was buried in the same spot in 1841 and each member of his family in turn has been laid with him. Dr. Seagle read the committal ritual of the Episcopal Church and the vault was sealed.

Mr. Warren disclosed afterward that Miss Wendel was preparing to leave her town house for Irvington-on-Hudson when stricken last Monday. She preferred her home there to any of the other Wendel properties, and always looked forward to leaving New York.

She was conscious up to the time of her death, he said, but

was unable to talk. Along with other old friends of the family, Mr. Warren pointed out that Miss Wendel was not a miserly old woman, as she has been pictured, but was actually a quiet and gentle soul who had chosen to live the way she did and liked it.

She was once quoted as saying that she did not know how to spend money, because she had never been given any money to spend as a girl. She loved Tobey to the exclusion of everything else, and the custody of the little white poodle is one of the problems that has to be settled by her lawyers. Miss Koss, who was with her when she died, was her most intimate friend. She visited Miss Wendel constantly during the years that the aged spinster lived as a recluse overlooking one of the busiest spots in the world.

Her will is to be filed for probate today or tomorrow.

## Frank Ward O'Malley

Frank Ward O'Malley ("O'Malley of the *Sun*") died at the age of 56 in Tours, France, and was buried there according to his wish. He was born in Pittston, Pennsylvania, and studied painting and architecture at the Art Students League in Washington. Later he attended Notre Dame University. He came to New York in 1902 and made a living as an illustrator and a writer of light verse until 1906, when he joined the staff of the *Sun*. In a sketch of himself he once described his newspaper career thus: "Reporter, New York morning *Sun*, for fourteen years, thirteen of which were spent in Jack's Restaurant." In 1917 he married Grace Dalrymple. They had two children, and in educating them he discovered Europe, where he passed most of his later years. In 1931 he came back and tried to settle down at Brielle, New Jersey, but prohibition, bigotry and other annoyances drove him abroad again. He is supposed to have coined the phrase "Life is just one damned thing after another," and the word "brunch," to describe the morning newspaper man's breakfast-luncheon combination. In his last years he did an occasional special article for newspapers and magazines, but he belonged essentially to the period of the old *Sun*. The story reprinted here was not a great news story, and it probably would not be printed in a New York paper if written today, but it is an example of the peculiar "feature" story for which O'Malley and a few others on the *Sun* became famous in their profession.

### GLAD NEWS FROM THE *WABBLE*

Waterfront Rejoices
that She Saved the *Ponce*

Well Known Here as a Sister Ship of the *Kron Prinz Hofbrau III*—Captain Once Commanded the Noted *Peruvian Bark Calisaya*—She Sails from Liverwurst.

(Apologies to the cow)

*I've never seen the Wabble boat,*
*I never hope to see 'er.*
*But, correspondents, kindly note,*
*I'd rather see than be 'er.*

There was almost as much joy among nautical persons about town last evening over fresh news from the good ship *Wabble* as there was in other quarters over the information that the famous German tramp steamer had towed the belated *Ponce* into St. George's Bay. Some time after the evening papers had published authentic cable dispatches describing the remarkable hobo steamer *Wabble* and her good work in towing the *Ponce* into safe haven all the folks in the Maritime Exchange sought to throw discredit upon the *Wabble* by making sworn statements that there was no such ship. "*Wabble*," insisted the Maritime Exchange scoffers, is merely a word in the A B A code that means, "Shall we act as your agents?"

Cable editors or Bermuda correspondents, said the experts, had jumped at conclusions when dripping cable messages began coming in to the effect: "Steamer *Ponce* in tow off Bermuda of tramp steamer wabble."

"The cable operator was too tired to make a period after the word steamer," said one of the Broad Street nautical seers, "that's all. When the Bermuda agent who sent that cable to the New York and Porto Rico Line here added the word 'wabble,' he merely wanted to know whether he was going to get a job."

"Piffle," answered the wise ones about town, who had heard of the *Wabble* and her famous cruises long before Cattle Kate— the Western lady bandit who was killed for the eighteenth time last October in Medicine Hat—was born. Furthermore, the *Evening Mail's* cable "beat" that told of the exploits of the *Wabble* left absolutely no doubts in the minds of the admirers of the noted tramp steamer.

As a matter of fact, the good ship *Wabble* is one of the most interesting craft that ever sailed the Seven Seas. Her commander is the well known Capt. Heinrich Hassenpfeffer, one of the most trusted skippers of the Royal German Frankfurter Line, whose home offices are at Liverwurst on the south coast of Saxony. She is a sister ship of the German hobo steamer *Kron Prinz Hofbrau III.*, which sailed from the Bay of Hoboken with a cargo of empty kegs aboard on either the first or second Friday in May, 1887, and is still overdue at Liverwurst. The *Kron Prinz Hofbrau III.* has probably gone down with all her souls, but that is neither here nor there.

The special cable to the *Evening Mail* yesterday afternoon announced that the *Wabble* would get "about $100,000 for her salvage job." The money will be a regular windfall to Capt. Hassenpfeffer, as he was said to be in straitened circumstances the last time he was spoken off the western coast of Milwaukee in the late fall of 1899 while returning with his ship from the Spanish War. "Her tail shaft is broken," continued the special cable, but this may have referred to the *Ponce*.

According to the cable dispatches "The *Wabble* towed the *Ponce* for five days. The sea was smooth throughout," continues the special cable message, "but the *Wabble,* a craft much smaller than the *Ponce,* had all she could do to lug the crippled liner along."

"Thank God, my brother, Capt. Heinie, is heard from once

again already," exclaimed Mrs. Lena Katzenjammer exclusively
to *The Sun* last night when Capt. Hassenpfeffer's sister was discovered exclusively by *The Sun* at her home, 2323 Wurzburger
Strasse, Hoboken, shortly after the news of the *Wabble* was
cabled to this port. "That man yet the death of me will be.
I hope this is a lesson to my two little boys, Hans and Fritz,
who with their Uncle Heinie to sea want to go."

It was learned from Mrs. Katzenjammer that her brother,
Capt. Hassenpfeffer, has sailed the seas for over sixty years.
Her pretty little parlor was decorated with odds and ends of
bric-à-brac of a nautical flavor that had been picked up by
Capt. Hassenpfeffer at out of the way places around the world.
The captain first sailed on the Peruvian bark *Calisaya* as wheel-
wright in the summer of 1842, when the *Calisaya* sailed for
South America with a cargo of artesian wells.    Later he was
assistant janitor of the deck on the clipper ship *Watercart* when
that old English flier brought the *Cardiff Giant* to America.

Capt. Hassenpfeffer was a past assistant chauffeur on one of
the California night boats that started the daily trips between
New York and Sacramento in the early 80s, when he first
thought of designing a boat on the *Wabble's* lines.    The California night boat used to arrive nightly in Eleventh Avenue before the city ripped up the tracks recently and she was the first
of the amphibious boats to go over the New York-Keokuk-
Sacramento route in less than twenty-four hours.

Capt. Hassenpfeffer worked a long time to get New York
capitalists interested in his plan of the *Wabble*.    For the benefit
of those who have never seen the ship it might be mentioned
that the *Wabble* and her sister ship, the *Kron Prinz Hofbrau
III.*, are the only seagoing liners that have only a single sidewheel, with the exception of the *Lactea*, which sails between
here and Brest, carrying condensed milk.    Because of ice the
single paddle wheel principle was found to be useless in North
Pole dashes.    It was tried and found wanting on the good ship
*Cuspidor*, which sailed for Baffin's Bay.    The pole could not be
found because the barber moved away.

Some local ship men finally grew interested in Capt. Hassenpfeffer's design when he proved to them that a boat with only
one sidewheel and no screw could be operated at only half the

cost of a two wheeler or a twin screw craft. After the *Wabble* was completed in Hank's popular Ship Yards at Pasquag, Ohio, she was towed to a point off Sandy Hook for her trial run. Early in the initial spin it was seen that unless something was done immediately the *Wabble* would sail around and around and around. Far from being disheartened, Capt. Hassenpfeffer straightway got on his thinking cap and long before the seventh lap was completed he hit upon the scheme of having the crew hold the tiller down hard until she got underway and sending her stern foremost for a spell.

In this way he got along swimmingly but wabbled a bit. Hence the name. But as Capt. Hassenpfeffer grows older his discipline relaxes and he hasn't the heart to make the crew reverse the ship every few minutes. As a result the *Wabble* circles about the ocean a great part of her time and rarely makes port.

The *Wabble* is equipped with duplex, open faced, stem winding, rotary engines and has a marked overhang on the keep haul. Her port lee scuppers are set well aft of the stern and she can be recognized at almost any distance by her square rigged starboard revolving storm doors.

The correspondent at Bermuda mentioned in his special dispatch about the *Wabble* that he had got some information from a passenger on the *Ponce* named P. T. Kidd, whom he had found well. Inquiries yesterday elicited the fact that the passenger's name is really P. T. Kidder.

## Robert B. Peck

Robert Barton Peck was born in Clinton, New York, on February 4, 1885, was graduated from Hamilton College in 1907 and got a job on the New York *Sun* that July. He was a reporter there until March, 1912, when he went to the New York *Tribune*. It soon developed that, although not a gifted reporter, he was an excellent rewrite man. In 1934 he was still going strong on the New York *Herald Tribune*. He never liked reporting, although as a youth he covered almost all types of assignments in New

York. Year in and year out he has sat at his desk, pounding out stories sent in or telephoned in by reporters outside the office, or revamping other articles. He has been called by many who have worked with him, "the greatest rewrite man ever born." He can write three columns in an hour when pressed for time, and it is all perfect. He is quiet, unruffled, and has few outside interests except his country place in the Catskills and his library on American colonial history. The story reproduced here, which was printed in the *Herald Tribune,* April, 1934, is only one of many items written by Peck for that same issue.

Jacob Maged, slightly bewildered and incredulous, was sentenced yesterday in the Court of Quarter Sessions, Jersey City, to serve thirty days in jail and pay a fine of $100 because he charged 35 cents for pressing a suit of clothes. The minimum charge permitted by the cleaners' and dryers' code of New Jersey is 40 cents.

Mr. Maged, who is forty-nine years old, has had a tailor shop at 327 Palisade Avenue, Union City, for a good many years. It is a neighborhood shop. Mr. Maged depends on cleaning, pressing, sewing up rips, sewing on buttons and making alterations for a livelihood for himself, his wife and their three children.

He has no helper. He starts work early in the morning and, if there are jobs to be done, he works late in the evening. He doesn't get around much. Changing social orders don't interest him so much as changes in the price of thread.

His observation had led him to believe that the only reason one man gets more business than another is that he gives more value for the money. Application of that principle has permitted Mr. Maged to survive in a world which seems to him unnecessarily full of tailors. It is a theory of business which seems to Mr. Maged incontrovertible.

Talk of unfair competition went right over Mr. Maged's head. To him, competition was competition and the man who gave most for the money got the business. Higher standards of living meant equally little to Mr. Maged; all he asked was a living for himself and his family and whatever work was necessary to yield that living he felt capable of doing.

Talk of codes and combinations of cleaners and dyers to fix prices was regarded by Mr. Maged as of little importance. That, he opined, was for the big corporations, the fashionable tailors; for him, all that was necessary was to go on as he had been doing, working much and saying little.

Several weeks ago they had him in Quarter Sessions and Judge Robert V. Kinkead had talked of changes in the world, of unfair competition and, more specifically, of the charge of 35 cents advertised by Mr. Maged as the price of pressing a three-piece suit. Judge Kinkhead had said the price wasn't high enough. He had said something about prosecution if Mr. Maged didn't raise his prices.

Even that didn't impress Mr. Maged very profoundly. It seemed far from likely that a man could be put in jail for charging five cents less than his competitors. That was business, not law. State inspectors went around to his shop and talked threateningly also, but Mr. Maged didn't have time to give them much attention. They were not customers.

So, on January 24, Mr. Maged charged William J. Morgan 35 cents for pressing Mr. Morgan's coat, waistcoat and trousers, and yesterday, having pleaded guilty to the charge, Mr. Maged, his own suit freshly pressed but a little shiny at the seams and his cravat distinctly frayed where his chin rubbed against it as he bowed his head to stitch, was in Judge Kinkead's court again.

His offenses were related by Atwood C. Wolf, Assistant Prosecutor. J. Raymond Tiffany, Assistant Attorney General of the state, spoke feelingly of his sympathy for the little tailor. But, said Mr. Tiffany, however his own personal feelings might be lacerated, his duty compelled him to ask the imposition of a prison sentence. If this defendant went free, said Mr. Tiffany, chiselers would be encouraged, unfair competition would arise in the fair State of New Jersey and the cleaners' and dyers' code would be held in low esteem.

Judge Kinkead spoke then. He too, he said, sympathized profoundly with the wife and children of the prisoner, but no one, Judge Kinkead pointed out, was at fault save the prisoner himself. He had been warned repeatedly, said Judge Kinkead; he himself had warned him.

It was not, said Judge Kinkead, the money, for the sum involved was small. There was, said Judge Kinkead, a principle at stake, a principle of vital interest to the state. The country, said Judge Kinkead, was in the midst of a changing social order; state and Federal authorities, to reduce unemployment and raise standards of living, were regulating industry by means of codes.

Infringement of the provisions of a code, said Judge Kinkead, were a menace to the welfare of the community. Steps must be taken to guard against such infringements, steps severe enough to deter others from reckless disregard for the humanities. Again Judge Kinkead said that he had profound sympathy for the family of the prisoner, but it was necessary to be severe in such cases; it was necessary for Mr. Maged to go to jail for thirty days and to pay a fine of $100.

## W. O. McGeehan

William O'Connell McGeehan died at the age of 54 on November 29, 1933, in his cottage on Sea Island Beach, St. Simon's Island, on the coast of Georgia. He was born in San Francisco, and as a youth knew "Lucky" Baldwin, the prize-fighting Britts and the amazing Mizner family. He was a student at Leland Stanford when the Spanish-American war started. He enlisted and was sent to the Philippines. On his return he became a reporter for the San Francisco *Examiner*. Later he was managing editor of the *Bulletin*. He covered the Gans-Nelson fight in Goldfield, Nevada, in 1906. He received the title of "Sheriff," for an old exploit in helping chase escaped convicts. He came to New York in 1914 and went to work on the *Evening Journal*. In 1915 he was writing baseball for the *Tribune*. During the war he was a captain of infantry. In 1921 he was managing editor of the *Tribune;* then he went to the *Herald* to write sports. When the *Herald* was merged with the *Tribune* in 1924 he remained with the sports staff. He was an erratic traveler. He liked moose and duck hunting, and fishing. Always he was hitting against the bunk in sports and sports writing. Outwardly a cynic, he actually was a sentimental Irishman, and had his heroes, among them Gene Tunney and Wilbert Robinson. He was always helpful to promising young journalists; he regarded the "good old days" of journalism as a delusion. In 1910 he married Miss Sophie Treadwell, then a reporter, who later became a playwright. In 1925, with Forrest Davis, he covered the Scopes trial at Dayton, Tennessee, for the *Herald Tribune*. One of his stories of that trial is reproduced here.

Dayton, Tenn., July 16—They never come back. The great moment in the case of the people of the State of Tennessee versus John Thomas Scopes has come and gone. William Jennings Bryan, the Plumed Knight of the Fundamentalists, the Prince of Pacifism, the Champion of the Chautauqua, was given the floor and in exactly one hour and ten minutes he was lying on it horizontally in a figurative sense.

For a week the citizens of Dayton, Tenn., have been haunting the vicinity of the Rhea County Courthouse and Fundamentalists all over the country have been waiting with their radio sets tuned up to catch the golden echo of the speech that would dim the Cross of Gold oration.

There was a tense hush in the sweltering room as Judge John Raulston made the most important announcement as far as this congregation was concerned, "Mr. Bryan will speak."

The Great Realtor arose, revealed stripped to the white starched shirt with the wing collar and the little black bow tie of the true believer. First he reached for his three-gallon graniteware jug and drank deeply. He walked to the center of the inclosure where the lawyers were huddled. Then, waving in one hand the palm leaf fan of the Florida Realtor and in the other the iniquitous Foster's "Civic Biology," he began.

But it was only the ghost of the voice of the Cross of Gold. The corrosion of nearly three decades became apparent at once. Once the voice had in it the qualities of brazen trumpets, but

the resonance had gone from the brass. Once it had at times
the qualities of a stringed instrument, but today the strings
were loose and discordant. Once it had the booming note of
the drum, but today the drum showed that it had been punc-
tured in many places and its hollowness was evident.

The Great Realtor was working to a climax when the soft
voiced Mr. Clarence Darrow slipped in an objection in dovelike
tones that seemed to disconcert Mr. Bryan.

"I do not intend to prejudice the court," said Mr. Bryan
mildly, caught off his guard.

"I assure you the court will not be prejudiced," said Judge
Raulston.

"Then what is the use of talking?" demanded Mr. Darrow.
There was a faint snicker in the rear of the courtroom and it
started with the true believers, the brethren and sisters. It
became epidemic despite the rapping for order on the part of
the court attendants. And that was the figurative knockout
punch, catching Mr. Bryan below the belt with the silver buckle
that he persists in wearing without regard to the sartorial dogma
of Rhea County.

After that it was merely a question as to how long Mr. Bryan
would last. At the conclusion Mr. Bryan tossed aside the iniquitous Foster's "Civic Biology" and sought consolation in another
draught from the three-gallon graniteware jug. There was
applause of course—applause that was not checked; but it was
not inspired applause. Mr. Bryan seemed to feel that he had
swung and missed. The brethren and sisters in the rear of
the courtroom looked sorrowful and disappointed. They were
still applauding Mr. Bryan, but it was the applause that is
given to an ex-champion. It was evident that the spirit was
not strong in Brother Bryan today. It was a terrible anti-
climax.

Then up stepped Mr. Dudley Field Malone, his eyes snapping
with a fine frenzy. For the first time since the court opened,
and what Mr. Bryan had called the duel to death between science
and the literal interpretation of the Bible, Mr. Dudley Field
Malone removed his coat. He stripped to a pongee shirt and
bright blue tie. He scorned the appeal of the galluses. His
keynote was fairness, and it would have sounded discordant if

he had armed himself with galluses while Mr. Bryan was defense-less in the matter of suspenders.

As Mr. Bryan sat there dejectedly waving his palm leaf fan, the faded ghost of the Boy Orator of the Platte, Malone, con-fident and self-assured, faced the judge flanked by a solid and stolid phalanx of the local Fundamentalists. Malone has a power-ful voice always. He started gently—for him—and worked up to a crescendo which indicated that he would overwhelm Mr. Bryan with sound if he did nothing else.

He came introduced as a foreigner and a Northerner from that seat of iniquity, one of the leaders in the war to prevent the intellectual secession of the State of Tennessee. The at-mosphere was one of hostile silence. But it was soon evident that, though Mr. Malone was allied with the unbelievers and could not have the gift of tongues, he had what his own people would call the gift of gab.

One Patrick Henry of Virginia must have had a voice of that quality. There was a note in the speech that seemed to echo the same impassioned appeal. The Tennessean is the easy prey of an orator of this type. The voice of Dudley Field Malone boomed louder until it seemed to reach every corner of the Tennessee Valley in the call for intellectual freedom. Even the lawyers of the prosecution listened. When a voice of that carrying power is ringing there is nothing to do but listen.

Hundreds had been barred from the courtroom at the start and were gathered on the lawn. They heard every word of that speech. He accused William Jennings Bryan and his asso-ciates of backing away from an issue. He shouted that Bryan had led all of the foreigners into the State of Tennessee. He challenged Bryan on the issue of the duel between science and interpreted religion.

"Mr. Bryan always has been a fighter," he said. "I know Mr. Bryan well and I never knew him to back away from an issue before."

The brethren and sisters craned forward. They looked at Malone, erect and vehement, and at the faded champion of the Chautauqua waving his palm leaf and evading the challenge that the voice of Malone carried with it in words and in tone. It was made to appear that the great old warrior of rhetoric was dodging a debate.

Mr. Malone's voice rose higher and higher. Suddenly, Mr. H. L. Mencken, the mercurial editor, fell off his chair with a crash that startled the courtroom.

"It is a jedgment," said one of the sisters. "The walls are falling in and Mr. Mencken is the first to go, and he won't go to glory either."

But above it all rang the voice of Dudley Field Malone crying through the hills for intellectual freedom. He was waving a book, the Koran, which he had brought with him to have read into the records if necessary. Mr. Bryan sat in his corner in the attitude of the defeated gladiator. The blow that the soft-spoken Mr. Darrow had dealt him had pierced the Starched Shirt of Righteousness. After that he was rhetorically groggy and mixed when the belaborings of the vehement oratory of Dudley Field Malone, his former Assistant Secretary of State, battered him more and more horizontal.

Mr. Malone reached a climax that stirred the distant herds drowsing under the hackberry trees in the distant hills. There was the fraction of a second of silence of the same sort that is felt at the Metropolitan Opera House after the tenor has reached the high note. It was the sort of silence that indicated that every note sung by Mr. Dudley Field Malone had reached the ears if not the minds of every brother and sister in the congregation.

Then the applause broke out in a volume that shook the courtroom.

All of the batons of the police beat on the pine for order. But it was in vain. The last effort of the orator of the "Cross of Gold" had been what they called, on Godless Broadway, a "flop." Translated into the same language the speech of Dudley Field Malone was a "wow."

Mr. William Jennings Bryan had been beaten at his own game on more than friendly soil by an invader from the North. Of course, the cause of Mr. Bryan goes marching on. Judge Raulston is seeking guidance tonight for his decision on the admissibility of scientific experts, the subject that caused the oratorical eruptions this afternoon. The fundamentalist army proceeds, but William Jennings Bryan lies horizontal on the field, mortally wounded in his vanity. He crossed jaws with a younger and better man. Oratorically, like many a champion of a less intellectual game, he went into the ring once too often. Once more, as the boys say, youth was served.

With a leonine mane shaking, young Mr. Stewart, the earnest and impulsive heir of the elder secession, spoke in fiery tones for the newer secession, the secession of intellect. At first he stuck to the law of the state, and he knows the state well, but gradually he worked himself into the emotionalism of the evangelist.

He made of this trial with its preacher-judge and its boyish defendant the Verdun of Fundamentalism, and he shouted that the forces of knowledge should not pass. These foreign lawyers were invading holy ground. It was the South against the North. He waved no bloody shirt, but he certainly waved an en-sanguined skull cap. He sounded the call to arms to the hill people of the Cumberlands to stand in their galluses with staves of hackberry in their hands to repel the invasion of the brutal and bespectacled professors from Yale, Harvard and Johns Hopkins, who were coming to invade the green hills of Tennessee and to shackle the free born Tennesseans with thought.

It became more and more impassioned. The young Attorney General, who has the forehead of a thinker and is calm and logical when he is talking law, was overwhelmed with the fervor of the camp-meeting. He bent to the floor. He made wide flourishes with his arms. When he warmed up to his work he looked like Joe Leffrew, presiding elder of the Holy Rollers, with the ecstasy upon him.

His eyes blazed with the fanatical light of the crusader. He was ready to make a Thermopylæ out of any pass in the Cumberland Mountains through which the invading scientists might attempt to march. He raised a cry that was calculated to inflame his auditors to hanging the professors in their own galluses. He rose to stand between Jonah and the whale, despite the charge that the whale was a mammal, and to perish for his faith.

When he finished there was another burst of applause mixed with a little awe. The young orator had painted such a picture of the hell fires of evolution and made his warning so realistic that it seemed as though the army of scientists already were hammering at the city gates.

This ended the bitterest outburst of oratory that has been massed into one day since the Scopes case opened. Through it all Judge Raulston beamed through his spectacles. He has been under many spells, first the spell of Mr. Bryan, which was disappointing. Then he sat back astonished while Mr. Dudley Field Malone made the courtroom quiver. Last of all he heard the impassioned plea of the young crusader, Tom Stewart, who was voicing his own beliefs, the beliefs of the Fundamentalist preacher. It was a hectic and confusing day for Judge Raulston. He was limp when it was over and he was given an opportunity to seek guidance.

There was some light comedy relief in the morning. General Ben McKenzie furnished it. The general is the local wit and storyteller. The general did a dialect piece which cannot be reproduced by any instrument but the phonograph.

He attacked the scientist with satire. "You are asking us to believe that God took this cell thing from the sea, some sort of protoplasm, a thing that looks like a dishrag, and said to it, 'You wait around here about six thousand years and maybe I will make a man out of you!' "

General McKenzie continued to scoff in dialect at evolution. The general had an elementally good idea. It struck a sympathetic chord in the hearts of the brothers and sisters and he made much more effect as a humorist than the funniest man on the Chautauqua circuit. It is not considered in the light of levity to laugh at evolution in these parts. Of course, when the laughter became too loud they rapped for order, but even the policemen seemed to feel that the general certainly was making monkeys out of those lawyers from the North.

Mr. William Jennings Bryan, Jr., who labors among the realty developments of southern California while his sire labors among the town lots of Miami, made his first appearance in the case today, reading a brief against the admission of science in any form into the sacred hills of Tennessee. His voice was inaudible. "Hain't nothin' like his pappy," was the general version.

They have dubbed him William "Begat" Bryan, this young man from southern California. Later the Attorney General announced that the brief was a masterly work. It might have been, but nobody outside the rail of the court heard a word of it. "Begat" Bryan sat by his parent during the whole day. At the conclusion of the proceedings, both William the elder and "Begat" the younger, seemed to evidence a feeling of personal defeat. The children of darkness seemed to have proved wiser and more vehement in their day and generation than the children of light among whom the most prominent are the Bryans—William and "Begat."

But all of this oratory means nothing. Judge Raulston is seeking guidance tonight. From the attitude of all of this section of Tennessee it is impossible to conceive how the right kind of guidance would permit Judge Raulston to render any decision tomorrow, following the opening prayer, than one forbidding the scientists to enter Rhea County.

If this is the decision it will not be long before young John Thomas Scopes is found guilty of the heinous offense of telling the salacious story of mammals and revealing the salacious theory of evolution to the children of the Rhea County High School. This seems to have been as plain as the boyish freckles on the nose of Mr. John Thomas Scopes.

While Mr. Dudley Field Malone was melting the memory of Mr. Bryan's cross of gold before the aging face of the former commoner, Mr. Malone's wife sat beside John Thomas Scopes. She may not be called Mrs. Dudley Field Malone, for she is even in the Tennessee hills a member of the Lucy Stone League, and she is here as Miss Doris Stevens.

When this news reaches this stricken town I rather fear for the consequences. Certainly the sisters of the community will be up in arms against the introduction here of strange goings-on by ladies from the North. I look for something of an uprising of indignant ladies in meeting bonnets. The quiet that broods over these hills tonight is the lull before the storm that is sure to come.

Your correspondent is dubious as to his own standing before the law. During one of the periods when the oratorical batteries were silent a pretty young ingénue of the Cumberlands seated herself in a chair next to your correspondent.

"What is the theory of evolution?" she demanded.

It was a tense moment for your correspondent. Before the plea of the beauteous young belle of the Cumberlands, he could not take refuge behind the law or claim its protection. He was not being paid in whole or in part by the taxpayers of Rhea County. He could not retort that he was a God-fearing man.

Consequently, your correspondent, in a husky whisper, repeated in part some of the details of the nebular hypothesis as revealed by little Howard Morgan, the precocious pupil of John Thomas Scopes, yesterday. You can rest assured that your correspondent did not go too far. He was too much of a gentleman instinctively to mention even the word mammal.

Your correspondent regrets to record, however, that Mr. William Jennings Bryan did not show the same delicacy or chivalry. He spoke right out there in meeting before the ladies of the congregation on sexual selection. What happened to him at the end of the speech I felt served him right after that.

Of course, Mr. Bryan wanted to expose the horrible theory and to place that salacious and prurient-minded Mr. Darwin where he belonged, among the writers of the sex stuff, which recently has been inundating our libraries. But he should not have done it in the presence of the ladies of the Rhea County congregation. At least, he might have been gentleman enough to ask the ladies to leave the gentlemen to their cigars and their stories of evolution.

If Mr. Bryan is wise he will enter the oratorical arena no more. He was bested. He should have basked in the shadow of his Cross of Gold. There is sorrow and disappointment in Dayton tonight and the lamentation is caused by the fact that the oratorically mighty hath fallen and fallen quite horizontal. There never was such obvious a sense of disappointment since John L. Sullivan was knocked quite as flat.

You can take it from your correspondent that this was no small feat achieved by Mr. Dudley Field Malone this afternoon. He won Tennessee from its idol in a fair battle of the jawbones.

Come to think of it, the battle was not quite a fair one at that. It was framed against Malone at the start.

Of course this will win for him the undying enmity of the great pachyderm of politics, but Mr. Bryan never will orate against Malone. He will carry on the feud from ambush and in whispers. The golden voice that came from the Platte today is revealed as having been only plated all along and the plate has worn off.

The populace is shaking hands with Dudley Field Malone and there are Fundamentalists among the handshakers, plenty of them. Mr. Buckshot Morgan is present assuring your correspondent that it was the greatest speech he ever heard and that it put it all over Mr. William Jennings Bryan.

It may prove to have been the speech that battered the way for the spectacled brigades of scientists awaiting word to march through the passes of Tennessee. It may be the forerunner of a branch of the Lucy Stone League itself in Dayton, Tenn. But that is dipping very far into the future.

Nothing at all may come of it for as a thunderstorm starts to break over these hills, Judge Raulston seeks guidance. The Pastors' Association is sitting in the back and Buckshot Morgan is humming:

> "Come, all you ladies, and from me take warning,
>    From this time now and on.
> Never speak harsh words to your true, loving husband,
>    He may leave you and never return."

It sounds ominous, indeed, for if Judge Raulston rules that evolution may be explained to the jury, your correspondent will have mountaineer's whiskers down to his knees before it is over. Let us hope for the best.

### Alva Johnston

Alva Johnston was born in Sacramento, California, in 1888. He tried high school but gave it up to go to work for the Sacramento *Bee* at the age of 16. Although he never got through geometry at school, he became known in later life as one of the best-educated of all reporters. He came to New York in 1911, worked at a telegraph rewrite job on the *Herald* for a few days, and then, armed with a letter from a California publisher, got a chance on the *Times* staff. He remained with the *Times* until 1923, when he jumped to the *Herald*. In 1924 he went back to the *Times*, and then in 1928 he joined the staff of the *Herald Tribune*. During his four years on the *Herald Tribune* he became one of the most widely known reporters in America. He went to the *New Yorker* in 1932. He also has done much work for other magazines. His experience as a newspaper man covers every variety of story. He was a leg-man on the Rosenthal murder case; in 1922 he won the Pulitzer prize for his report of the convention of the American Association for the Advancement of Science. Many observers have called him the best all-around reporter in the country; certainly his wide knowledge and versatility have given him a high reputation. The story reproduced here is an "interview" of a type which can easily be botched. Needless to say, this story, as is true of more than half the stories concerning Mr. Fellows, is the result more of the ingenuity of the reporter than of Mr. Fellows.

Dexter Fellows, the publicity man with whom the Ringling Brothers and Barnum & Bailey circus has been connected for the last forty years, arrived in this city yesterday wearing a long black beard with oiled ringlets and an expression of discontent, which proved to be due to his failure to buy Storm King Mountain for a billboard.

Mr. Fellows passed the winter touring the country buying mountains, which are to be sawed up into precipices for the new granite billboards, ranging in size from 140 acres to a square mile and chiseled over with adjectives which Mr. Fellows has been a lifetime in selecting. Some of these will be visible to the naked eye at twenty miles on clear days and the circus is now manufacturing thousands of cheap telescopes which will bring them up nicely at fifty or sixty miles. Mr. Fellows took an option on Mount Shasta, but found the all-year-round snow there a serious problem. He said he would either have to warm up the mountain or find some less pretentious peak for the northern California public.

"I snapped up sixty-seven of the choicest alps in the country scattered from the Coast Range to the White Mountains," he said. "Beautiful fellows that spring right out of the ground and shoot straight up in the air several thousand feet. A few hundred tons of dynamite, and they will be a credit to the Greatest Show on Earth. It has been very interesting but you have to have your wits about you all the time. You have to know your stuff when you buy mountains. There are mountains and mountains. I have to have nice, abrupt ones with big open faces that look out on distant railroads and highways. You have no idea how many things can be wrong with a mountain. Some of them have clouds around them most of the time. Then there is snow. Some of them are always crumbling away and sliding off in avalanches. And look out for those mountain dealers. They're the greatest set of David Harums in the world. Don't trust any man that tries to sell you a mountain. They'll misrepresent every time. The majority of the mountains of this country are no good. Either they're made of the wrong material or they're in the wrong location. Before I learned the business they outsmarted me a few times and I got stuck with a few defective ranges, but I'll pass them on to the next man.

"The thing that struck me most was the way the mountain owners and jobbers all stick together. I started in California and intended to sneak all the best peaks before the trade got wind of my intentions, but before I had cleaned up the Coast Range the news was out. In the Sierra Nevadas the prices jumped from $50 a peak to $1,000 and I had to play one mountain against another to get them for anything like a reasonable figure. Then the racketeers got after me with forged titles and fake mountains.

"After my first experience in buying mountains by the map I never bought another without going to look it over. If you let them work on you with a map they'll sell you Yosemite Valley or Death Valley for a mountain. These gyp mountain brokers never think anything of doctoring a government survey. They'll palm off a foothill or a canyon for a Mount Everest. There are absolutely no ethics in the mountain traffic. Once or twice to make them reasonable I had to threaten to throw all my mountains—and I own enough to stock two or three Switzerlands—all on the market at once, which would have knocked the bottom out of every range in the United States. I made that threat to the biggest mountain dealer in the West.

" 'You'll ruin me,' he gasped.

" 'I'll ruin you all,' I replied. 'I'll hit your mountains a blow they'll never recover from. I'll make you think the Himalayas fell on you.'

"I took out my watch and gave him two minutes in which to accept my terms. He accepted. That had a valuable effect. When I came East I found they had heard of it from the Blue Ridge to the Catskills and there was no more gouging. I was trimmed once in the Adirondacks where they sold me a mountain that looked all right and was round geologically, but I found that, in the summer, the roads are so screened by trees that tourists can't see it."

Mr. Fellows said that he had spent a month looking for some adequate summit near New York and had finally decided on Storm King Mountain, which was to have been trimmed down to a cube, with each of its four sides carved in circus language and illustrated in pastel shades. But he found the mountain in the hands of all kinds of selfish interests, and was beaten.

"It's the only mountain that I went after that I didn't get," he said. "You may want to know why I have been working so fast. The reason is more or less of a secret. It is because we have something this year so astonishing, so paralyzing, so staggering to the imagination, that the ordinary billboard is utterly unable to cope with it. It is ridiculous to try to give any conception of it through the billboards. Radio, sky-writing, the press and all means of communication are unable to do it justice. We were driven to the mountain-peak method of expression by the epic nature of the subject.

"I wish that I could give some inkling about this year's unparalleled headliner, but we can't be responsible for causing so much excitement all at once. It has to be revealed gradually. We have no right to cause business to be suspended and all other topics to be driven out of the public mind. The work of the world must go on.

"All that I can say at present is that this great secret is of an ethnological nature; that it is now on the high seas; that it will be here in due time; that no one need be frightened, as the public's interest is being carefully guarded."

Mr. Fellows was badgered into a confession that the circus will open at the New York Coliseum in the Bronx on Thursday afternoon, March 27, for a ten-day engagement, after which it will move to Madison Square for a limited engagement. Mr. Fellows then left to complete arrangements for his lectures at the School of Journalism.

"The secret of writing is six adjectives to a noun," he said. "If a noun is not worth six adjectives it should be left out of the sentence. Modern literature is admittedly in a bad way and that is why I have consented to give my series on Ringling Brothers and Barnum and Bailey prose. Let's get away from the anemic, half-dead style and write like men."

### *Thoreau Cronyn*

Thoreau Cronyn, known to his colleagues as "T Cronyn," was born in San Diego, California, and was the son of a Unitarian clergyman. At Stanford University (class of 1903) he edited the college daily and made a living as college correspondent for the San Francisco *Chronicle*. He worked one month on the *Chronicle*, then came East to the Springfield *Republican*, where he worked for three years. As a child he had acquired a desire to do newspaper work from reading the Springfield *Republican* to a blind man for 25 cents a week. As a reporter in Springfield, he read the New York *Sun* and wanted to work for it. Finally Chester S. Lord, the managing editor, wrote: "If you want to come to the *Sun* and take your

chances at $15 a week, come ahead." For the first three
years he read copy; then he became a reporter on space at
$8 a column. He covered City Hall, politics, Theodore
Roosevelt's Bull Moose campaign in 1912, the impeach-
ment of Governor William Sulzer, coal strikes in Pennsylvania and West Virginia, Roosevelt's speaking tour for
Charles Evans Hughes in the Presidential campaign of
1916, and the funeral of Roosevelt. He had been city
editor of his paper (then called the *Herald*) for about a
year when, in 1923, he went to *Collier's* as associate editor.
Later he was managing editor. He went into advertising
in 1925, and is now with Batten, Barton, Durstine and
Osborne, where he is regarded as one of the ablest practitioners of that recondite art. The story reproduced here
is from the old *Sun*.

In the days when Chatham Square was the sailorman's Sar-
gasso Sea, long before Nigger Mike's and the Chatham Club
and the Fleabag enticed the slummer to their brief day of glory
and then the stifling police, there was a singing waiter on the
Bowery known as Bull Johnstone. In Callahan's place he held
the world's record for skidding schooners across wet, glary tables
without spilling a drop. When, between rounds, he stood beside the piano with the towel of his profession draped gracefully
within his crooked elbow and lifted his tenor in the monstrous
ballads of that day and hour the crowd in Callahan's slung their
dimes at Bull Johnstone. For he was good, boy, he was good!
    From Callahan's he went to McGurk's Suicide Hall, where he
not only was singing waiter for young men with creamless tarts
but was bouncer as well. As he had been a prize fighter and
baseball player and came up through the streets with hard
muscles and harder eyes, he was the Bowery's best bouncer.
    In short, the Bull whatever vocation he elected was at the
top of it. He was a thief, he dealt faro for Jake Rosenthal in
Jake's Grand Street dive, he was a crooked umpire in a crooked
baseball league, he was a pickpocket and a gambler and a convict, and most of all he was a rummy—oh, such a rummy was

Bull, christened William H. Johnstone by his hopeful parents when he received the holy water on Cherry Hill.

On December 4, 1909, Bull was pegging along Water Street. The old lays had petered out, but as a certain feeling in the throat persisted he had to make a touch. Seeing a lot of men in the McAuley Mission he wandered in and cast an appraising eye over the assembly to size up his material.

As they used to say in the double-decked novels, eight years pass by. December 4, 1917—last night. Again the mission is crowded. There is prayer and a song and a voice. "This meeting tonight, friends, is to celebrate the eighth anniversary of the conversion of the well known singing evangelist, the man who goes from prison to prison and gets the boys where they live because he talks their own talk and has been through more than they have."

Introducing, of course, our old friend from Suicide Hall, Bull Johnstone. Yes, sir, the baldish, clear eyed, crooked nose (from a fight), happy faced man with the gimp leg (from trying to pretend he could play baseball after all that stuff) and the black cutaway coat and the voice that led all the hymns and out-hymned everybody else, is none other than old Bull Johnstone, the singing waiter of the Bowery.

On a bench up in front sits Mrs. Johnstone and the three girls —all acquired since McAuley's mission retrieved the Bull eight years ago. The youngest, Jeannie, won't stay put. She hollers "That's daddy up there" right in the middle of a prayer and runs up to the platform and tries to pull his toes.

Bull Johnstone, favoring his right leg but with plenty of spring in the other, hops from his chair when the prayer is ended and begins his experience.

"There seems to be quite a bunch here tonight," he says. ("You keep quiet, Jeannie, or I'll give it to you when I get home.) Well, I was born right around here, men. I got my education in a house of refuge.

"All I got out of it was hatred of authority, for you know a kid catches holt of everything by the wrong handle. And I grew up and I was a wise guy. I had been knockin' around the Bowery, slingin' beer in the back room of Mike Callahan's in the days when Mike was the maker and breaker of police captains.

"The cream of grafters came in there. Some people will tell you these fellers are all hard, but to people like them at Callahan's they're the grandest men ever seen. It was my way of thinkin' too, and I got to livin' that way. Men, you remember Chew Tobacco Mike, that copper on the Bowery? He says to me one day, 'Bull, if you don't get out I'm going to put you where they throw the key away.'

"So I says to myself, 'I'll go up to Albany to clean out the soft yaps.' We hit the rattler for a caser apiece and landed among the joy factories of the Gut in Albany—you remember the Gut, men. Yaps, I said? I found the wisest bunch of thieves I'd ever broke up again.

"They had me covered to a spot, and I had many a good drunk with the real grafters in them little burgs. I had opportunity to learn all that was goin' in my line, but I got sick and put on the bum. I goes to a lieutenant of police and says to him, 'George, I want the fare on the old river boat so's I can get home to croak.' He let me have it.

"My wish was to sponge on my old aunt when I got to New York and put my feet three times under the table. When I walked in she looks me up and down. She never says a thing but thinkin' she was goin' to I asks her to direct me to Uncle Chris—you know him, men, Lucky Baldwin. Well, she told me he was here.

"It was disgustin' to think of me goin' into a mission, but huntin' Uncle Chris here I come and Charley Stewart—he's here tonight, praise be—and John Tyler sat alongside. Well, they got to singin' out loud all them hymns and I says to myself, 'This sure is some squirrel factory and I'm the only wise guy.' Then right alongside me Charley Stewart gets up and says he's been on the Bowery seven years.

"I see this guy was lyin'; when I was in Callahan's seven years I didn't know 'm. If he'd said one word to me I'd a knocked 'm down. Then up gets this Tyler and says he's been on the Bowery forty-two years. I says, 'You big stiff,' but he never looks at me and sits down.

"Well, they tells me to get up and Christ will make a new

man out of me. I got up—me, without a clean thought in my head. Then says the superintendent, 'Kneel.' I says, 'I can't kneel; my leg is on the bum.' He says, 'Fall down then,' and I did.

"When it come to repeatin' the prayer, 'Be merciful to me, a sinner,' I couldn't; whether it was because I was mulled or not I dunno. I finally got up the same old red tad I was when I fell down, but, men, here's the part I always emphasize: When I went out of that door there I had a clean heart and it's been clean ever since. That's eight years ago tonight, men."

Bull's daughter Jeannie was trying to reach his toes again. Her dad reached down for her.

"Sunday week they took her to Sunday school and she started to clean up the dump," he said proudly.

One by one, to the number of about thirty, other graduates of McAuley's Mission got up to say:

"Bull"—or "Billy," or "Bill," or "Brother Bill"—"I want to congratulate you on your eighth anniversary and to say for myself that it's been two years, six months, and eleven days tonight (or some other carefully calculated period) since I was saved here by grace, and I thank God."

"Amen," responded Bull to each of these avowals. The superintendent, John H. Wyburn, testified that Bull was indeed "a pretty rotten sort when he came in here eight years ago."

He said that Bull—or maybe it was some other sinner—who, when asked to repeat the prayer of the publican, replied, "I can't; I'm a Dimmycrat."

And Charles Tyler, now spruce and prosperous, got up to say that the reason Bull didn't know him on the Bowery was that he, Tyler, was drinking whiskey with cherries in it with the boss in the front room of Callahan's, while Bull was slinging beer in the back room. There are castes on the Bowery, explained Tyler, and Bull Johnstone wagged his head in approval of the sentiment.

The Bowery Caruso filled a chink between the speeches with a song, and a racetrack bookmaker who "hit the trail" with Billy Sunday told his story and at the very end Bull Johnstone bowed his head and talked very softly to five gray penitents who shuffled from the back bench to the front when the ex-singing waiter called for volunteers in the fight that he's making.

## Martin Green

Martin Green was born in Burlington, Iowa, on August 28, 1870, in the period of the prairie schooners. He left school at the age of 15; at 20 he was Iowa agent for an insurance company. The company blew up, owing Green $5,000. He went to work as a reporter on the Burlington *Gazette*, remained there for four years and then went to the St. Louis *Star;* and then to the *Republic.* In 1896 he was offered a job on the New York *Journal*, then a morning paper, which had been purchased by William Randolph Hearst. In 1901, in response to the urgings of Charles E. Chapin, he went to work for the *Evening World*. He remembers Chapin as a man who dealt fairly and even considerately with his efficient men. He remained with the *Evening World* until it suspended publication in 1931, when he went to the *Sun*. At an age when most reporters are long since retired or in some other business, Mr. Green is able to cover all sorts of assignments. He is known as an all-around news man, though on the *Evening World* he conducted a humorous column for a time. The story reprinted here is a recent one from the *Sun*.

Among the attendants at the American Bartenders Institute, at 53 East Twenty-fifth street, last night for the championship contest for bartenders, was a young woman in a Scotch plaid dress. The material was of red and black checks and stood out like a bandaged finger in a symphony orchestra.

She wore a cap of the same material and looked like a walking checker board. She attracted the attention of all beholders and especially of one who was the guest of Prof. A. H. Payne, the dean of the faculty. Prof. Payne's guest, when he first entered the gigantic barroom, could almost count the checks in the dress and hat, so vividly were they marked. But the professor urged a Scotch highball on his guest and turned his attention to the bar, behind which a line of whitejacketed bartenders were doing their stuff for a silver cup.

The girl in the plaid gown was seated on a table pensively absorbing gin rickeys. Prof. Payne suggested to his guest that he try a Jamaica rum cocktail. The guest tried one and immediately called for an encore. After three or four rum cocktails Prof. Payne's guest glanced at the table on which the girl in the plaid dress was sitting.

He could tell the difference between the gown and the cap, which were separated by the girl's face, but the plaids were not so distinct as they were when he first went in. They had run together. He had another rum cocktail and watched with fascinated gaze the performance of Aldo Piantino of the "Round the World" bar at the Park Lane Hotel, who ultimately won the championship cup and the honorary degree of "Master Mixologist" awarded by the American Institute.

Mr. Piantino learned his trade in Venice in his native Italy and he can do more things with a glass, a mixer and an assortment of liquor than a juggler ever dreamed of. What won him the championship was his feat of mixing a drink in two glasses, one in each hand, by passing the liquor from one glass to another in an arch over his head—or at least it seemed so to Prof. Payne's guest. The cup was presented to him by Horace D. Meyers, the "Jamaica Rum King," who donated it, and Piantino made a speech of thanks in the Scandinavian tongue or it at least sounded that way to Prof. Payne's guest.

The guest drank a couple of rum cocktails to Piantino's health and again glanced at the table on which the girl in the plaid dress was sitting. Peculiarly enough she was now robed entirely in red and had on a red hat. The black lines separating the red squares had entirely disappeared. However, that was all right and the guest cordially shook hands with the winner of the second prize, a gold medal. He is Mr. Gormley and tends bar in the Park Central Hotel.

Mr. Gormley is what is known as a close mixer. Seemingly carelessly he pours the ingredients of a mixed drink for four or five people into a large glass or shaker, and when he pours out four or five drinks there is not a drop left over nor a drop too much.  Mr. Gormley is good, but not as good as a bartender Prof. Payne's guest once knew in Lipton's on Park Row.  He always mixed drinks so that he had just exactly one over, and he drank that himself.

At the urgent solicitation of Mr. Meyers the guest had another Jamaica rum cocktail.  Happening to glance at the table where the young woman in the red dress had been sitting he was almost floored to find that she was gowned entirely in black and had a black hat on.  She was still absorbing gin rickeys.

By that time the crowd in front of the bar was about ten deep and Prof. Payne and his guest had all they could do to hold their places in the front row.  Long experience in the subway rush hours stood the guest in good stead now and by using his elbows and feet in a way never intended by nature he managed to stick right against the bar rail as long as he could stand up.

"Where is the girl with the plaid dress?" he asked a couple of men who were holding him up with difficulty because they had all they could do to hold themselves up.

"You're nutty," said one of the men and that was that because the guest made a solemn promise when a small boy that he would never fight, but he still asserts that the aforesaid young woman had on a plaid dress when he first saw her and a black dress when he lamped her last and that some time during the evening she was robed from head to foot in red.

## Meyer Berger

Meyer Berger was born on the East Side of New York on September 1, 1898, one of eleven children.  He attended public school and passed two terms in the Eastern District High School in Brooklyn.  He quit school at 12 to run messages for the Brooklyn office of the New York *World*.  He had sold newspapers along Broadway beginning at the age of 8.  He became night telephone operator of the *World*, then head office boy.  He fought in France and Belgium with the 106th Infantry.  After the war he was a police reporter for the *World*, then a reporter and rewrite man for the Standard News Association. He went to the New York *Times* on March 8, 1928. Since then he has been recognized as one of the best reporters on the *Times*. The Capone trial, one story of which is reproduced here, was his first important out of town assignment. His specialties are crime and human interest stories. In 1932, assigned to cover a spelling bee of the Catholic Actors Guild, he entered the contest and won.

Chicago, Oct. 16.—Impassioned oratory, punctuated with jury-rail thumping for emphasis, echoed today in the sunny, high-ceiled Federal court chamber in the old Postoffice Building as defense counsel pleaded with a farmer jury for the acquittal of Al Capone. He has been on trial since Oct. 6 for evasion of income tax from 1924 to 1929.

"Delenda est Capone!" cried Michael Ahern, one of the lawyers. "Do you know what that means?"

The rural gentlemen blinked owlishly at him, held by his sharp eyes.

"It means 'Capone must be destroyed!' " the lawyer translated. "These censors (waving a hand at the staff of United States Attorney Johnson) cry out: 'Capone must be destroyed!' "

Thump!! (on the rail). The fat juror with a sad face, who sat nearest the descending fist, drew back. Mr. Ahern pinned him with a glance.

"Why do they seek conviction on this meager evidence?" the lawyer went on. "Because he is Alphonse Capone; because he is the mythical Robin Hood you read so much about in all the newspapers. They have no evidence, or what they have produced here discloses only one thing—that the defendant Al Capone is a spendthrift, that he was extravagant."

Slap! (on the rail).

"But the government itself is also guilty of acts of profligacy," Mr. Ahern resumed. "It has spent thousands upon thousands in the investigation and prosecution of this case when it might better have spent the money, in these times, for the establishment of soup kitchens." Thump!

So it went all morning and all afternoon. Rich, manly phrases poured from the lips of the slim, dynamic Ahern and rolled sonorously from the mouth of Albert Fink, his older associate, as they raised the cry that their client was the victim of government persecution. The jury had it after breakfast and after lunch, and the impassioned words were still holding their attention as the shadows crept further down the white marble court room walls.

And Capone drank it in. A mint kept his ponderous jaws moving as he gave ear to the word painting of his counsel. Even the parts about the Punic Wars, about Cato, about the Arabian Nights and the Old Man of the Sea held him in rapt attention, though there seems to be a reasonable doubt as to whether he grasped the full meaning of it all. It sounded good.

Both Mr. Ahern and Mr. Fink contended that the government had failed to prove that Capone had an income. Mr. Fink further maintained that there was no evidence of "willful failure" to pay the tax or of "attempt to evade" payment of tax.

"In order to sustain the charge that he willfully failed to make a return they must establish, first, that he had a gross income in excess of $5,800—income gained from any source," said Mr. Fink, as he leaned over the jury box. "Secondly, they must show that there was a 'willful failure' to make a return; that such willful failure was motivated by evil design, by intent to defraud.

"Now, when Capone went to Philadelphia in 1929 he was put in jail for carrying a gun. Glory be to Philadelphia! I don't think its conscience had been so shocked for years as when Capone came there with a gun in his pocket. I strongly suspect, however, that if the man's name hadn't been Alphonse Capone, it wouldn't have been done.

"Well, he got out on the seventeenth of March, two days after the income tax was due. He went immediately to get this tax matter settled. That was shown by the government's own evidence. Now, if you believe that, how in the world can you find any 'willful intention' to defraud the government of the tax for 1929? What have they got to prove the evasion count in the indictment?

"Suppose we take up the character of what I am forced to

characterize as the 'chaff'—the government evidence. Is there
a scintilla of proof? No.

"The government seeks to stow Capone away, but don't let
yourselves be drawn away from your duty with an argument
that this man is a bad man. He may be all that you read in
the newspapers, but don't find him guilty of something of
which he is not guilty. You are the only bulwark against
oppression in times of public excitement."

Mr. Fink admitted that Capone was a gambler, even that he
may have derived some income from a gambling business in
Cicero, as the government contended.

"But he may have lost everything he ever made in that gambling business. They have not proved that he had net income
in any single, solitary year named in these indictments. If his
name wasn't Al Capone there would be no case, gentlemen."

Mr. Fink strode up and down before the jury box. When his
memory failed as to names or sums involved in the evidence, he
would turn to opposing counsel with a benevolent smile and
ask for data, explaining: "As I get older my memory gets
poorer."

In his argument before Judge Wilkerson yesterday, in the
absence of the jury, Mr. Fink dwelt at length on the legal meaning of the term "attempt" as read in the indictments. He went
over the same ground today in his summation.

"What is an attempt?" he asked. No help, of course, from
the twelve good men and true. "An attempt is an act done in
part execution of a given design, something short of accomplishment. I don't think you can make an 'attempt' by doing
nothing. I don't think you can 'attempt' to evade a tax by
failing to pay it."

Judge Wilkerson interrupted with a question:

"Do you think, Mr. Fink, that one could 'attempt' to defraud
another by remaining silent when it was his duty to speak?"

Mr. Fink turned from the jurors to direct his answer to the
bench.

"I do not think you could call it 'attempt,' because I think
'attempt' connotes a physical attempt," he said. "Failure to
speak when it is a duty to speak would be motivated by 'intent.' "

Mr. Fink turned to the jury box again. The judge got out of his seat and paced up and down behind his high backed chair for a few moments as if in deep thought, while the lawyer continued to harangue the jurors.

"Suppose Capone believed that money he received from so-called illegal transactions was not taxable," he asked; "suppose he was under that impression, and suppose he discovered to the contrary and tried to pay what he owed, would you say he ever had an 'intent' to defraud the government of that tax?

"No—and neither would I. Capone is the kind of man who never fails a friend."

It was hard to be certain, but something suspiciously like a lump bulged Capone's throat. And it seemed his eyes filled at the tribute. His whole face showed deep self-pity.

"There is not a man in this court room," said Mr. Fink, "who doesn't know that Al Capone never had intent to defraud the government of that tax. He is not that kind of a man. A tin horn or a piker might, but no one ever accused Capone of being a piker. If he owed a tax you may be sure he didn't pay it for some motive other than to defraud the government."

Mr. Fink's final argument to the jury had to do with the part played by Lawrence Mattingly, the Washington lawyer who undertook to settle Capone's debt to the Treasury Department and who provided figures and facts as to Capone's income as he had gathered them from "Capone's business associates." These data were the backbone of the government's case, more or less.

"I think this is the first time a jury has been asked to convict a man on the uncorroborated 'confession' of his lawyer," said Mr. Fink. "I insist that they were Mattingly's statements, not the defendant's."

Then he went on to charge that his client had been "betrayed" and "lured" into making damaging statements before Internal Revenue men. Both he and Mr. Ahern contended that Mr. Mattingly's statements and Capone's could not be used against the defendant, because "it was not supported by other and independent evidence."

Mr. Ahern opened the afternoon session, taking up the argument where his partner had left off. He seemed to put into his

words every ounce of power that he had.  His voice grew hoarse
and he went to the water cooler for a drink.

Every time he brought in a sharp point he hammered it down
with a thump on the rail or with a sharp clap of the palms.
He had the jury's attention every second, and the attention of
all others in the court room as well.

He referred to one Miami witness for the government, put on,
according to an admission made at the time by Jacob I. Gross-
man, assistant prosecutor, "to prove the humble origin of the
defendant."

"To show the humble origin of the defendant," Mr. Ahern
repeated, soothingly.  "Why, gentlemen, that was mild decep-
tion.  They wanted to show that the defendant in 1920 was a
bartender in Coney Island."  And he slapped the jury rail
sharply three times.

Eventually, he began to talk about the corpus delicti.  In
simple language he explained to the farmer jury the meaning of
the term, used in his argument that the "extra judicial admissions" wrested from Capone by Florida authorities could not be
used against the defendant "unless there is other and independent evidence" to corroborate it.  Swiftly he went back over
the testimony in an attempt to prove that no such evidence had
been introduced.

Bitterly Mr. Ahern referred to "hypocritical Miamian officials" who called Capone for questioning when he wanted to
establish his home on Palm Island.

"They called him so they could trap him for the Washington
authorities," charged Mr. Ahern.  "It was all a plot, gentlemen,
to get this defendant to make admissions that he had a tax
liability.  The cry had gone out. 'Delenda est Capone!'—
'Capone must be destroyed!' "

Thump!  Thump!  It stirred the echoes in the profound
stillness of the chamber.  The day was growing old and the
shadows were deep in the corners near the ceiling.  Capone
hunched forward in his seat, still held by the vibrant voice of
his "mouthpiece."

But at last it was over.  The last words died away.  Feet
shuffled and chairs creaked as the listeners relaxed.  Capone
smiled.

Mr. Johnson and the defense counsel huddled before the bench and arranged for tomorrow's session. The government will spend an hour or more with its final argument, then the charge will be delivered by Judge Wilkerson. The case should be in the jury's hands early in the afternoon.

# MEMORANDUM FOR TOMORROW

IS there any sense in the idea that a respectable, high-class, sophisticated newspaper of tabloid size, morning or evening, could find a place in New York? Since the war little groups of newspaper men, and ex-newspaper men, have discussed this dream, but nobody ever does anything about it. It is a sort of newspaper man's dream of a paper. Most of the papers of standard size are too bulky or unwieldy; the sensational tabloids don't cover the news. The circulation of this theoretical paper, it is argued, need not be great to make it profitable. Some wealthy man, tired of losing money in Wall Street, in keeping up yachts or racing stables, may attempt this venture some day. He can lose lots of money and have a great deal of fun proving his point.

\* \* \*

It is strange that most of the good newspaper cartoonists, particularly those who draw political cartoons, are old or outmoded. Rollin Kirby and Jay Norwood Darling are occasionally effective, but few of the younger generation, with the exception of Edmund Duffy of the Baltimore *Sun,* seem to have many ideas. Is it possible that political cartoons belong to the adolescent period of American life, and that their appeal to grown-ups has lost its potency? Most of the really competent cartoonists are either professional radicals or foreigners. Not one approaches Nast or Daumier.

\* \* \*

One school of thought argues that all good journalists, like all good prizefighters, "come out of the gutter." This idea is as foolish as the corollary that no rich man's son has any business becoming a newspaper man.  Many of the best journalists, to be sure, started life under great handicaps, and they may have gained some strength of character in battling adversity, but there is nothing to prove that, with better advantages, they might not have been even better men.  It is unfortunate for the business of getting out a newspaper that the more literate and thoughtful sons of rich men don't invest their time and money in it.  They could help enormously, and the investment might even increase their wealth.

\*    \*    \*

What is the best training for a young man who wants to break into newspaper work in New York?  There is no completely satisfying answer.  Some school of journalism graduates are ready for it; some ordinary college graduates, particularly those who have helped edit their college papers, are well equipped to start; for others, a few years on a good small town paper is excellent training. The smaller towns give the young man a wide variety of experience.  They teach him the meaning of grinding hard work, and iron out the rough spots in his technique.  On the other hand, if a young man remains too long in a small town he may lose his freshness, his writing and thinking habits may become set, and he will be useless in the larger cities.

\*    \*    \*

In "The Crock of Gold," James Stephens, the Irish author, has a passage which might be the text for every young journalist who wonders about writing:

"A thought is a real thing and words are only its raiment, but a thought is as shy as a virgin; unless it is fittingly apparelled we may not look on its shadowy nakedness; it will fly from us and only return again in the darkness crying in a thin, childish voice which we may not comprehend until, with aching minds, listening and divining, we at last fashion for it those symbols which are its protection and its banner."

\*   \*   \*

Racial inheritance probably has little to do with journalistic expertness, and yet most men who have got ahead in American journalism have been of Irish, English or Scottish blood. There have been a few Germans, and fewer from the Scandinavian countries. French blood? Sometimes, but not often. And a good Italian newspaper man is so rare that he belongs in the Smithsonian Institution. Of all reporters, the Irish, if they have a poetic streak in them and can stay reasonably sober, probably make the best. Jewish reporters are impossible to classify; some are cloddish, some brilliant, some level-headed, some itching with messianic afflictions, some profligate, and some close-fisted and scheming. One thing surely may be said about them: most Jews know enough not to drink too much.

\*   \*   \*

The system of having news stories which start on page one and then jump to page thirty-seven of the second section, causing the reader to maul and tear his paper and lose all interest by the time he finds the continuation, are an affront to the reader. It would be possible to have virtually every story complete on one page. True, the idea is revolutionary, and would require drastic changes in make-up, but it could be done. The Manchester *Guardian* does it without losing any of its reputation. Some day a paper will abolish "jumps" and gain many devoted readers by that simple act of thoughtfulness.

\*   \*   \*

It is true that the more important branches of newspaper work require a high talent and a quality of brains which would not be in the slum section of any of the other professions or businesses.   But the newspaper man who says, "If I had gone into some other work when I was younger, I could have made millions; now look at me," usually is deluding himself.   The man who says this is most often one who has always had a sneering attitude toward newspaper work, and who, in all truth, had no business taking up the noble profession in the first place.   If he had become a banker, he would have lived to curse that business.   And he probably would have failed.

*   *   *

The traditional attitude of the old-fashioned newspaper man toward what is known as "culture," was a pose to begin with, and was not shared by the better men.   It is no longer any disgrace to read a book, and yet as late as 1932 a graduate of a school of journalism tried to impress himself upon a city editor, from whom he sought employment, by boasting that he had not read a book in four years.   Although reporters in 1934 appear better educated, in general, than ever before, they still do not read newspapers enough.   Many New York newspaper men have not read a British paper, or an out of town American paper, in years.   And many of them never read such publications as "Editor and Publisher" and the "American Press," the periodicals which deal with newspaper work. There is an appalling lack of curiosity on the part of many of the younger men as to the history and personalities of the business.   The better ones keep their eyes open.

*   *   *

Of incalculable value to any large newspaper is its "morgue" or library.   Hardly an hour passes that some situation does not arise which requires reference to previous items.   Books, clippings and indexes should be arranged so that the information desired may be available instantly.

Filed away under the names of persons, as well as under subject-matter, there may be a treasure of necessary information. One of the difficulties in the way of starting a new paper in a city like New York would be the lack of such a library. Keeping a "morgue" is in itself an important and not sufficiently appreciated branch of newspaper work.

*    *    *

When Jake Lingle was shot and killed in Chicago, and the story of how for years he had been a crook gradually came to light, some of the critics of journalism asked whether there were not a great many Lingles in the business. Could any large newspaper afford to subject its staff to a rigid ethical examination? Weren't there a great many reporters who took graft, who would sell out their papers to politicians, or criminals, or sports promoters? The answer was that Lingle was almost in a class by himself. Some newspaper men exert considerable influence, and have the opportunity to make shady money, but few of them take advantage of these chances. Sports writers, who still accept too many favors, are much more honest than they were even ten years ago. Some newspaper men may live a long lifetime without ever having the chance to turn down a picayune bribe.

*    *    *

In the popular mind, a newspaper man is one who drinks a great deal. It is true that most newspaper men drink; it is also true that booze takes many of them to a pathetic ending. But the majority of newspaper men today are careful about their liquor; they have to be. Liquor is good for relaxation, and for stimulating fresh ideas. Indeed, many men would be the most insufferable dullards were it not for an occasional strong drink. Liquor also may be of infinite help in reading copy. However, the stories of reporters who wrote just as well on twelve high-balls as when cold sober are utter bunk. A man may stagger horribly through writing a column while groggy and get by with it, but he would have done much better if he had had nothing to drink.

# INDEX